9/15/12

Shirley —

I'm sure you'll enjoy this ride down Rt. 7 with me. You may learn from me; and I from you! Thanks!

John Tait

Roads, Rivers, and Rails

The Delaware & Hudson's Susquehanna Division Heritage Trail
Volume 1: Albany/Schenectady to Oneonta

John Taibi

DEPOT SQUARE PUBLISHING
LOVELAND, OH
2012

Roads, Rivers, and Rails
  The Delaware & Hudson's Susquehanna Division Heritage Trail
  Volume 1: Albany/Schenectady to Oneonta
Copyright 2012 by John Taibi

First printing 2012
First edition
10 9 8 7 6 5 4 3 2 1

Manufactured in the United States of America
by Jostens, Inc., Clarksville, TN

Library of Congress Control Number: 2012934964

ISBN: 0-9651364-7-7
978-0-9651364-7-1

Printed on acid-free paper.

For more information on this or other books, please address all correspondence to:
John W. Hudson
Depot Square Publishing
6683 Loveland Miamiville Road
Loveland, OH 45140-6953
e-mail: depotsquarepub@fuse.net
www.depotsquarepublishing.com

With the Main Street crossing and business district just a few yards to the left and a small engine terminal to the right, the unique architecture of the Delanson, NY station warmly welcomes visitors to its village. The position of the lower quadrant train order board indicates there are no orders for trains in either direction.
EDWARD P. BAUMGARDNER COLLECTION.

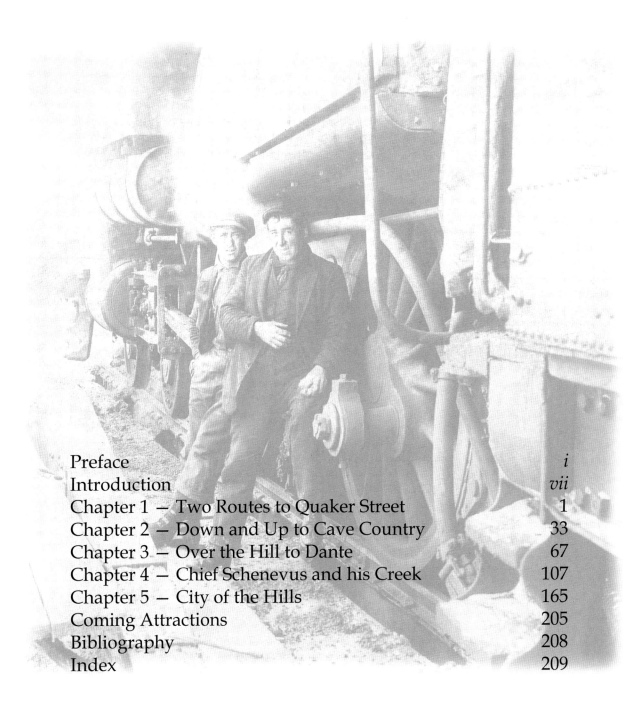

CONTENTS

This book is dedicated to the memory of

Walter G. Rich

Railroad Executive, Historian, and Friend

DEDICATION

While attending high school at Franklin, NY, an English teacher asked all the students to prepare a biography on someone they admired. For his subject, Walter chose Joseph H. Nuelle, ninth president of the Delaware & Hudson Railroad that ran through nearby Unadilla. Another railroad close to Franklin was the New York, Ontario & Western Railway. The O&W had a creamery located along its line at Merrickville where Walter's father delivered cans from the family farm's daily milk bounty. Growing up between the D&H and O&W gave Walter a great appreciation of — and interest in — railroads in general, and Delaware-Otsego county railroading in particular. Mr. Nuelle, by the way, had been president of the O&W before going to the D&H in 1938.

ACKNOWLEDGEMENTS

Afton Historical Society
Afton (Town) Historian
   Charles Decker
Robert Arrandale
Bainbridge Historical Museum
   Gary Darling
   Mary Drachler
   Ernest Whittaker
   John Bates
Edward P. Baumgardner (*)
Paul Beck
Charles A. Bilby
Joe Boyd (*)
Bridge Line Historical Society
Broome County Historical Society
   Gerald Smith and Monica
Broome County Public Library
Fred Cannistra, Jennison Power
   Station caretaker
Tom Clough
Cobleskill Historical Society
   Peter Bent
   Karen Wilson
Cobleskill Library
   Richard Churchill
Robert F. Collins (*)
Robert (Fagan) Collins
Clyde R. Conrow (*)
Lambert D. Cook (*)
Gerald Coyne
Elise D'Andrea
Paul D'Andrea
Steve Davis
William Davis

Depot Square Publishing
   John W. Hudson, II
   Suzanne C. Hudson
Michael Elwood
Esperance Museum
   Ken Jones
Walt Forsythe
Tim Frederick
Jim Georges
Al Gorney
Barry Gottshall
Greater Oneonta Historical Society
   Bob Brzozowski
   Tom Heitz
John M. Ham
Hamilton Public Library
   Barb Coger, Director
   Sandy Crumb, Assistant Director
Jeff Handy
Bob Harris
William M. Hayes (*)
David Haynes
George Hockaday (*)
Jean and Howard Hontz
H. J. Humphrey (*)
Jack Humphrey
Todd Humphrey
Howe Caverns, Inc. and Cave House
   Museum of Mining & Geology
   Robert Holt, General Manager
   Shane Jones, Tour Guide
   Richard Nethaway, Curator
   Sara Pratt, Tour Guide
   Guy Schiavone, Tour Guide

Joseph B. Radez Elementary School
   (Richmondville)
   Laura Gagnon, Librarian
John Krause (*)
Leatherstocking Chapter, NRHS
   Jim Loudon
Len Kilian
Ernie Mann
Robert E. Mohowski
Jack Nagle
National Archives & Records
   Administration
   David A. Pfeiffer
Harold Nozak
Oneida City School District
   Gary Hoole
   LeAnn Youngcrans
Oneida Public Library
   Tom Murray
Otego Historical Society
   Carol Beckman (*)
Richard F. Palmer
Melissa Patterson
Brad Peterson
John Pickett
Jim Purdy
Walter G. Rich (*)
Richmondville Historical Society
   Ann Lape
   Harold Loder
   Dennis Shaw
   Joan Sondergaard
Scott Roland
Joan and Jim Royston

Jim Shaughnessy
Sidney Historical Association
   Graydon Ballard
Lester A. Sittler, Esq.
Henry Sollman (*)
Dean Splittgerber
Susquehanna Valley Chapter, NRHS
   Bob Pastorkey
Allen Bruce Tracy
Herbert V. Trice
Tunnel Historian
   Pam Brown
Unadilla Historical Association
   Polly Judd, Town/Village Historian
   Charles Reichardt
Unadilla Valley Railway Historical
   Society
   George Wolfangle
Utica & Mohawk Valley Chapter,
   NRHS
Vestal Public Library
George E. Votava (*)
John V. Weber
Worcester Historical Society
   Marilyn DuFresne
   Larry DeLong
   Gynger O'Connor
Worcester—White House Inn
William S. Young

(*) Deceased

Uncredited images are from the Author's
collection or are his original creations.

John and Sue Hudson of Depot Square Publishing (www.depotsquarepublishing.com) edited and amplified the manuscript. They provided design and layout, digital improvement of most images, and production. Tom Turner, of Seaber-Turner Associates, provided technical assistance and manufacturing oversight at Jostens, Inc., Clarksville, TN.

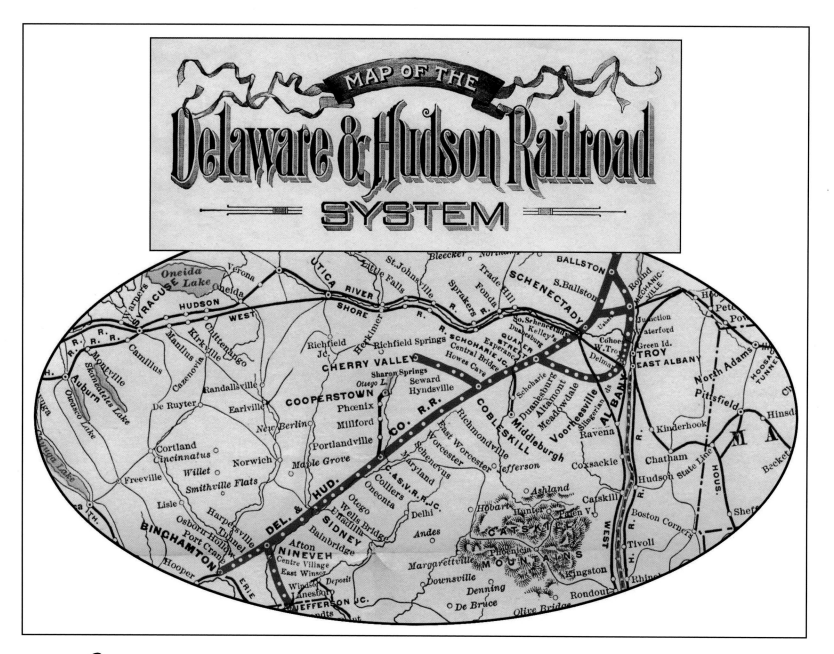

As shown in the map above, the Susquehanna Division of the Delaware & Hudson Railroad extended from Albany and Schenectady, NY southwest to Binghamton. This route is presently the property of CPRail, which operates it as their Mainline Freight Subdivision of the Northeast United States Division.

PREFACE

Shortly before his death on August 19, 2009, Don Hewitt—creator of television's popular news documentary show, 60 Minutes—was asked to what he attributed the show's success. Hewitt responded, "That's easy. I can answer that question using only four words: tell people a story. People love having a story told to them."

Roads, Rivers, and Rails is a story I am pleased to tell you. But first I want to inform you that I am a Baby Boomer, a part of the nation's populace who were born shortly after the cessation of World War II hostilities. I am equally pleased to admit to you that I am a member of a sub-section of Boomers known as "Sunday Drivers." No, this is not the old fogies whose foot can't seem to find the accelerator, but a person who grew up by enjoying a Sunday afternoon drive through the countryside.

During the 1950s, a Sunday drive in the Taibi household almost always followed a 1 PM dinner, and then a quick nap. After Dad finished "resting his eyes" he would announce, "Who wants to go for a ride?" Mom, Rich (my brother), or I never ever replied in the affirmative or negative, we all just headed for the jalopy, which was—depending on the era—a golden-tan Nash sedan, or a jet black Pontiac coupe or sedan. A two-tone, four-door 1956 Plymouth Belvidere, the latter employing a push-button automatic transmission selector on the dash, came next. This was our first car with only two pedals. In no way could it be called a "jalopy." My brother described it best: it was "snazzy." He and I had two good reasons why we liked going on a Sunday drive, both of which had nothing to do with never knowing which direction Dad was going to point the car. The mystery of our "destination" was part of the lure of the ride. I always felt Dad never really pre-planned an itinerary; he just drove along a spontaneous route letting his compass guide our path. (Dad always equipped his cars with a dash-mounted compass. He used to say that folks who had a St. Christopher's medal dangling from the rear view mirror knew where they were going, and by employing his compass, so did he!)

Living in Uniondale, Long Island, and depending on the season, we might head over to Eisenhower Park or Jones Beach. If Dad had enough money for gas—which was about 18 cents a gallon then—maybe he would point the hood ornament due east and head for the "country"—

ABOVE LEFT: *John S. Taibi, 9th Armored Division, 73rd Field Artillery forward observer, prisoner of war, and father.* ABOVE: *Dad with his nearly-new 1956 Plymouth Belvidere in Brentwood, NY during summer, 1956.* BELOW LEFT: *The author in 1947, Springfield Gardens, NY.*

Suffolk County. Some Sundays we'd cruise along Sunrise Highway visiting model homes that were being sold in post-war Levittown-sized developments. At other times we would watch the pine barrens slip by as we toured the then unpopulated areas where housing projects such as Robin Hill, Sunset Village, or Charter Oaks would blossom areas of Brentwood into World War II veteran neighborhoods. We eventually moved into a Robin Hill home when Dad's Post Office Department salary couldn't keep us in the home he had built in Uniondale.

But, no matter where we went on those Sunday jaunts, it always seemed we did two things, which curiously enough were the Taibi brothers' favorites. We'd stop for gas—where the smell of leaded gasoline was a treat for our nostrils—followed by a stop at a Carvel Ice Cream stand where a vanilla cone satisfied the taste buds and punctuated the end of a perfect day. I still like vanilla ice cream best.

ABOVE: *Margaret Orlicky Taibi—Mom—with the Belvidere.* BELOW: *John (left) and Richard Taibi. Both photographs were taken at the Bayard Cutting Arboretum in Great River, NY on Easter Sunday, April 1, 1956.*

Sunday drives started to become a thing of the past about 1960. Rich and I were teenagers then, preferring studying and playing baseball—respectively—as opposed to riding around the countryside in Dad's snazzy turquoise and white Plymouth. I suppose he may have still wanted to drive us around in that great car but the fact was he just could not afford to do so anymore. Janice—a sister—came along the same year as the Plymouth. And there was always the mortgage to pay for our house at 210 Claywood Drive in Brentwood, Long Island.

When I got my driver's license in 1964, I occasionally went out on a Sunday drive all by myself, or sometimes with a girlfriend, but never again with Dad behind the wheel. For the Taibi family, Sunday drives—much like attending church—had become a thing of the past. Carvel ice cream, however, was still a staple in the Taibi diet. For nearly forty-five years my desire to drive around willy-nilly Sunday-style lay dormant. My love of doing so, however, never died. It just took maturity, age, and an understanding of a good story's components to awaken the Sunday drive mentality from dormancy. But, before that happened, I drove many miles—wearing out many cars—before realizing that I had been missing the fun of a "Sunday" drive.

Suspending Sunday drives wasn't my fault entirely. There was a four-year hitch in the military, a marriage and children (several of both) and, despite the fact that I was a railroad photo bum, I continually used the road only as a means to get to work or to the next picture location. Getting there, I had forgotten, was supposed to be part of the fun. I was only using the roads—not enjoying them.

Roads had changed though; so had the number of cars using them. Randomly meandering on the highways of the '70s, '80s, and '90s had devolved into a hectic, high-pressure, and expensive affair. Interstate and super highways eased the pain of motoring somewhat, but in using them, the "back roads," as Dad called them, were forsaken. The old main roads of Long Island Avenue and Sunrise Highway on Long Island were usurped by the Long Island Expressway, the nation's longest parking lot! In nearby upstate, Route 17, the original, was replaced by Route 17, the "Quickway." Routes 9 on both sides of the Hudson River were laid waste by the Thomas E. Dewey Thruway.

As my years wore on, a degree of sentimentality for the good old days began to settle into my motoring consciousness. I suppose (and hope) that it is common for older folks to reminisce about their youthful experiences and desire to attain once again—and relive—the joys of those earlier years. For me, this reawakening, that desire to drive the "old roads," occurred during 2008, my 61st year.

I first set tire to asphalt on New York State Route 7 during February 1969. I was home on leave after a tour of duty in Vietnam and was with a fellow rail fan when we came upon Oneonta. We had our sights set on photographing American Locomotive Company (ALCo) diesels leading Delaware & Hudson Railroad freight trains. So Oneonta—the Susquehanna Division headquarters city—was a natural starting point. The first train our cameras encountered, though, was led by three (Electro-Motive Company) SD-45s (Nos. 801-803) arriving from the north. I have enjoyed seeing SD-45s in action ever since. It would take quite a few years to notice that I enjoyed Route 7, too.

Sporadically, over the years I visited other D&H photographer hangouts, such as Brooker Hollow and Pony Farm roads, Harpursville Trestle, Nineveh Junction, and Delanson. All were conveniently situated adjacent to Route 7 or via a short drive down an intersecting road. This was during the time when Route 7 was still King of the Road, before Interstate 88 was completed in 1989. Route 7 was the thoroughfare that made it possible to chase—and photograph—D&H trains during these early years. It was quite simply a means towards that end.

By the time I returned to Oneonta in 2008, Interstate 88 was the new King of the Road. Clocking 65 mph or more, autos and tractor trailers screamed non-stop by old Route 7 communities, such as Sanitaria Springs, Bainbridge, Unadilla, Schenevus, Worcester, and Richmondville! There were, however, exits for all these villages that sat squarely abreast of the "old" road. Frankly, it is a good thing that the Senator Warren M. Anderson Expressway (I-88) had been built because

On February 18, 1974, I stood upon the Brooker Hollow Road highway bridge for the first time and photographed this southbound D&H manifest train that was being led by three ALCo C-628 locomotives. At the time, I did not know that the bridge was built in 1924 to eliminate a grade crossing; that the cleft in the background was where the Cobleskill and Schenevus creeks got their start. Cobles Kill flowed north; Schenevus, south. This train will follow Schenevus Creek all the way to Colliersville where the creek will deposit its water into the Susquehanna River. At the time of this writing (2011) the old Brooker Hollow Road bridge is being replaced by a new span.

BELOW: *Long before Interstate 88 was a twinkle in New York State's eye, Route 7 curved through Richmondville's business district. At this four corners, if you were going to Summit, NY, you turned right. Headed for the railroad depot? Turn left. I-88 changed the roadways to both places. RICHMONDVILLE HISTORICAL SOCIETY. LOWER RIGHT: Cobleskill Creek flows through this glen not far from its source.* COBLESKILL HISTORICAL SOCIETY.

that old scenic Route 7 which passed through each village, could never support the number of vehicles that now traveled upon the "new" road.

Because human beings prefer things they are familiar with, I remained loyal to Route 7. Maybe that was because of earlier exploits that the "old road" had made possible. Maybe it was because the Interstate was too much of an "urban" road. Whatever the reason, Route 7 was like a comfortable pair of shoes; it felt just right.

Little by little I renewed my acquaintance with Route 7 as it wended its way out of Schenectady County and into Schoharie, then on through the counties of Otsego, Delaware, Chenango, and Broome. From the magnificent high Helderberg area in the east to the junction of the Chenango and Susquehanna rivers at Binghamton, the road had descended to Schoharie Creek then inched its way up in elevation until it encountered Dante—between West Richmondville and East Worcester—where the Hudson River and Chesapeake Bay watersheds went their separate way. From there, Cobleskill Creek flowed eastward, while Schenevus Creek went west. Only a few steps off the shoulder of Route 7 a person could straddle each creek as it rose from its birthplace and watch as water flowed to the Susquehanna or Hudson, both ultimately ending up in the Atlantic Ocean.

From Dante it was downgrade all the way to Broome County. Along the way, the old road kept company with Schenevus Creek until it emptied into a fledgling Susquehanna River at Colliersville, but by the time the Susquehanna reached into Delaware County it had matured into one of America's wonderful rivers. The addition of the Unadilla's water played an important role in the Susquehanna's success. Yet, Route 7 remained true to its two-lane birthright.

Through Chenango County, the old road and the mighty river continued to hold hands as they coursed through a widening and fertile valley, with the railroad crossing and re-crossing the river a handful of times. When Broome County was reached at Nineveh, however, the twosome bid each other *au revoir*. The waterway continued on its descending course, while the highway ran headlong into Belden Hill where a steep ascent had to be undertaken. Both the river and the road would meet up once again at Binghamton, the Parlor City, with Route 7 getting there in fifty fewer miles.

For the entire distance from Schenectady to Binghamton, Route 7 stayed mostly in close proximity to the railroad. It is said that proximity helps to make hearts grow fonder so it must be true that the highway and the railway were deeply in love.

They ran side-by-side, the road crossing over the rails and vice versa, so that the two transportation systems appeared to be frolicking just as a human couple does once struck by Cupid's arrow. While the waterway vied for the highway's affections it abandoned the roadway at Nineveh. Not so with the railway. It remained true to the highway's path, hopefully not just for saving fifty miles distance but to continue courtship with the friend it got to know after miles of traveling together.

As I became familiar with Route 7's territory once again, I realized that traveling upon its macadam path was made more enjoyable because of four-lane Interstate 88 that had usurped the former highway's existence. Commercial trucking, families going on vacation, employees going to work, and shoppers heading to the mall all used the interstate highway, which left old Route 7 for local travel, sightseeing, and "Sunday driving." And certainly Route 7 was handier for taking train pictures too. Sure, you could see trains from I-88, but from the old road it was a singular experience. You could almost touch the trains. They were so close you could smell their exhaust; hear the squeal of steel on steel on a super-elevated curve or that distinctive sound of a flat spot on a wheel; and feel the earth literally vibrate to the cadence of their horsepower and weight. Proximity made that possible.

In a manner similar to the way small creeks contribute water to the Cobleskill, Schenevus, and Susquehanna, lesser roads intersecting with Route 7 made it possible to more completely enjoy the presence of the railroad. Brooker Hollow Road (East Worcester), Tannery Road (Schenevus), Pony Farm Road (Oneonta), and Tunnel Road (near Sanitaria Springs) all delivered a Route 7 traveler to a more up-close-and-personal vantage point where train watching could be more fully appreciated. Conversely, being a great distance from the railroad could also be enjoyable too. Standing atop the outcroppings of Table Rocks, high above Route 7's West End in Oneonta, provided an extraordinary vista. From there, the relationship of the Susquehanna River, Route 7, and the D&H railroad could best be discerned, examined, and contemplated by the viewer.

Route 7 today, along with its water and rail-riding neighbors, is a wonderful Sunday — or any day for that matter — driving experience. You do not have to be a Baby Boomer to appreciate the great sights, sounds, architecture, and history that this New York State roadway can provide. All you need is an appreciation of Americana and you will marvel at how these Roads, Rivers, and Rails can entertain and provide enjoyment throughout their 140-mile journey down a wonderful transportation corridor.

Let me take you for a drive along New York State Route 7 from Albany and Schenectady to Binghamton. I'll drive; you can ride shotgun. Together, we'll admire the creeks and river, keep an eye peeled for trains on the railroad, and enjoy the historic and interesting thoroughfare that Route 7 still is today. If you haven't participated in an old fashioned auto tour recently, just turn the page for the experience to begin.

Hey, does anyone know where the nearest ice cream stand is?

From Route 7 in Schenevus, Tannery Road is a side street that leads to the nearby railroad, making it easy for both to keep in touch — and cameramen to ply their trade. Until 1964, old Delaware & Hudson track No. 2 (earlier, No. 4) ran to the right of this crossing gate at Tannery Road. Here, train 930 with General Electric C40-9W No. 9219 on the head end splits the crossing gates with a freight on the drawbar on June 18, 2010.

High above Oneonta's West End, Table Rocks provides a platform to contemplate and enjoy a geological setting that took millions of years to create. Standing upon this stage of rock, the railroad (center) can be discerned alongside the four-lane Interstate 88. The Susquehanna River lies hidden beyond the copse of trees at left while Route 7 passes at the base of this geologic formation. Through this scenic valley runs our "Roads, Rivers, and Rails."

INTRODUCTION

Before we hit the road, I thought it may be important to provide you with historical information regarding the transportation corridor that we will be following from Albany-Schenectady (New York's Capital District) to Binghamton. There will be much more to tell you along the way, but this will provide you with insight as to how the "Roads, Rivers, and Rails" of today came into existence.

Suffice it to say that our good old Earth has undergone a myriad of changes over the last few billion years as it evolved into the planet we occupy today. While a vast number of books have told the story of the evolution of our Earth—and this narrative is not intended to revisit or make short shrift of those works—it is not our intention to delve into that arena in depth here. Rather it is important to say that New York State has been the recipient of its own share of that change in the region covered in this tale. Upheavals in the Earth's crust spawned majestic mountains of the Catskills and Adirondacks while glaciers carved deep scars in the ground leaving behind drumlins, kames, moraines, and the beautiful deep valleys that became the Finger Lakes. Even the courses of our major rivers, such as the Susquehanna, have been completely changed from whence they started.

So what did the Albany & Susquehanna founders face when they began to survey and construct the fledgling railroad? Desiring to build from Albany to Binghamton, the obstacles faced included the Helderberg Mountains, the northeast shoulder of the Catskills, the high plateau around Quaker Street, and the breathtaking hills surrounding Richmondville among others.

The Susquehanna itself, or rather what we refer to today as the North Branch of the Susquehanna, was once much different in origin and destination. It formerly rose in the Adirondacks and emptied into the Mississippi River. The continual reshaping of the topography of central New York created the Mohawk River which forever severed the original headwaters of the Susque-

Susquehanna River at Bridge

During the Nineteenth Century, sailing and rowing in one's Sunday-finest couture were a form of recreation upon the placid water of the Susquehanna River. Ladies wore dresses and fashionable hats while men donned suits, ties and straw "boaters." Today, sail is no more, but a yearly rowing regatta still takes place. This view is from Oneonta's old Main Street bridge. GREATER ONEONTA HISTORICAL SOCIETY COLLECTION.

hanna from the Adirondacks and moved them south of the Mohawk Valley. Now, the Susquehanna flowed into what eventually became the Atlantic Ocean—formed after the Susquehanna—making this one of the oldest rivers in the world.

With the departure of all continental ice, the Susquehanna assumed its present course with its source now located at Otsego Lake in Cooperstown. As it traveled south, the river picked up water from local creeks, such that it began to grow in size. Of note were Schenevus Creek which joined at Colliersville and the Unadilla River which emptied into the Susquehanna at Sidney. Keep in mind that when all this happened, none of these names had yet been given. South of Sidney, NY,

The thin layer in this image is known as Manlius Limestone, a very fine-grained sedimentary rock. The thick coarse layers are called the Coeymans Formation; they are infused with quartz sand. Strata such as this took millions of years to build. Limestone is calcium carbonate, created by adding layer upon layer of fossils to ocean or stream beds. This photograph comes from the Helderberg Cement Company at Howe's Cave in 1906.
LEN KILIAN COLLECTION.

At Cooperstown, the Susquehanna River (foreground) rises from Otsego Lake (beyond) to begin its 444-mile journey to the Atlantic Ocean. The lake is the Leatherstocking Region's "Glimmerglass."

the Susquehanna valley benefitted from the enormous amount of sediment from glacial erosion that had been brought to it by its tributaries, especially the Unadilla.

From its union with Route 7 and the railroad at Colliersville, the Susquehanna descends from 1,180 feet to slightly over 900 feet by the time it diverges from traveling companions at Nineveh. Between the same two locations, Route 7 and the D&H change in elevation by almost the same amount. Later, a railroad would be built south from Nineveh into Pennsylvania, following the course of the Susquehanna, but the A&S did not build this segment.

Of the roads, rivers, and rails pertinent to this story, it is the waterways that are the oldest. Next came the roads, which were made necessary by the presence of humans. It was the Red Men who first located pathways that White men improved into roads. These same men gave names to the waterways and villages important to

this story, some of which have already been mentioned. It was the Iroquois Indian tribe, *Susquehannock*, that gave its name to the river.

Footpaths along waterways and overland between villages were the earliest form of roads; the main artery for commerce was the rivers. Villages conducted business with only their nearest neighbors. By the end of the Eighteenth Century, foot, horse, and wagon travel had developed to such a degree that turnpikes were laid out and constructed. The earliest relating to this story was the First Great Western Turnpike (1799) that connected Albany with Cherry Valley, which at that time, was an important interior business center and a crossroad for commerce. Then, within a dozen years, came the Troy & Schenectady (1802), Schoharie (Schoharie and Schenec-

tady, 1807), Unadilla (1806), Otsego & Broome (1807), and Schoharie & Duanesburg (1808) turnpikes. The Troy Turnpike connected the Collar City with the Vermont state line. All of these roads played a part in developing the modern Route 7. New York State helped in the development of Route 7, too, but years of fine-tuning the route's classification varied the destination of Route 7's northern end.

At the beginning of the Twentieth Century, New York State took over the maintenance of its early highway system. In 1909, New York's Highway Law went into effect. It lumped together the early connecting roads between Binghamton and Albany and designated this amalgamation as NY State Route 7, with Route 7A diverging off the main route at Duanesburg, terminat-

In the early Twentieth Century, riding along Route 7 in a convertible near Sidney (below right) or roughing it on a bicycle outside of Worcester was a dusty affair for travelers. New York State began to improve the highway with concrete and macadam in the late 1920s and continued to do so throughout the 1930s. During that period, the route was temporarily renumbered to "9" as reflected on the telephone pole (right) located at the corner of North Grand Street and Route 9 (Main Street) in Cobleskill.

SIDNEY HISTORICAL ASSOCIATION

ROADS, RIVERS, AND RAILS

LEFT: *At one point in its history, the Cherry Valley Turnpike had been designated by New York State as Route 7. This section of highway, built as the Cherry Valley Cut-Off, has always been a part of US 20. Although the highway sign in the distance directs motorists to turn right to gain Cherry Valley, the community is actually to the left. The bridge was a part of the D&H's Cherry Valley Branch, which at the time the cut-off was constructed had already ceased operations.*

ABOVE AND LEFT: *The passage of time is reflected in these images of Route 7 in downtown Unadilla, NY in the 1930-1940s and 2010. Despite the different eras, many of the stores appearing in the older image are now restored, either hosting new businesses or awaiting new occupants. Note the image at left advertises such name brands as Coca-Cola, Bendix home laundry, Philco electronics, Gulf Oil and Canada Dry's Spur Cola which sold for just 5¢ per bottle.*

LEFT, UNADILLA HISTORICAL ASSOCIATION.

ing in Schenectady. To continue on to Vermont, New York State routes 42 and 22 connected Schenectady to Troy, and Troy with the state line near Hoosick.

When New York first began to place signs along its roadways in 1924, the preceding route was changed from an Albany destination to include Route 7A and NY State Route 2 (Latham-Troy) and was re-designated as NY State Route 9. This was done so that the number coincided with Vermont's Route 9. Earlier, New York had combined what had been the First (along with the Second and Third) Great Western Turnpike(s) (Cazenovia-Albany) with the Rensselaer & Columbia (Albany-Massachusetts state line) and designated that roadway as NY State Route 20. But, when the state re-named Route 7 to 9 it also changed Route 20 to Route 5 so that it would become a part of the Yellowstone Trail.

The following year, 1925, the state reconsidered its Route 5 designation and re-assigned that number to the more northerly Seneca Turnpike and then gave the Cazenovia-Massachusetts road the number 7. The following year, the national highway numbering system, which was also being developed, came into play and used similar numbers for different routes. This confused New York's roadway number system. The federal numbering system dictated that its US east-west roads would be even numbered, while US north-south roads would be odd numbered. Consequently, during 1926 the Cazenovia-Massachusetts New York State Route 7 was changed to United States Route 20.

Because there was some number duplication between NY and US highway numbering, the Binghamton-Vermont road was also changed, in 1927, from NY State Route 9 to NY State Route 7. This was done primarily to minimize any confusion between NY Route 9 and US Route 9 that ran north-south in the Hudson River valley. At this same time, the roadway connecting Binghamton with the Pennsylvania state line was also designated as the southern end of NY State Route 7.

During the 1930s, state engineers realigned portions of Route 7. At some locations the improved highway received new tangent sections so that automobiles would not have to negotiate endless curves. These cast-aside sections of Route 7 are still used today as local roads.

Some examples of them are Pearl Street Extension in Bainbridge, Beiby Road near Otego, and Stevens Road between Maryland and Schenevus. Improving Route 7's alignment — and protecting its motorists — also caused several grade crossings with the railroad to be eliminated by erecting new overpasses. The Route 7 bridges over the railroad both north and south of Unadilla are examples of Route 7's new crossovers of the railroad undertaken during this same period.

By the end of the Twentieth Century's fourth decade Route 7 had finally reached its modern form from Pennsylvania through New York State to Vermont.

While it is the modern Route 7 that we will be following in this story, the ancestral segments of the route will also be explored in this tale. Much like the Susquehanna and the lesser waterways, Route 7 has been shaped, defined, and refined in its own way. The process took private individuals and state/federal managers only a little over one hundred years to accomplish, whereas the formation of the route's paralleling waterways by tectonic and glacial forces took billions of years. The railroads relating to this story were brought to fruition in an even speedier manner, beginning on April 19, 1851 when the Articles of Association incorporating the Albany & Susquehanna Railroad were filed with the legislature. That same day, Edward C. Delavan was elected as the road's first president.

The A&SRR was allowed to form under Chapter 140 of New York State's Laws of 1850. It was the terms of this Chapter with which all of New York's future railroads had to comply. Doing so meant that the railroad would be able to solicit construction aid from the townships through which it desired to pass. It was this aid from local municipalities, along with the sale of stocks and bonds, and maybe even financial aid from the state, that allowed construction of a road to commence. While some railroads, such as the New York & Oswego Midland, determined their route by the availability of municipal aid, such was not the case with the A&S. Its sights were set on running directly from Albany to Binghamton from the outset. In doing so it connected Albany with the developing west via the New York & Erie Railroad (reorganized as the Erie Railroad in 1860) thereby bring-

ing continued and increased prosperity to Albany.

By 1870, $2,870,000 in state and municipal aid had been pledged or obtained by the A&S (see table on Page *xii*). Remember, this total of nearly 3 million dollars was in Nineteenth Century currency. That would be substantially higher in today's money. It was a big investment then, especially for smaller communities that may have wondered how their aid to a fledgling railroad might increase their well-being. The decade prior to Chapter 140 of the Laws of 1850, Schenectady desired to connect itself with Binghamton by a similar route to that of the A&S below Quaker Street. But, the future community that "lights and hauls the world" — a reference to Schenectady's General Electric and American Locomotive companies — could not finance the road's construction with only private capital. Chapter 140 of the Laws of 1850 made it more feasible for the A&S to do so. Yet, it got off to a rocky start, too. It was not until six years after the A&S was incorporated that surveying and construction commenced. It took another six years or more for the above townships to agree to provide the road construction aid via town bonding.

Referring to the list of municipalities that financially aided the A&S, there are several other aspects to note. First, all of the townships and cities were situated along either the ancestral or modern Route 7. Secondly, the one million dollars offered by Albany was only a loan which the railroad — most likely A&S successor Delaware & Hudson Canal Company — repaid. And, thirdly, the amount of construction aid provided by the state showed something that did not happen very often: New York State actually contributing money to construct a railroad.

The reason that New York enacted Chapter 140 of the Laws of 1850 in the first place was so that they would not have to be burdened with monetarily backing the construction of railroads like they did canals. Frankly, the canals were New York's investment; it did not desire to finance competition. So, the New York State legislature purposefully did not support railroads with money, even though the state's political machine did so with enabling legislation, knowing full well that railroads were the wave of the future.

State of New York		1863-67	$750,000 (donation)
Albany County	Albany	1865	1,000,000 (loan repaid)
Broome County	Binghamton	1867	50,000
	Colesville	1858	50,000
Chenango County	Afton	1864	30,000
	Bainbridge	1865	30,000
Delaware County	Davenport	1865	100,000
	Harpersfield	1870	100,000
	Sidney	1869	50,000
Otsego County	Decatur	1857	20,000
	Maryland	1862	70,000
	Milford	1862	60,000
	Oneonta	1862	70,000
	Otego	1862	70,000
	Unadilla	1862	70,000
	Westford	1862	30,000
	Worcester	1862	65,000
Schenectady County	Duanesburg	1862	30,000
Schoharie County	Cobleskill	1862	60,000
	Esperance	1862	30,000
	Richmondville	1862	50,000
	Schoharie	1864	30,000
	Seward	1864	30,000
	Summit	1862	25,000
Total			**$2,870,000**

The three-quarters of a million dollars the A&S received from the state was the second largest sum contributed to railroads. The largest amount was $3,015,000 to aid the New York & Erie Railroad and the Erie had to beg for every dollar they received over many years. Only thirteen other railroads ever received financial aid from New York; three of which later became properties of the D&HCCo as would the A&S itself.

On November 17, 1857, Cobleskill native Joseph H. Ramsey (shown at right) was elected vice-president of the Albany & Susquehanna Railroad, and it was due to the efforts of this man that the surveying and construction of the road finally got under way. Seven years later, on September 9, 1864, he became the fifth president of the A&S. Not only had he ascended to the road's top position, he was its moving and kindred spirit. "For more than ten years past he has haunted the capitol from the beginning to the close of every session converting senators and assemblymen until the project of granting aid to the A&S became known as Ramsey's bills." (*Albany Evening Journal*, August 9, 1869.)

Under the new president's guidance—and arm twisting—construction of the railroad progressed so that it could be opened for business from Albany to Central Bridge on September 16, 1863. In 1865, the A&S reached Cobleskill on January 2; Richmondville, June 1; Worcester, July 17; Schenevus, August 7; and Oneonta, August 28. The following year saw Otego obtaining service on January 23; Unadilla, March 21; and, lastly, Sidney on October 22, 1866. The A&S continued to steadily push toward their ultimate goal of Binghamton in 1867, completing the line to Bainbridge on July 10; Afton, November 11 and Harpursville, on Christmas Day. But it was not until January 14, 1869 that the prize, the "Parlor City" itself, was finally reached.

The reason that it took a little over one year to finish the line between Harpursville and Binghamton was because of the need to excavate a 2,260-foot tunnel at the top of Belden Hill. When the Susquehanna River wisely turned to the south at Nineveh, Route 7 and the A&S said good-bye and struck out directly into the face of the geologic obstacle; the road took a more severe uphill path than the railroad. The A&S temporarily vacated the side of the road to circle around the hill in order to lessen the grade by adding distance. It caught up with the road on the other side of the hill, but not before cresting the grade inside of the tunnel.

On the day of the railroad's completion, another noteworthy event took place—the tri-transportation corridor extending from Albany to Binghamton that included roads, rivers, and now the railroad, became united in bringing commerce and prosperity to all of the communities along the route. All of a sudden, the money that the municipalities had provided in construction aid was looked upon in a favorable

The Albany & Susquehanna Railroad was built utilizing a six-foot broad gauge so that it could better effect interchange with the Erie Railroad at Binghamton, NY. Near Richmondville an early locomotive has tip-toed onto a timber trestle along the newly constructed line to have its picture taken. RICHMONDVILLE HISTORICAL SOCIETY COLLECTION.

light. It was President Ramsey's time to bask in the sunshine of success as it was he more than any other person who pushed the A&S to completion. If that was not enough to please the president, he could look to other accomplishments as well.

Ramsey entered into a contract with the Delaware & Hudson Canal Company—a formidable producer and shipper of coal from Pennsylvania's Lackawanna Valley—on February 14, 1866 to haul that company's coal to Albany upon the completion of the A&S. Coal was the most demanded commodity, being much needed by residents and industry lying along a newly built railroad; soon they would have it in abundance. President Ramsey was also pleased in knowing that the Cooperstown & Susquehanna Valley Railroad would soon be opening (on July 14, 1869), and that a revitalized Schenectady & Susquehanna Railroad was in the process of forming and would do so by the end of 1869. Also under con-

struction was the Cherry Valley, Sharon & Albany Railroad that had begun life on April 10, 1860 as the Cherry Valley & Sprakers Railroad then reorganized as the Cherry Valley & Mohawk River Railroad on July 15, 1868, receiving its final moniker on April 10, 1869. Two other roads had attached themselves to the coattails of the A&S in Schoharie County. They were the Schoharie Valley and Middleburgh & Schoharie railroads that had joined forces to provide service to their namesake county and villages when they assumed operation on January 4, 1867 and October 19, 1868, respectively.

The C&SV carried passengers to and from the A&S via Cooperstown Junction near Colliersville, while the S&S line would eventually connect the A&S at Quaker Street with Schenectady—after a change of name to the Schenectady & Duanesburg Railroad—during 1873. The CVS&A began operation on June 15, 1870, connecting Cherry Valley to the A&S at Cobleskill, and the

combined SVRR and M&SRR conducted passenger and freight interchange with the A&S at Schoharie Junction. All but the M&S would become properties of the D&H at a point in the future.

Ramsey could also look forward to the opening of the New York & Oswego Midland Railroad (June 15, 1870) whose Oswego to Sidney Plains segment intersected the A&S at the latter location. All of this railroad construction and completion was keenly watched and applauded, and was all undertaken and encouraged by the Albany & Susquehanna's president. There was much for him to be proud of. But, just when he should have been celebrating, he found himself in the midst of what we would call today a "hostile takeover." Ramsey's problem arose because he had done too good of a job. He had developed his railroad into such a promising financial property, even before its completion, that others desired to acquire it. The "others" were Jay Gould and Jim Fisk. What happened next has been written about, discussed, and analyzed to such a degree that it has become a chapter in the lore of nineteenth century railroading. It began with stock acquisition and manipulation, and ended in an all-out brouhaha and a Hollywood movie.

Gould and Fisk had recently gained control of the Erie Railroad, and during 1868 decided that the Albany & Susquehanna Railroad would make a nice addition to their growing railroad portfolio. So, they set about purchasing stock in the company to gain financial control. At the same time men were successfully placed on the railroad's board of directors that were sympathetic to Gould and Fisk. One of these men was Cobleskill banker Charles Courter. This was a particular irritation to President Ramsey since he hailed from Cobleskill, too. A proxy fight ensued. So did legal wrangling and courtroom shenanigans, which resulted in both factions at one point having been appointed receivers of the property by two different courts. While the consensus favored Ramsey and the A&S, Gould and Fisk were not about to give up without a fight, and a fight was what resulted.

On August 6, 1869, Fisk and Courter sent out messages to the officers and employees of the A&S that the

LEFT: *The completion of a 2,260-foot tunnel under the summit of Belden Hill allowed the Albany & Susquehanna Railroad to open its line to Binghamton on January 14, 1869. This view shows the tunnel's south end with a section-man's residence situated between the portal and a double-bladed upper quadrant signal mast.* A. BRUCE TRACY COLLECTION.

*As the Albany & Susquehanna Railroad was completed in a southwest direction, mostly large wooden board-and-batten combination stations, such as Bainbridge (*LEFT*) were erected. At three locations, however, more substantial stone depots were built. Cobleskill (*ABOVE*) was one of those locations, reflecting the fact that President Ramsey was a native of that community.* LEFT, BAINBRIDGE HISTORICAL SOCIETY COLLECTION. ABOVE, ROBERT HOLT COLLECTION.

Supreme Court in New York City had duly appointed them receivers of the line. That evening, A&S Superintendent Van Valkenburgh wired his officers and employees that R. H. Pruyn—who was loyal to the railroad—had been first appointed the line's receiver by Albany Judge Peckham, and that the office and books of the road were in Pruyn's possession.

For the next few days, each side attempted to reinforce their position through legal means, but physical action occurred that only served to escalate the bitterness felt by both factions. A&S men threw Erie men out of the Albany offices, and Erie men removed an A&S crew from an engine in Binghamton. Erie loyalists at Binghamton, it seemed, controlled that portion of the railroad, while men loyal to the A&S reigned supreme on the northern end of the line.

Finally, Van Valkenburgh had had enough. He telegraphed all stations on the line and instructed the agents to gather men to protect the depot and the railroad. "You are to remain on duty until further advised," he instructed. Then, he directed Master Mechanic R. C. Blackall to take a special train southward to meet, and overpower, any persons loyal to the Erie.

On August 9, Blackall's train highballed south with about 400 men. At Bainbridge they waylaid a northward trainload of Erie men and Broome County sheriffs, and quickly turned the chaos into an A&S victory. Then, the loyal train load of A&S men continued south as far as Harpursville where they learned what their adversaries were up to. Blackall telegraphed Van Valkenburgh that "Erie folks are preparing to move upon us. They have the militia with them." Without awaiting a reply from the superintendent, the A&S train cautiously headed southward through the night.

On Tuesday, August 10, 1869, a train loaded with 850 Erie men had come up from Binghamton and was positioned at the south portal of the A&S tunnel at the top of Belden Hill. Arriving at the north portal was Blackall's train. Late that day, the Erie train proceeded through the tunnel, and on a slight curve beyond the north portal, their train met that of the A&S. Although the A&S engine derailed in the ensuing collision with the Erie engine, loyalists of the road succeeded in scattering the Erie men back through the tunnel and up into the hillsides. When darkness came, Blackall—with his engine re-railed—proceeded through the tunnel to accost the enemy anew. At the south portal, both sides again fought with fists, clubs, and revolvers. But, this time, the fight was broken up by a detachment of the state militia that had been called out by Broome County officials to break up the insurrection. At this turn of events, Blackall's train and men retreated through the tunnel and, at Harpursville station once again, he telegraphed Van Valkenburgh stating that, "The Governor has charge of the road."

Peace returned to Belden Hill, but who would take possession of the line still remained to be settled. Towards that end, New York State Governor John Hoffman installed General James McQuade in charge of the road, as superintendent, and Colonel Robert Banks was made executive agent and treasurer. The gover-

At Harpursville depot, Master Mechanic R.C. Blackall telegraphed Superintendent Van Valkenburgh that: "Erie folks are preparing to move upon us." A creamery stands adjacent to the station. Cans of milk were loaded onto milk cars using the small wooden platform that fronts the team siding at the creamery. A. Bruce Tracy collection.

nor hoped that the ownership of the road would be resolved at a September 7 board of directors meeting, but all that happened was both Erie and A&S loyalists elected their own separate boards so that nothing had been decided. At that juncture, Governor Hoffman had the state's attorney general institute legal proceedings to end the fight for the A&S by establishing who would control the railroad.

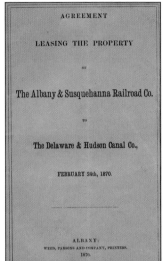

A trial took place in November in Judge Darwin Smith's courtroom in Rochester; in January he handed down his decision. The judge upheld the right of the A&S to remain in the hands of President Ramsey and his officers. It was a bittersweet victory for Joseph H. Ramsey; he and his railroad employees prevailed. The next month, on February 24, 1870, an emotionally fatigued Ramsey and his board leased the A&S in perpetuity to the Delaware & Hudson Canal Company (shown at left). The Albany & Susquehanna Railroad name would not be completely erased from the history books until it was officially merged into the D&H system on July 2, 1945. Fortunately for the D&HCCo, in 1867 it had successfully petitioned New York State to have its charter amended to add railroad operations.

Many years after the Battle of Belden Hill, the fight for control of the railroad was loosely immortalized by a Hollywood movie production based upon an Edna Ferber novel. The 1945 movie *Saratoga Trunk* starred leading man Gary Cooper and starlet Ingrid Bergman. Coop portrayed Superintendent Van Valkenburgh and Master Mechanic Blackall all rolled up into one man—Colonel Clint Maroon—while Bergman played Clio Dulaine, a mostly self-promoting, money-hungry woman in search of her man. Except for its well-known actor and actress, the movie was more a love story than a railroad yarn. In the end, however, Maroon captured Clio's heart, or maybe it was the other way around, but he did save the Saratoga trunk line railroad. It was the only movie in which Ms. Bergman sang.

The D&HCCo received its charter to operate a canal in Pennsylvania on March 13, 1823; in New York, on April 23, 1823. Nine years earlier, its founders, Maurice and William Wurts had acquired considerable acreage in Pennsylvania where they found anthracite or "hard" coal to be in abundance. On October 16, 1828 the 108-mile canal linking the coal field to the Delaware and Hudson rivers, hence the company's name, was opened to commerce. The first loaded coal boats reached the Hudson River port at Rondout (near Kingston, NY) on December 5. There was more to it than that, of course, like a gravity railroad to get the coal from the mines to the boats at Honesdale, PA, but that was how the Delaware & Hudson Canal Company got into the transportation business.

After it went railroading by leasing the A&S, the canal company began refining and improving its new property in much the same manner that four successive

On August 10, 1869, a trainload of Erie supporters stopped at the south end of the A&S tunnel to gather its courage for battle. An A&S scout would have seen them beyond this portal at left. Their train proceeded through the tunnel to meet Blackall's train head on, on the curve just beyond the tunnel's north portal. On this curve (shown below), the Battle of Belden Hill for control of the A&S commenced.

LEFT, LEN KILIAN COLLECTION.

glaciers created the features of the landscape through which it ran. The first thing the canal company did was to standard-gauge the six-foot width trackage that the A&S built to be compatible with its intended connection with the Erie at Binghamton. This change-of-gauge was accomplished by first laying a "third rail," which—in effect—made the railroad temporarily a dual-gauge line, and then removing the wide-gauge rail leaving only the 4-foot 8½-inch standard gauge rail width. All of this work was undertaken during the period 1871-76.

Because the D&HCCo was in the business of mining, transporting, and distributing coal efficiently, it desired to provide its black diamonds by a more direct route to central New York and Albany. Towards that end, it built the Lackawanna & Susquehanna Railroad that connected Nineveh on the old A&S with Erie's Jefferson Railroad at Lanesboro, PA. This line followed the course of the Susquehanna River for its entire distance and was, in effect, a cut-off that bypassed Binghamton. The L&S was put into operation on June 17, 1872.

Further improvements were centralizing the road's shops at Oneonta, double tracking portions of the line: Central Bridge-Richmondville in 1882; Quaker Street to Nineveh in 1895; and Delanson (Quaker Street) to Schenectady in 1908, after acquiring the Schenectady & Duanesburg five years earlier, and then triple-tracking from Schoharie Junction to Delanson (1916), Oneonta to Cooperstown Junction in 1918 (having acquired the Cooperstown & Charlotte Valley Railroad in 1903), and then putting into operation the "Low Grade Line" between Schenevus and Dante (Richmondville Summit) in 1921. Along the way, the D&H purchased the Schoharie Valley Railroad (1906) allowing it to remain an independent operation, and they even modernized their own title. On April 28, 1899, by an Act of New York's legislature, the Delaware & Hudson Canal Company was allowed to change its name to the Delaware & Hudson Company, and was permitted to "lease, discontinue, or sell its canal." It did the latter on June 13, 1899 when it sold the canal to S. D. Coykendall (president of the Cornell Steamboat Company) for $10,000. The D&HCo, however, remained in the railroad business until acquired by the Guilford railroad system eighty-five years later. The coal business petered out long before the company was sold; so did steam locomotives, giving way completely to diesels in 1953. Binghamton saw its last steam engine the previous year.

Within four years Guilford had brought the old D&H to its knees and the Albany & Susquehanna's successor filed for bankruptcy protection. Until then (1988) it had been the longest continually operated corporation in the United States. Delaware Otsego Corporation's New York, Susquehanna & Western Railroad was selected by the Interstate Commerce Commission to be the line's interim operator, with its president, Walter G. Rich, hoping that it would later become the line's new owner. Walter was an old D&H man, you know, having been tutored by President "Buck" Dumaine. He was disheartened, then, to learn in 1991 that for only $15 million,

The Lackawanna & Susquehanna Railroad was built by the D&H. It connected with the Erie's Jefferson Railroad at Lanesboro, PA. The L&S passed through an arch of the fabled Starrucca Viaduct so that both railroads would occasionally be able to get a good look at each other. A D&H Rouses Point (NY)-bound train has just arrived at the viaduct as an Erie-Lackawanna train soars overhead, headed for Port Jervis, NY. JERRY COYNE PHOTOGRAPH.

Walter G. Rich poses with D&H President Frederick C. Dumaine, Jr. and a photograph of Starrucca Viaduct. Behind Walt and "Buck" is Road Foreman of Engines, Marv Davis. WILLIAM S. YOUNG PHOTOGRAPH.

Canadian Pacific, a Canadian Crown corporation, became the Delaware & Hudson's successor.

Applying a degree of Monday morning quarterbacking, it is probably a good thing that CPRail did become the new owner/operator as its' pockets ran deeper than those of the Susie-Q. They have improved the property, and although the line is now mostly single track (with strategically located passing sidings) the operation of trains can be efficiently handled. Considering Norfolk Southern has in place a trackage rights agreement with CPRail, the number of trains run on a daily basis seems to be slowly increasing. The D&H may be long gone, but there's still some mighty fine railroading taking place between Albany-Schenectady and Binghamton.

During the time of Delaware Otsego's operation of the railroad, Interstate-88 officially opened, although portions of the route had gone into service previously. (It was originally proposed in 1968.) Automobile op-

erators, and especially truckers, were now free to rule the road without the village speed limits associated with Route 7. It was the road's namesake, Warren M. Anderson—a New York State Senator from Binghamton—who had lobbied for, and pushed forward, the construction of the new interstate highway. In a similar manner, he did what Joseph H. Ramsey had done earlier: he made transportation for individuals and commerce an efficient and modern form. Certainly, I-88 made it a more comfortable and timely commute for Senator Anderson to travel to Albany to transact state business and to visit his constituents back home. Still, despite frequent exits the highway largely bypassed the historic villages such as Cobleskill, Schenevus and Worcester that Route 7 and the Delaware & Hudson Company's railroad had brought prosperity to.

CPRail does the same thing. Aside from a handful of local businesses along the corridor, its trains, and those of Norfolk Southern, cruise through the region non-stop with freight going to and from more distant markets. It is almost disheartening to see today's trains pass through Oneonta, the D&H Susquehanna Division headquarters, without breaking stride. Unless, of course, the Minneapolis-based dispatcher sets up a meet there between northbound and southbound trains.

Change is certainly inevitable, whether it is Route 7 or the railroad. It could be a lot worse. I-88 could have been built so that it obliterated the Schohanna Trail—as Route 7 is called in places, and in 1988, the bankrupt railroad could have been abandoned. Considering this, we are quite fortunate that change has been kind to the area. By the way, although the Earth is billions of years

CP Rail is modernizing the old D&H property. Big-time railroading is back in the Albany-Schenectady-Binghamton corridor. Southbound train 252 nears SW Cabin, at Nineveh, NY on August 7, 2010.

old it is still changing too. Even with our hectic pace of life, we humans just do not live long enough to take notice of it.

Not long ago I was talking with the owner of the Quaker Street convenience store. "The day before I-88 opened," he said, "I stood out here (along Route 7) all day and counted over a thousand cars. The next day only sixty-six cars used Route 7; everybody else was on the new road. But," he continued, "there's more folks using Route 7 for local traveling today."

Maybe there are more "Sunday" drivers out there than I thought!

Let's join them.

Light snow covers the ground and right-of-way as a Norfolk Southern train 939 rolls southwest toward Oneonta and Binghamton. The image was made from the cab of an SMS diesel awaiting interchange with the NS . DEAN SPLITTGERBER.

ABOVE: *The head end for CPRail's "Super Local," train 514, sits crew-less upon a stub-end track just outside Mohawk Yard (beyond the background signals). This train will contain a rather lengthy consist (hence its nickname). Local switching will be undertaken between Mohawk and Binghamton. Less than a handful of businesses along the old Susquehanna Division require rail service: Lutz Feed Company at Oneonta; Blue Seal Feeds at Bainbridge; and McDowell & Walker Feed Company at Afton. CPRail company cars may be switched at Oneonta as required. Because there is not much switching to do, the train contains cars that need to be delivered to CPRail's East Binghamton Yard for distribution to other points. The lead locomotive for this January 5, 2011 train is ex-D&H GP38-2 No. 7312 that still proudly wears the color scheme of its original owner despite now being the* property of CPRail. Two other engines, Nos. 7303 and 7304, are similarly attired. In Glenville, Mohawk Yard lies adjacent to Stratton Air National Guard Base where the 109th Airlift Wing is stationed. One of that Wing's Lockheed C-130 Hercules is on final approach to the air base and, if its crew members are also railfans, then they are afforded a wonderful view of the railroad's Mohawk Yard. Train 514, re-designated 554 on January 17, 2011, faces (railroad) south with the single track mainline curving around the local and towards the Mohawk River bridge that is behind the photographer. The extension track that the local sits upon ends before the bridge and does not reconnect with the main track. South of the bridge lies Schenectady and the beginning of the Delaware & Hudson's Susquehanna Division Heritage Trail.*

DEAN SPLITTGERBER PHOTOGRAPH.

When the Albany & Susquehanna Railroad issued its August 28, 1865 timetable—the beginning of service to Oneonta—it noted that the village of New Scotland was ten miles distant from Albany but the name of that community had been changed to Voorheesville the previous year to honor lawyer Alonzo B. Voorhees. The railroad had built a depot and had been providing service to Voorheesville since the opening of the line between Albany and Central Bridge on September 16, 1863. That standard-design A&S edifice became a "union" station when the New York, West Shore & Buffalo Railway began service for its entire length on January 1, 1884. The station was sited within the northeast quadrant formed by the crossing of the two railroads. (By then, the A&S had become part of the D&HCCo.) By 1889, the two railroads decided that the original station was no longer satisfactory to properly serve them or the public; it was torn down that year and replaced by a unique design. The new 28′ X 72′ building was jointly built and maintained. The fortunes of the West Shore were diminished when the New York Central & Hudson River Railroad assumed control. The NYC relegated the West Shore to mostly mainline freight operations while maintaining its primary passenger service along the NYC&HR mainline to the east and north. Still, Voorheesville continued to see passenger trains, though mostly on the D&H. The three-story Friar's Grove Hotel (named for its proprietor) sat at the right, separated from the depot by the D&H mainline and Grove Street. Both the station and hotel are now gone. CSX mainline freights now use the West Shore. The sprawling Selkirk Yard lies not too far east of this site (to the left). The image is by Breakabeen's John H. Dearstyne. DEPOT SQUARE PUBLISHING COLLECTION.

CHAPTER 1
TWO ROUTES TO QUAKER STREET

It's a rainy, mid-spring, morning at CPRail's Mohawk Yard where we begin our tour—and story—of the former Delaware & Hudson Susquehanna Division. This yard, situated just across the Mohawk River from Schenectady runs parallel to Glenville's Maple Avenue. It is in truth a shadow of its former self. The D&H once used this nearly twenty-six-track yard (thirteen tracks on each side of the double-track mainline) to allow trains to set out or pick up cars to adjust tonnage for the grades that lie to the south. Today, only a hand-ful of very long sidings are used to manage: occasional interchange with Pan Am Railways (ex-Guilford Transportation, nee Boston & Maine); a crew change when the Hours of Service Law catches up with an engineer and conductor; or as a safe haven for CPRail's mostly-noc-turnal local freight when it is running late and gets in the way of higher priority trains. Tonnage is not so much of a consideration with today's diesel locomotives manufactured by General Electric or General Motor's Electro-Motive Division; two or three six-axle engines offering 4000 hp or more apiece suffice to drag most lengthy trains up Kelley's, Howes, Richmondville, or Belden hills. There is only one main track today too. Notably absent from the scene is New York State Route 7, which is located across the river and on the southeast side of Schenectady. We will meet up with Route 7 in about nine miles.

Despite downgrading Mohawk's earlier purpose as a tonnage-balancing yard, its main track still assumes a traditional role. First, it is a corridor for trains bound

ABOVE: *Delaware & Hudson Class K 4-8-4 No. 301 holds the main as it rolls a southbound merchandise train past Mohawk Yard's yard office (left). 2-8-0 No. 1072 acts as the yard switcher. Both engines hail from ALCo's erecting hall.* RIGHT: *Norfolk Southern train 930 departs a downgraded Mohawk Yard on May 3, 2010. Regardless of its change in status, Mohawk Yard is still CPRail's gateway to the south.*

Colonie Shops

Watervliet

Most D&H freight trains originating at Albany and destined for Binghamton travelled 'round the horn to Mohawk Yard in Glenville, directly across the Mohawk River from Schenectady. Along the way these trains passed the Colonie Shops, Watervliet, Cohoes, and West Waterford before turning west at Mechanicville. Colonie's main shop building cared for steam and diesel locomotives alike, with celebrated ALCo PA passenger engines Nos. 16-19 being the glamour girls of the fleet. One of the PAs is being groomed for Albany-Montreal service. The Watervliet station was erected in 1889-1890; Cohoes, in 1883, replacing a thirty year-old building that was connected to the freight house; and West Waterford, in 1882. In 1900, thirty-five year old Elmer J. Wyman was the station agent at West Waterford. Note that the Delaware & Hudson adorned its depots near Albany with shingles, dormers, gables, stained glass, wide canopies, and other architectural touches suitable for these important commuter stops. FAR LEFT, JOHN TAIBI. BELOW, DEPOT SQUARE PUBLISHING COLLECTION. OTHER IMAGES, NATIONAL ARCHIVES COLLECTION.

Cohoes

West Waterford

ROADS, RIVERS, AND RAILS

Coons

Alplaus

Schenectady

At Mechanicville, D&H trains encountered the Boston & Maine, turning west to run parallel through Coons, Usher, and Elnora, thence bending south to reach Alplaus before sidling into Mohawk Yard at Glenville. As one can easily see, many of these rural locations were served by a non-agency waiting room such as that found at Coons. These buildings were far more utilitarian than their kinfolk within the usual commuting range to Albany. Simple accouterments like the pair of finials atop the roof crest of the Coons depot gave these small structures a bit of elegance. A number of these structures were built in the 1880s-1890s. RIGHT: The original route taken by the D&H to enter Schenectady was to use the New York Central's bridge over the Mohawk River, Erie Canal, and Erie Boulevard, the latter shown here in this view which looks east. The NYC and D&H had nine grade crossings through downtown Schenectady which led to numerous traffic problems, especially when passenger trains made frequent stops at the depot. The city fathers decided to have these grade crossings eliminated by having the two railroads elevate tracks through the city. To that end, several years were spent completing the project which included building a new union station at State and Union streets. A D&H train approaches the new station complex opened in 1909.

ALL IMAGES, DEPOT SQUARE PUBLISHING COLLECTION.

Schenectady, NY in 1912

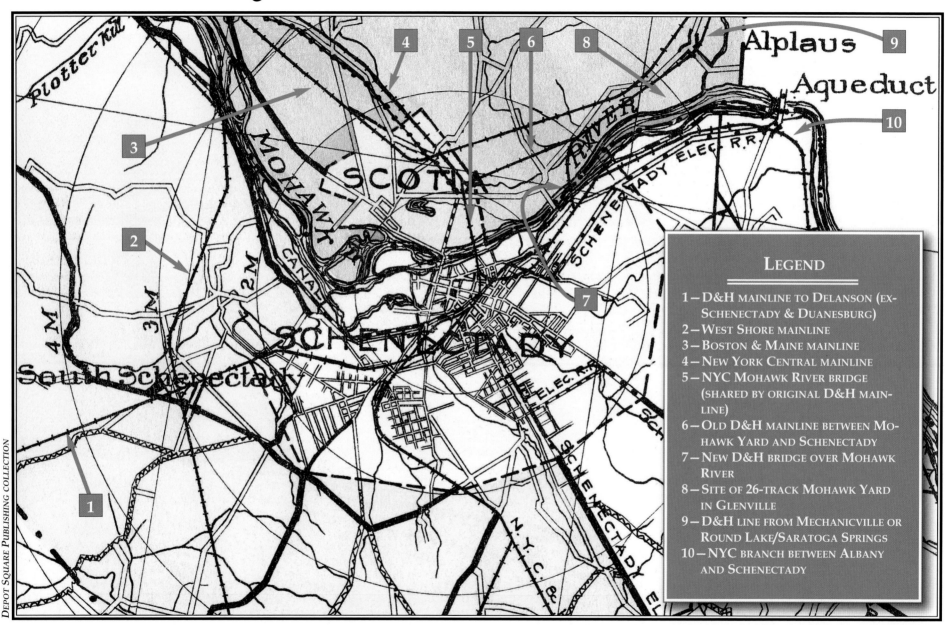

Alplaus

Aqueduct

LEGEND

1 — D&H MAINLINE TO DELANSON (EX-SCHENECTADY & DUANESBURG)
2 — WEST SHORE MAINLINE
3 — BOSTON & MAINE MAINLINE
4 — NEW YORK CENTRAL MAINLINE
5 — NYC MOHAWK RIVER BRIDGE (SHARED BY ORIGINAL D&H MAINLINE)
6 — OLD D&H MAINLINE BETWEEN MOHAWK YARD AND SCHENECTADY
7 — NEW D&H BRIDGE OVER MOHAWK RIVER
8 — SITE OF 26-TRACK MOHAWK YARD IN GLENVILLE
9 — D&H LINE FROM MECHANICVILLE OR ROUND LAKE/SARATOGA SPRINGS
10 — NYC BRANCH BETWEEN ALBANY AND SCHENECTADY

ROADS, RIVERS, AND RAILS

Born in Greece in 1878, Theophilus Peter Avlon immigrated to Schenectady in 1895, eventually opening a photographic studio at 525 State Street with his wife, Ada. Avlon, who Americanized his first name to Theodore, recorded many images of his adopted hometown including those of the major project to elevate the joint New York Central and Delaware & Hudson trackage through downtown and the erection of a new union station. This image looks east at the new depot standing beside the Edison Hotel. This was the third and last depot to call this site home. It was designed by St. Paul, MN-based architects Reed and Stern and built by William Wilgus, who had been chief engineer and later a Vice President for the Central. Unfortunately, this beautiful station was torn down in 1972 for nothing more important than a parking lot. DEPOT SQUARE PUBLISHING COLLECTION.

for Saratoga and Montreal to the north; for eastbound consists destined for Pan Am Railways' Ayer, MA intermodal terminal (via Mechanicville, an ex-B&M interchange point); and for southbound trains headed for either Binghamton or Albany's Kenwood Yard (also via Mechanicville). D&H freights originating from Kenwood or Colonie yards go "around the horn," so to speak, to Mohawk Yard, interchanging with the B&M at Mechanicville along the way. Although this was operationally longer—going north before heading south—its advantages were: more efficient interchange; optimum tonnage characteristics for all freight trains; and a route whose gradient became far superior to the old Albany & Susquehanna Railroad's line between Albany and Quaker Street. That is where trains had to slug it out to surmount the Helderberg Escarpment. Freight trains did, indeed, operate via the Albany main line of the A&S, but this was mostly passenger train territory. That was the wisdom behind the D&HCCo's acquisition of the Schenectady & Duanesburg and Rensselaer & Saratoga railroads. The combination affected a short cut to the north and an operationally less demanding route to the south, although the D&HCCo may not have fully realized all this at the time of their 1870s lease of these two regional properties.

The S&D and A&S routes to the south both consisted of a 1.06% ascending grade. A new line built in 1907 reduced the grade to 0.88% southward from Schenectady (on the old S&D). Further grade reductions and a new northbound line undertaken during 1930 and 1933 improved upon the old S&D such that the original line could be mostly abandoned during 1933.

The A&S line was not upgraded. Its character was operationally inferior to that of the S&D. It ran through the heart of seven residential communities (Elsmere, Delmar, Slingerlands, Font Grove, Voorheesville, Meadowdale, and Altamont), which made for an ideal commuter district to Albany from outlying Altamont. The renovated S&D, on the other hand, called on only one municipality: Duanesburg. The commuter trains, plus all the passenger trains bound to and from Binghamton, made it all the more difficult for freight trains to negotiate the single-track A&S main line between Albany and Quaker Street. Schenectady aside, the S&D line—and its upgraded rights-of-way—was rural in character. That was more beneficial for the operation of freight trains. Hence Mohawk Yard was important as a gateway to the south even though freight trains from Albany had to go north first to get there. This is substantiated by an Interstate Commerce Commission report (dated October 8, 1917) that states, "Traffic on the Schenectady Branch [the old S&D route] consists approximately of 3 passenger trains each way daily, except Sunday, and 21 freight trains each way daily. Traffic on the Albany line consists of 9 passenger trains each way during the week, 4 on weekends, and 2 freight trains each way daily." Then, twenty-five years later, D&H vice-president and general manager Glenn H. Caley advised a group of visiting railroad signal engineers that, "ninety-

A Boston & Maine Railroad employee mans the console panel in Mechanicville's Tower B in 1928. Both the B&M and D&H utilized expansive yards at Mechanicville to forward interchange freight destined for all regions: north, south, east, and west. LEN KILIAN COLLECTION.

nine percent of our freight trains are moved over the (Schenectady) branch between Delanson and Mechanicville," via Mohawk Yard. As you might imagine, Mohawk Yard was a busy place regardless of era.

The 131-mile railroad between Mohawk Yard and Binghamton (which mostly follows Route 7) is today a direct corridor, a "spine" if you will, without interchange. At its termini a multitude of routes diverge from the spine that lead to important east coast, midwest, and Canadian markets. From Binghamton, routes to the New York metropolitan area, Harrisburg and Philadelphia, PA, Washington, DC, Buffalo, NY, and Chicago, IL can be reached. Traffic flowing northward through Mohawk Yard can be destined for Montreal, Albany, and all New England via Ayer and Boston, MA (the old Fitchburg, later Boston & Maine route). These same markets could also be attained by the Delaware & Hudson's "Bridge Line," but many more independent railroads would have been involved to do the same thing that today's merged railroads accomplish.

Mohawk Yard, at CPF (Control Point Freight line) 483, witnesses the passage of at least a dozen CPRail and Norfolk Southern (via trackage agreement) trains that carry merchandise, coal, intermodal trailers and containers, and an occasional ethanol tank car train. They all operate over CPRail's Freight Mainline Subdivision of the Northeast United States Division that is controlled by CPRail dispatchers stationed in Minneapolis, MN, and operated by CPRail crews whose home terminals are at Saratoga and Binghamton. It is this freight train activity that we will witness along our tour—once we get to Route 7. To do that, we first have to cross the Mohawk River via the Freeman's Bridge; the railroad crosses just to the east using a five-span deck-truss-deck bridge where a single track mainline has replaced former double-track iron.

Once we have reached the other side of the river, another obstacle for the railroad has to be crossed: Amtrak's passenger mainline at Schenectady's downtown station. But first trains pass the site of one of America's premier steam locomotive and third largest diesel locomotive manufacturer: the American Locomotive Company. It is very disheartening to view the vacant, derelict buildings and grounds of this one time railroad institution that gave Schenectady the right to say that it helped to "haul" the world. At the zenith of its steam locomotive building operations the ALCo complex contained forty-four buildings on sixty-five acres of land, and paid wages to over 3,300 employees. Today, all is silent there.

The passenger mainline at Schenectady station, situated adjacent to Erie Boulevard, is a component of Amtrak's Empire Service corridor, but is certainly better remembered as the New York Central's "Water Level

D&H class G-5 4-4-0 No. 456 poses for its official builder's photograph after being outshopped by American Locomotive Company in 1904.This double-cab Camelback can look forward to a long career of prancing at the head of passenger trains until being retired and scrapped thirty years later. ALCo was traditionally the builder of choice for D&H steam and diesel locomotives as its erection halls sat astride the railroad's Susquehanna Division trackage in Schenectady.

ALCo HISTORIC PHOTOS COLLECTION.

Route." Getting across this busy mainline artery at grade by CPRail and Norfolk Southern trains requires coordination between Amtrak and CPRail dispatchers. Until a window of opportunity presents itself, southbound trains may lie in wait at Mohawk Yard. But, if the dispatchers strut their stuff—and they generally do— trains will proceed unimpeded.

Beyond Amtrak's rails, our trains pass under Interstate 890; then skirt the vast grounds of the General Electric Company. This well-known corporation once supplied electrical apparatus for ALCo's diesel locomotives, but mostly it allowed Schenectady to brag that it "lit" the world. GE got its start when the Edison Electric Company moved from New York City to Schenectady in 1886. It merged with Edison General Electric Co. (1889) and then Thomson-Houston Electric Co. of Lynn, MA (1892), becoming General Electric Company. Its facility dwarfed the layout of ALCo. 301 buildings sat on 523 acres. Thirty-two miles of standard and narrow gauge railroad track criss-crossed the property. At one time over 26,000 people were employed here. GE is today's number one locomotive manufacturer but not, unfortunately, in Schenectady. At one time, however, both ALCo and GE were treasured shippers and consignees for the Delaware & Hudson Railroad.

TIME TABLES
OF
PASSENGER TRAINS
ON

THE DELAWARE AND HUDSON CANAL CO'S RAIL ROADS.

BETWEEN

MONTREAL,
PLATTSBURGH, SARATOGA,
ALBANY, TROY,
Binghamton,   Carbondale,
SCRANTON and WILKESBARRE,
Connecting for Philadelphia.

Issued from the General Ticket Office.

SEPTEMBER 18th, 1876.

Trains are run by Albany Time.

S. E. MAYO,
Gen'l Pass. Agent.

Trains West. SUSQUEHANNA

LEAVE	11		1	3	5	7
	A.M.		A.M.	P.M.	P.M.	P.M.
Albany	6.00		8.10	3.00	5.00	6.25
Adamsville	6.27				5.15	6.38
Slingerlands	6.35		8.32	3.21	5.20	6.42
New Scotland	6.56				5.32	6.54
Guilderland	7.10				5.41	7.02
Knowersville	7.30		8.55	3.40	5.50	7.10
Duanesburgh	8.15				6.11	7.32
Quaker Street ...Arrive	8.33		9.20	4.00	6.19	7.40
						P.M.
Saratoga ...Leave						
Ballston						
Schenectady				7.50	2.40	
Quaker street ...Arrive				9.10	3.50	
Quaker Street ...Leave	8.33		9.20	4.00	6.19	
Esperance	9.04				6.35	
Central Bridge	9.43		9.43	4.21	6.48	
Howe's Cave	10.04		9 50	4.28	6.56	
Cobleskill ...Arrive	10.45		10.04	4.40	7.10	
Cobleskill ...Leave			10.05	4.45	8.00	
Hyndsville			10.19	5.08	8.17	
Seward			10.30	5.16	8.30	
Sharon			10.45	5.35	8.48	
Cherry Valley ...Arrive			11.10	6.10	9.20	
Cherry V'y (for west)..L've			6.30	11.25		
Sharon			7.02	11.50		
Seward			7.20	12.03		
Hyndsville			7.34	12.12		
Cobleskill ...Arrive			7.50	12.25		
Cobleskill ...Leave	10.45		10.04	4.40	7.10	
Richmondville	11.15		10.16	4.52	7.22	
East Worcester	12.02		10.33	5.08	7.40	
Worcester	12.22		10.44		7.52	
Schenevus	1.08	9	10.56	5.30	8.05	
Maryland	1.35				8.14	11
Junction	2.12		11.18	5.50	8.27	
Colliers	2.20				8.31	
Oneonta	3.00		11.43	6.15	8.45	11.50
Otego		7.50	12.00	6.37		12.45
Wells' Bridge		8.12				1.18
Unadilla		8.26	12.19	7.01		1.49
Sidney		8.40	12.27	7.14		2.20
Bainbridge		8.56	12.37	7.28		2.53
Afton		9.14	12.50	7.45		3.30
Nineveh		9.30	1.00	8.00		4.00
Carbondale ...Arrive			3.20			
Scranton "			4.10			
Tunnel ...Leave	10.00		1.20			4.50
Osborn Hollow	10.22					5.28
Port Crane	10.35		1.45			5.50
Binghamton ...Arrive	11.00		2.00	9.00		6.30
	P.M.		P.M.	P.M.	P.M.	P.M.

Nos. 1, and 5 connect at Central Bridge for Schoharie and Middleburgh.

No. 1 and 3 at Junction for Cooperstown; at Binghamton with Erie Railway for West.

No. 3 and 9 at Sidney for Oxford and Norwich.

No. 1 connects at Scranton with D. L. & W... Philadelphia 9.45 P.M.

DIVISION. Trains East.

LEAVE	2	4	12	6	10	12
	A.M.	P.M.	A.M.	A.M.	P.M.	A.M.
Binghamton	8.40	1.30		4.30		6.30
Port Crane		1.45		4.58		6.53
Osborne Hollow		1.53		5.13		7.07
Tunnel		2.07		5.40		7.30
Scranton	6.30					
Carbondale	7.10					
Nineveh	9.30	2.27	6.15			8.00
Afton	9 40	2.38	6.45			8.15
Bainbridge	9.52	2.53	7.20			8.33
Sidney	10.04	3.05	7.55			8.50
Unadilla	10.14	3.16	8.26			9.05
Wells Bridge		3.27	9.00			9.19
Otego	10.34	3.37	9.40			9.35
Oneonta	11.05	4.10	10.25	6.30	10.00	9.00
Colliers		4.23		6.41		9.40
Junction	11.18	4.26		6.45		9.50
Maryland		4.37		6.55		10.30
Schenevus	11.40	4.45		7.04		10.56
Worcester	11.53	4.56		7.15		11.30
East Worcester	12.02	5.08		7.25		12.02
Richmondville	12.16	5.24		7.40		12.57
Cobleskill ...Arrive	12.27	5.36		7.53		1.40
Cobleskill ...Leave	4.45	8.00		10.05		
Hyndsville	5 03	8.17		10.19		
Seward	5.16	8.30		10.30		
Sharon	5.35	8.48		10.45		
Cherry Valley ...Arrive	6.10	9.20		11.10		P.M.
Cherry Valley (for East) L've	11.25			6.30	6.25	
Sharon	11.50			7.02	6.57	
Seward	12.03			7.20	7.15	
Hyndsville	12.12			7.34	7.28	
Cobleskill ...Arrive	12.25			7.50	7.45	
Cobleskill ...Leave	12.27	5.36		7.53	1.40	
Howe's Cave	12.39	5.49		8.05	2.23	
Central Bridge	12.45	5.58		8.12	2.45	
Esperance		6.09		8.24	3.28	
Quaker St. ...Arrive	1.05	6.19		8.33	4.00	
Quaker St. ...Leave	1.10	6.25				
Schenectady ...Arrive	2.10	7.35	8			
Ballston	6.20					
Saratoga	7.00					
Quaker St. ...Leave	1.05	6.19	7.00	8.33	4.00	
Duanesburgh			7.07	8.38	4.16	
Knowersville	1.30	6.40	7.30	8.55	4.55	
Guilderland		6.47	7.40	9.02	5.14	
New Scotland		6.54	7.50	9.09	5.32	
Slingerlands	1.55	7.03	8.01	9.17	5.50	
Adamsville		7.07	8.05	9.20	5.58	
Albany ...Arrive	2.15	7.25	8.20	9.35	6.25	
	P.M.	P.M.	A.M.	A.M.		

Nos. 2 and 4 connect at Junction for Cooperstown.

Nos. 2, 4 and 6 at Central Bridge for Schoharie and Middleburgh.

No. 2 at Sidney for Oxford and Norwich.

Nos. 2, 4 and 6 at Albany with Trains for New York.

No. 8 with Day Boat on Hudson River.

No. 4 with Night Boat for New York.

Nos. 2 and 6 for Boston and East

CONNECTIONS.

At **SCRANTON**—with diverging Railroad Lines.

At **BINGHAMTON**—with Erie, and Delaware, Lackawanna and Western Rail Roads.

At **SIDNEY**—with New York & O. M. Rail Road.

At **JUNCTION**—with Cooperstown & Susq. V. R. R.

At **COBLESKILL**—with Cherry Valley Branch.

At **CENTRAL BRIDGE**—with Schoharie Valley and Middleburg & Schoharie Rail Roads.

At **SCHENECTADY**—with New York Central & H. R. R. R.; Junct'n of Susquehanna and Saratoga Divisions.

At **ALBANY**—with New York Central & Hudson River Rail Road, Boston & Albany Rail Road, and Hudson River Steamers; Junction of Susquehanna and Saratoga Divisions.

At **TROY**—with New York Central & Hudson River and Troy & Boston R. R's, and Hudson River St'rs

At **BALLSTON**—Junction of Schenectady Branch.

At **SARATOGA**—with Adirondack Co.'s Rail Road.

At **FORT EDWARD**—with Glens Falls Branch.

At **GLENS FALLS**—with Stages for Caldwell.

At **WHITEHALL**—Junction of Saratoga and Champlain Divisions.

At **RUTLAND**—with Central Vermont Rail Road, Junction of Eagle Bridge Branch.

At **EAGLE BRIDGE**—with Troy & Boston Rail Road.

At **FT. TICONDEROGA**—with Lake Champlain St'r.

At **BALDWIN**—with Lake George Steamer.

At **CROWN POINT**—with Rail and Stage Line for Schroon Lake.

At **WESTPORT**—with Stages for Elizabethtown, North Elba, &c.

At **PORT KENT**—with Stages for Ausable Chasm and Keeseville.

At **PLATTSBURGH**—with Ausable Branch and Lake Champlain Steamer.

At **AUSABLE**—with Stages for Paul Smiths, Martin's, and Saranac region.

At **MOOERS JUNCTION**—with Cent. Vermont R. R.

At **ROUSES POINT**—with Grand Trunk and Central Vermont Railroads.

In 1876, the Delaware & Hudson Canal Company's timetable (ABOVE) listed adequate, convenient, frequent, and connecting passenger train service to and from all Susquehanna Division locations. For persons who had limited traveling means just a few years earlier, a schedule such as this must have been a godsend. LEN KILIAN COLLECTION. RIGHT: On March 20, 2011, Amtrak's southbound *Adirondack*, train 68, crosses the Mohawk River from Glenville to Schenectady with newly repainted GE P42DC No. 156 leading the way into the city that "Lights and Hauls" the world, a reference to General Electric and American Locomotive companies. This engine is one of four selected by Amtrak to be attired in a heritage paint scheme that had been applied to earlier Amtrak engines in celebration of its 40th anniversary. Mohawk Yard, the official starting point for this story lies within one mile to the north (left) of this bridge. RIGHT, DEAN SPLITTGERBER PHOTOGRAPH.

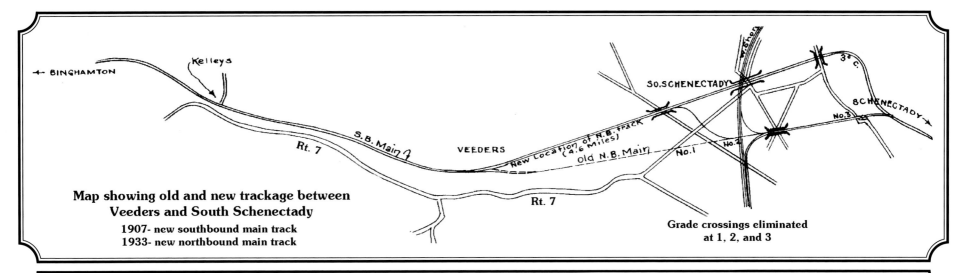

Map showing old and new trackage between
Veeders and South Schenectady

1907- new southbound main track
1933- new northbound main track

Grade crossings eliminated
at 1, 2, and 3

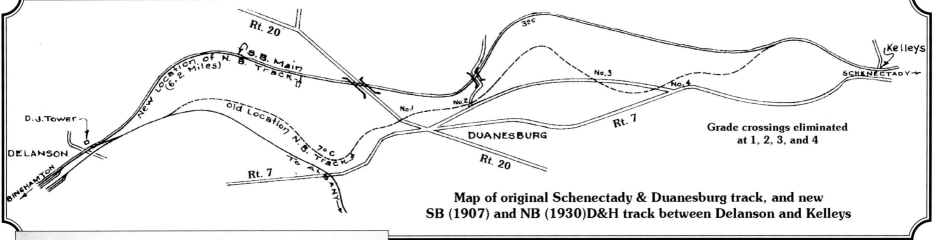

Map of original Schenectady & Duanesburg track, and new
SB (1907) and NB (1930)D&H track between Delanson and Kelleys

Grade crossings eliminated
at 1, 2, 3, and 4

The above maps display the work undertaken by the D&H to lessen its southward grade by constructing a new northbound track between Delanson (Quaker Street) and South Schenectady. This work was completed in stages during the years 1907, 1930, and 1933, with seven grade crossings being eliminated during the latter two years. The result of this new construction was a southbound grade of only 0.88%, reduced curvature throughout the line, and the near total abandonment of the original Schenectady & Duanesburg right-of-way. The S&D route is marked as being "Old N. B. Main" on both maps. Bridge Line Historical Society collection. Left: High above Route 7, which is situated down the embankment at right, a southbound freight works upgrade. It is about to pass the small wood frame depot at Kelley's. A. Bruce Tracy collection.

Just before Rotterdam, CPRail's ex-D&H trackage encounters CSX's mainline freight artery from massive Selkirk Yard. Ownership of this line dates to the building of the New York, West Shore & Buffalo Railway during the early 1880s, and its becoming a New York Central & Hudson River Railroad property within two years of completion in 1884. Selkirk Yard replaced an earlier yard at Ravenna, while Penn Central and Conrail followed New York Central into the history books. CSX here, and Norfolk Southern in other locales, did the same to Conrail. CPRail bows to CSX by diving under the latter's line and continues on to an overpass over the New York State (Thomas E. Dewey) Thruway. It is right about here that New York State Route 7 comes abreast of CPRail, but between the two lies Interstate 88. Isn't it just like a Johnny-come-lately to come between old friends? In about two miles, Route 7 crosses under its four lane replacement and pulls alongside of its railroad. From this point, the road and the rails play tag and cavort all the way to Binghamton. They may not always be within sight of each other, but the absence makes their hearts grow fonder for the next reunion.

By the time Route 7 has caught up with Delaware & Hudson's old Susquehanna Division, the highway has already seen its fair share of railroading. Not long after leaving the Vermont border, the road passed over the Rutland Railroad's old branch to Chatham. Both the branch and the railroad are now only a lovely memory; the branch, abandoned in 1953; the railroad in 1962 after many months of inactivity. Not much further along, Route 7 crosses over Pan Am Railway's Mechanicville-to-Ayer line at Hoosick, NY. Maybe it would be more appropriate if Pan Am "flew" over the road. Pan Am Railway is the latest name for the Guilford ex-Boston & Maine line that was built by the Fitchburg Railroad. This line, which Norfolk Southern is helping to rehabilitate, is commonly referred to as the Patriot Corridor.

From Hoosick's 473-foot elevation, Route 7 continues in a southwesterly fashion, descending and curving to and fro, until Troy — and a Hudson River crossing — is attained at a height of seventy-three feet. Today, our road crosses over the location of Boston & Maine's one time passenger line to Troy Union Station and uses the Collar City Bridge to cross the "Rhine of America." Many years before this bridge was completed in 1981 and a new multi-lane roadway on the west side of the river was opened to it in 1986, Route 7 crossed the river via Route 2's bridge further to the south where it got a look at the location of New York Central's line to Troy Union Station.

On the west side of the Hudson, no matter what era, our road next crossed D&H's Saratoga Division line which hosted passenger trains from Albany to Saratoga and beyond, and freight trains to/from Mechanicville, Colonie, and Kenwood yards. This corridor is also a component of CPRail that Norfolk Southern uses as an intermodal route to the Port of Albany. During our road's ancestral time (when Route 2 west of the Hudson was labeled Route 7) it was barely possible to get a glimpse of D&H's massive Colonie yard where its main shops were located. Situated adjacent to the yard/shops was the Watervliet Arsenal that supplied the U.S. Army with much of its large artillery, gun tubes/barrels for mortars and tanks and other ordinance for America's great wars.

Route 7 then continues on across the Capital District suburbs but, as it approaches Schenectady, it turns to the southwest where it eventually crosses Amtrak's Empire Corridor, then CSX's main freight line just as the D&H had done earlier and CPRail does today. Our road then cozies up to our railroad after meeting its arch enemy: Interstate 88.

This portion of D&H's Susquehanna Division that is now in full view on our right, follows an alignment originally built by the railroad in 1907 when a second track was added between Veeders and South Schenectady. The other track, which was on the original Schenectady & Duanesburg alignment to South Schenectady, was abandoned in 1933. It was replaced with a new southbound track parallel to the 1908 northbound track, also doing away with three grade crossings in favor of overpasses in the process.

Between Veeders and Kelley's both tracks (but only one today) remain on their original S&D location. Just beyond Kelley's, however, new trackage built in 1907 (southbound) and 1930 (northbound) allowed the railroad to abandon the old S&D route while saving 0.18% of southbound ascending grade. Four more grade crossings were eliminated during the construction for the new north track in 1930. Far fewer crossings at grade also helped to develop this line into the railroad's main freight route as opposed to the A&S line which featured numerous road and rail crossings..

This section of CPRail's route is known as Kelley's Grade, which benefits from the D&H's new track alignment(s) so that the 1.06% grade built by the S&D was reduced to 0.88%. Route 7 follows along this new right-of-way but the road and railroad are on separate elevations so that neither gets to see the other. Kelley's Grade is somewhat of a proving ground for locomotive performance. Engineers feel that if their power lash-up handles a train well here, then they can make it any-

The original Schenectady & Duanesburg depot for its namesake Duanesburg village was located along what would become the northbound Delaware & Hudson line to Schenectady. In this pre-World War I postcard view, the depot stands silent. The semaphore blades are down indicating there is no need for any train—freight or passenger—to stop. Not so much as a box of express waits on the platform. A. BRUCE TRACY COLLECTION.

RIGHT: *When south and northbound tracks were still separated at Duanesburg, a waiting room located inside the agent's dwelling provided accommodations for passengers heading south. From the front porch a view of trains passing on the northbound track—such as seen here—could be visualized. Roy Knowles was the agent in 1920.* LOWER RIGHT: *A one-story structure replaced the earlier Schenectady & Duanesburg depot on the northbound track and was moved to a nearby location as well. This Type 2PW2 station was 14' x 28' in dimensions. In 1918, the Interstate Commerce Commission commented that "…its size is identical to the railroad's standard tool house." Water tanks at the far right in both pictures were also sited near each station to handle thirsty engines on the slope. Both were Type WT1. The northbound tank held 50,000 gallons of water while the southbound unit provided only 37,000 gallons.* BOTH, A. BRUCE TRACY COLLECTION. LOWER LEFT: *On April 30, 2010, Norfolk Southern train 939, a Kenwood Yard (Albany)-to-Binghamton intermodal train, has gone 'round the horn and is now assaulting Kelley's Grade at Duanesburg. The steel girders carry what was once double-track over US Route 20. Just one pair of steel ribbons follows our route now with the exception of strategically-located long passing tracks.* INSET: *The yellow and blue Delaware & Hudson shield logo still adorns the sides of this girder bridge over US 20.*

where. That may be true, but the engines will have to dig deep into their horsepower ratings for the next three grades, as Howes Cave, Richmondville, and Belden hills all have a gradient over one percent.

Stations along this section of the railroad are infrequent. South Schenectady (telegraph call NE) had a small shelter at one time but that became a thing of the past when the old main track there was done away with during the 1933 grade crossing elimination project. A small frame building served as a depot for Kelley's where a community was non-existent. At Duanesburg separate structures were provided for the south and northbound tracks. These three buildings were not traditional depots, merely providing shelter for waiting passengers. They were primarily telegraph offices. (Kelley's call was KY; Duanesburg, RG.) That is because passenger trains were mostly directed from Quaker Street towards Albany rather than Schenectady; freight trains were routed vice-versa. Schenectady did see passenger trains, such as numbers 386 and 389 in 1930 for example, but boxcars far outnumbered coaches in the old S&D territory. These two trains did not stop at Duanesburg, Kelley's, or South Schenectady. By 1930, folks were driving their own cars locally. Three decades earlier, however, there were three passenger trains each way over this route and they made calls at all three depots. On the Albany line, by comparison, there were twenty-two passenger trains being operated into and out of the Capital city.

At Duanesburg, routes 7 and 20 cross each other. If you look to the west when negotiating this angled intersection you can see where the original S&D line crossed Route 20 at grade and, just beyond, the grade-separated overpass that took the 1907 and 1930 tracks across the Great Western Turnpike. CPRail's single track mainline is still there.

Not much further along, our road passes over the old Albany main line (INSET). This is where Route 7 and the Albany & Susquehanna Railroad first say hello to each other. The D&H named this junction between road and rails Duane, after James Duane had purchased an astonishing 60,000 acres. Duanesburg and the Town of Duanesburg are also named for him.

Duane's depot was a more traditional board-and-batten combination station than any on the Schenectady line, yet, it was not much to brag about. Its plainness was its charm. It was not even listed as a stop in the D&H 1901 Susquehanna Division timetable. Duane, by the way, sat at an elevation of 743 feet, 700 feet more than Albany. Right around the corner, Duanesburg's elevation was 433 feet above Schenectady. That differ-

ence of 267 feet of grade between the two routes is what helped to substantiate the use of the old S&D as a freight route and the A&S primarily for passenger service.

From Duane to Quaker Street it is a mere three miles of Route 7 driving. (This portion of the highway was once known as the Danforth Turnpike.) The railroad still lies off to the north, beyond our ability to keep track of it. We enter Quaker Street upon passing Gibby's Diner (RIGHT), a fine remnant of the old silver flute-sided art deco diners that are a landlocked version of Budd Company's post-war streamlined passenger cars. At Quaker Street's main intersection we meet up with the Schoharie Turnpike, which predates the arrival of the railroad. Back then, the village, which was settled in 1820, did not have to share its identity with anyone. It sat mostly on the shoulder of the Helderberg Escarpment with its "suburbs" lying at the bottom of the hill nearly equidistant from Route 7 and the Great Western Turnpike. When the A&S came along, opening for service to Quaker Street on September 16, 1863, it built a depot down in the hollow just to the east of Main Street, and appropriately named the station Quaker Street. Joshua Whitney was the railroad's

first agent. That was the beginning of the end for Quaker Street's singular identity.

Six years later, the Delaware & Hudson Canal Company leased the A&S in perpetuity and began to improve its Quaker Street terminal that sat near the junction of the S&D and A&S. A freight house and roundhouse were built so that in addition to the station's personnel—ticket agent, telegraph operators, and baggagemen—a freight agent, transfermen, hostlers, wipers, mechanics, and train crewmen were added. All of these men lived near the railroad down in Quaker Street's hollow. It was only natural for a business district to sprout up there, too; dry goods, apothecary, groceries, a saloon or two, and the Shoudy House Hotel all catered to either railroad men, travelers, or both. This section of Quaker Street blossomed and prospered while the section up on the hill—along the state highway and turnpike—seemed to be content to view all this activity from a distance, and to not become mired with all the hustle and bustle, noise, smells, and confusion associated with the railroad's operations.

The time finally came, in 1893, when the community that had sprung up along the railroad became more prosperous and purposeful than the settlement up on

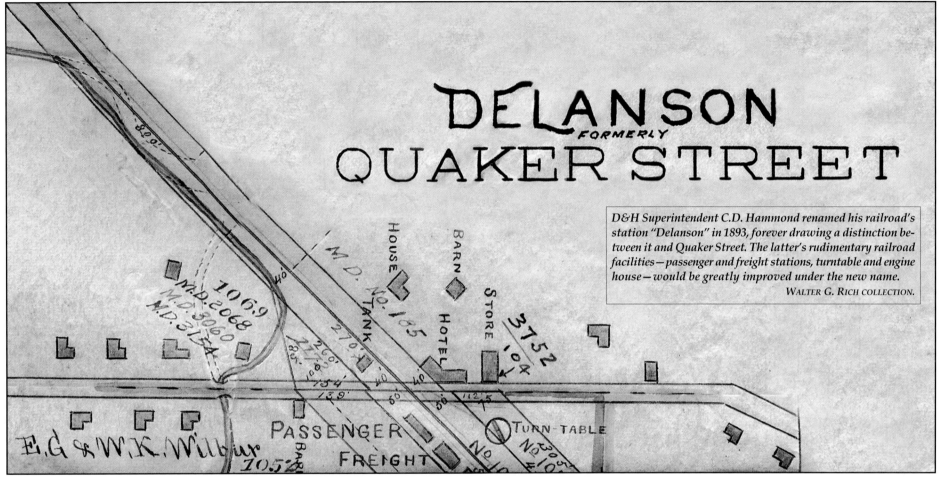

DELANSON
FORMERLY
QUAKER STREET

HOUSE No.185

BARN HOTEL

STORE

3752 -04

TURN-TABLE

PASSENGER

FREIGHT

E.G & W.K. Wilbur

106.9
M.D.2068
M.D.3060
M.D.3154

M.D.TANK

the hill. At that time, the railroad decided that it desired to give the "community" it helped to build its own identity, so its superintendent, C. D. Hammond, renamed that station "Delanson." The name derived from select portions of the railroad's own name: <u>Del</u>aware <u>an</u>d Hud<u>son</u>. Forever after, Delanson and Quaker Street assumed separate identities, with the railroad's community greatly usurping the prosperity of the original village. Delanson was successful in doing this because the railroad connected it to both Albany and Schenectady, and points beyond.

The other way to get to Quaker Street, er, Delanson, is via an ancestral Route 7 or by the original Albany &

Susquehanna Railroad route. The highway — today's US Route 20 — is more direct than the railroad that first drops to the south to gain the Normans Kill valley before turning northwesterly to reach its first station: Elsmere. For the twenty-six mile distance between Albany and Delanson, the old Route 7 and the railroad are unknown to each other. Beyond Duanesburg, where the old and new Route 7s cross, the road and railroad introduce themselves to each other at Duane, as previously mentioned.

The passenger facilities at Elsmere consisted of a simple wood frame waiting room with an attached canopy. No agent, or other conveniences for travelers

could be found there. Less than a mile further on, the railroad's station at Delmar provided all the traditional services undertaken by an agent-equipped depot: ticket sales, baggage handling, money orders, and Western Union telegraph service. A nearby freight house stood ready to receive and dispatch freight, so that in its own way, Delmar became the quintessential country depot, albeit one sited in a residential community. In 1929, T. W. Hall was the Delaware & Hudson's ticket and freight agent at this location.

Slingerlands was the next agent-manned station, with Font Grove lying exactly one mile beyond. At the former location, a combination freight and passenger

Named for a character in a book called **Elsmere**, the hamlet of the same moniker was located within the Town of Bethlehem on the opposite side of the ravine drained by the Normans Kill, this was one of the first stations on the climb south out of Albany. The large canopy suggests a significant patronage by local commuters to the Capital. A. Bruce Tracy collection.

The original A&S Albany station was built at Steamboat Square, which was appropriately named for the property which abutted the Hudson River's steamship dockage. Beginning in 1912, the city pursued redevelopment of the area at nearly the same time that the Delaware & Hudson Company desired to put up a new office building. The collaboration resulted in re-naming the area "The Plaza" and the construction of a Flemish Revival style office building (Top) whose focal point was a thirteen-story Gothic tower. That tower was capped by a weathervane portrayal of Henry Hudson's ship the **Half Moon** that had docked at this location during Hudson's exploration of the river. The building was designed by Marcus T.

Reynolds who had earlier studied classical architecture in Europe. The building's design called for occupation by the railroad in the tower and north wing, while the Albany **Evening Journal** newspaper owned and occupied the south wing. Since 1978, the building has housed the ad-ministrative offices for the State University of New York (SUNY) college system. Above Left: D&H passenger trains used the lower level of Albany Union Station after the Plaza was created. It is from there that a southbound D&H train is about to leave for Binghamton.

Both, National Archives collection.

LEFT: In 1838, Nathaniel Adams built a hotel at what became known as Adamsville. In 1866, the A&S erected this board-and-batten station. Half the funds for its construction were reportedly contributed by Adams' descendants. The hamlet was renamed Delmar in 1891. A Grand Trunk truss-rod boxcar rests on a siding behind the depot. In 1930, Thomas A. Hall was the station agent while Raymond Cromwell was the chief clerk. LOWER LEFT AND RIGHT: In 1888, the Albany & Susquehanna built a handsome structure to serve as Slingerlands' new depot. Built of stone, its roof-mounted dormers were unusual for the D&H-built stations. Consequently, this building's class was termed "Special." It replaced a standard combination station which was converted to just a freight house. Originally known as Normanskill, the largely residential village was renamed for its founder, William Slingerland, in 1891 with the tacit approval of D&H President Olyphant. LOWER LEFT, A. BRUCE TRACY COLLECTION. LEFT AND LOWER RIGHT, DEPOT SQUARE PUBLISHING COLLECTION.

depot was put up by the A&S. The D&H improved upon this lone facility by erecting a modern stone passenger station (with canopies) and remodeling the old depot into a freight house. Both modernizations were done during the late 1880s. Today, only the board-and-batten freight house, one time depot, remains. The waiting room for Font Grove passengers was only thirteen feet square, and was not even owned by the railroad. No accommodation other than the shelter, which was owned by Charles T. Terry, was provided here, its purpose simply to protect passengers from the elements.

At nearly eleven miles from Albany, the union station at Voorheesville sat snugly within the southeast quadrant formed by the crossing-at-grade of the Delaware & Hudson's Albany mainline with the former New York, West Shore & Buffalo Railway thoroughfare that became a property of the New York Central Railroad in 1886. The A&S, of course, was there first, but the NYC had a more significant presence due to a major classification facility at Selkirk Yard, lying not far to the south. Besides the union station, there was also a joint freight house situated here along the NYC line. The D&H accessed the freight house via connecting interchange trackage. Because of the grade crossing, and the A&S being first on the scene, the D&H held priority at the diamond. Yet it was Central freight trains that predominated here, which created another impediment for efficient operation of D&H freight trains. At the junction, one could stay at the Grove Hotel (also known as the Friar's Grove Hotel) managed in 1900 by John Vines for just $2.00 per night or "in town" at the Harris House for the same daily rate.

Through a succession of companies (Penn-Central and Conrail) CSX freight trains still use the

ABOVE RIGHT: *Named after railroad lawyer, Alonzo B. Voorhees, this village was once not much more than a junction between two railroads, the West Shore and the Delaware & Hudson. A village eventually settled around this point, with hotels, a bakery, cider mill, and a foundry to start. This view shows the side of the building along the D&H tracks. One of Voorheesville's primary industries around 1910 was the Phoenix Foundry Company which employed sixty-five men in 1913. Charles L. Canton was the owner.* DEPOT SQUARE PUBLISHING COLLECTION. RIGHT: *This image was taken from the West Shore's right of way where a camelback-led passenger train has stopped to exchange travelers. Note the unique smashboards used to protect the crossing for both railroad lines. They are anchored to the ground to prevent accidental movement unless directed by the agent.* A BRUCE TRACY COLLECTION.

ex-West Shore as a main component of its New York-Buffalo-Chicago line, but the D&H Albany mainline is noticeably absent. CPRail had used the line to reach the Northeastern Industrial Park at Guilderland Center (an ex-US Army depot) until $6,000,000 worth of repairs were needed to fix the ailing Normans Kill bridge. The cost of repairing the bridge was not deemed justifiable considering the meager amount of traffic run over the line so it was taken out-of-service after a final run to NIP on June 8, 2000. CSX stepped in, happily, to serve the park via a new connection located on the old Albany mainline west of the diamond in Voorheesville. That service, however, did not last long.

In 2004, CPRail abandoned the Albany mainline east of Voorheesville with rail removal undertaken during May and June of that year. At that time, the crossing of CPRail and CSX was removed so that trains of the latter company could run unfettered and non-stop past the former site of the Voorheesville station. Although the depot is gone, the freight house does survive. Previously, CPRail had taken the line out-of-service west of the Northeastern Industrial Park during 1995. Fortunately, that single track line remained in place so that it could be used as a round about route

SMS or SNY, whichever initials you prefer, handles mostly tri-level automobile rack cars laden with Ford Motor Company products between Delanson and the Northeastern Industrial Park at Guilderland Center via the old D&H Albany mainline interchange at Delanson. While auto racks dominate, the occasional box car sneaks into the consist, such as in the scene above photographed at Duane on January 27, 2010. The new bridge carries Route 7 over the old D&H Albany mainline.

to service the NIP via Delanson. Today, SMS Rail Lines, a Bridgeport, NJ-based short line operator uses this Delanson-NIP segment of the ex-Albany mainline to shuttle loaded tri-level auto racks laden with Ford Motor Company automobiles to the park. The loaded and returning empty tri-level cars have been switched into and out of Norfolk Southern trains at Delanson since early 2010. Loaded cars are cut out of Kenwood Yard-bound train 938; the empties go south in train 939. SMS operates its connection to NIP as SMS Rail Lines of New York, LLC, using "SNY" as its reporting mark. This service was started on November 1, 2006. SNY operates about eighteen miles of track in the area.

At rural Meadowdale, a wood frame board-and-batten depot provided station services for passengers and freight, but those services were later reduced to that of a simple waiting room. Three miles beyond—at milepost 17.2—a superior terminal was provided for the travelling public at Altamont. As was the case at Slingerlands, a standard board-and-batten style depot (Type W103) was erected here by the A&S in 1864. Thirty-three years later, the D&H improved the station grounds with a new depot, remodeling the old one into a 135-foot-long freight house and, still later, adding a single-stall enginehouse and a 90-foot turntable. The enginehouse and turntable were on opposite sides of the main track, but both still admirably served the commuter train service to and from Albany; this being that operation's outlying terminal.

In addition to catering to the commuter and regular passenger trains, Altamont also hosted special trains for groups desiring to vacation at the nearby Helderberg Mountain resorts. After all, for its entire distance of seventeen miles from Albany, the railroad had been climbing the grade of the Helderberg Escarpment, first via the valley of the Normans Kill, then Black Creek. Thus, the Altamont depot was the ideal jumping off place for capital district residents to get a lofty breath of mountain fresh air. You can bet your boots that Ticket/Freight Agent R. B. Safford was kept busy instructing passengers and handling baggage destined for the Helderbergs.

Seven miles beyond, Duane depot and Route 7 are reached. Within three more miles the original route of the Albany & Susquehanna Railroad arrived at Toad Hollow, as this section of Quaker Street was referred to at the time of the railroad's arrival. By the time Superintendent Hammond devised the name "Delanson" the earlier unflattering name had been cheerfully forgotten. Regardless of the moniker, the railroad's station sat nearly equidistant from routes 7 and 20, with Route 395 connecting both and serving double-duty as Delanson's Main Street where it crosses the railroad at grade. Before Delanson station was reached via the Albany mainline or Schenectady Branch, a junction of the two lines was made nearly a mile to the northeast. That was where the old Schenectady & Duanesburg and Albany & Susquehanna either joined forces or separated, depending on the direction under discussion. The importance of that junction was lessened when the D&H built its new southbound line from Schenectady.

The railroad desired to improve upon the 1.06% southbound grade of the Schenectady & Duanesburg Railroad so, beginning in 1906, it began work on a new line (except for a short section at Kelley's) that was located specifically to lessen curvature

ABOVE: *The village of Altamont, 17.2 miles distant from Albany, was the southern limit of the railroad's commuter district that served the capital. The community's station played host to legions of folks who desired to vacation within the nearby Helderberg Mountains, such as at the Helderberg Inn (INSET). Built in 1886 on the ridge above town as The Kushaqua, a summer-only resort, the structure measured 75x150 feet. It had its own private reservoir. After its tenure as the Helderberg Inn, it became a seminary in 1928 under the LaSalette Fathers. Unfortunately, it succumbed to fire October 18, 1946. The hotel at right was built in 1867 by George Severson who named it after himself. In later years, it became the Union Hotel, then the Commercial Hotel, as it is in this image. A northbound passenger train lies in wait for its departure time across from the station. The agent between 1900 and 1910 was Justin L. Smith; Adam Sitterly was the gate tender, visible in the tower.*
A. BRUCE TRACY COLLECTION. INSET, DEPOT SQUARE PUBLISHING COLLECTION.

LEFT: *Montford Sand was one of the prominent citizens of Altamont, serving for a time as Mayor. Among other things, Sand owned a bottling works, a coal dealership and a feed and grain business. Just to the right of the station—and down the tracks in the main image on the previous page—Sand's coal, feed and grain complex can be seen. In subsequent years, this facility was owned by Frederick Keenholts and Frank Becker, then Plank & Righter. It burned in March 1980. Between the* port cochere *attached to the coal dealership office at right and the right side of the depot can be seen the second story of the Altamont Soft Drinks bottling works (just above the box-car roofline) in the background. The station is the second building to serve Altamont; it was built in 1897.* LOWER LEFT: *Directly across the tracks from the station sat the Commercial Hotel, managed here by Dutch Cornelius. Accommodations could be had for just $1.50 per day around 1900.* BOTH, DEPOT SQUARE PUBLISHING COLLECTION. LOWER RIGHT: *This scene depicts what the site appears like today. Looking northwest from a compass standpoint but southbound operationally the restored depot now serves as the town library. SMS trains still pass by here almost every day, as evidenced by the shiny rails.*

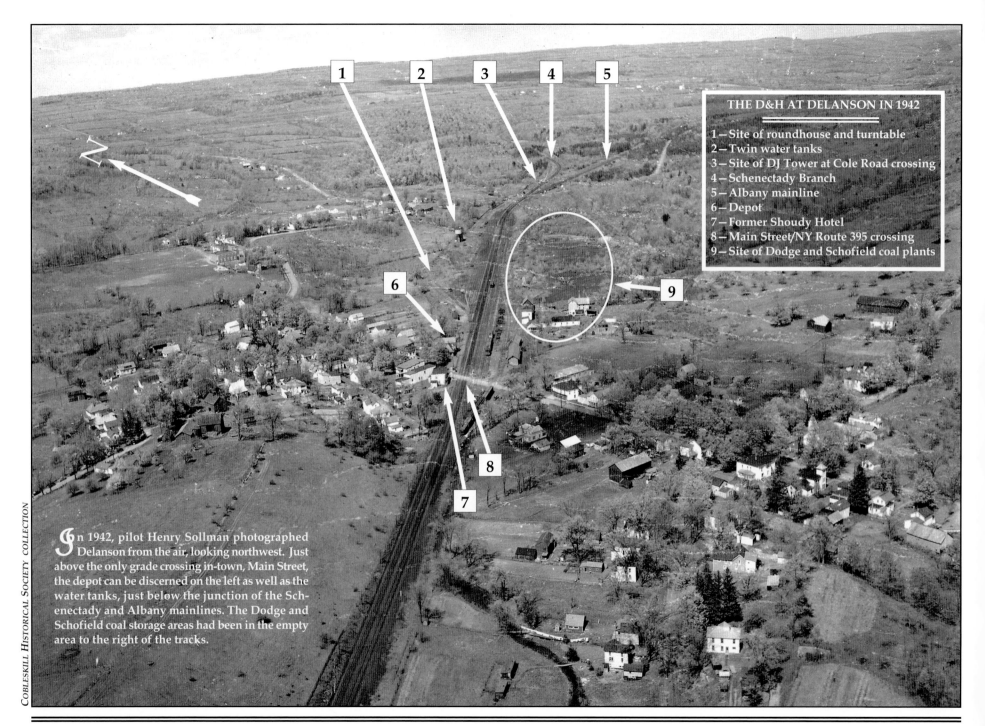

THE D&H AT DELANSON IN 1942

1 — Site of roundhouse and turntable
2 — Twin water tanks
3 — Site of DJ Tower at Cole Road crossing
4 — Schenectady Branch
5 — Albany mainline
6 — Depot
7 — Former Shoudy Hotel
8 — Main Street/NY Route 395 crossing
9 — Site of Dodge and Schofield coal plants

In 1942, pilot Henry Sollman photographed Delanson from the air, looking northwest. Just above the only grade crossing in-town, Main Street, the depot can be discerned on the left as well as the water tanks, just below the junction of the Schenectady and Albany mainlines. The Dodge and Schofield coal storage areas had been in the empty area to the right of the tracks.

and reduce the grade to 0.88% for southbound trains. During early 1908, at a cost of $29,105.15, the new line for all trains headed south was opened for service. This new line made its junction with the old A&S closer to Delanson, at Cole Road, than the original S&D/A&S junction. A new signal tower, designated DJ, was built (1908) to preside over this new connection. When the D&H built and implemented a new northbound track along the same grade as the southward line, during 1930, the original S&D line and junction was abandoned and the new connection controlled by DJ Tower became the only Schenectady Branch junction in town.

By the time this change of junctions took place, many more "betterments" had come to Delanson. A new station replaced the original depot in 1882, and by the turn of the century a second story addition was built. But, these upstairs rooms were not for the convenience of the agent and his family, they were used for the yard-master's office. The core of the yard was the construction of an anthracite and bituminous coal storage facility, at the time, the largest in the nation. Hard coal was stored in (four) piles using the James M. Dodge-designed system, while soft coal (which could not be piled as high) was placed in a separate contiguous area. (Soft coal, by its own properties, tended to self-combust if it was piled higher than 12-15 feet.) The two storage facilities became known as the Dodge Coal Storage Plant and the Schofield Coal Storage Plant: Dodge for hard coal; Schofield, for soft.

Besides mineral hardness, the Dodge and Schofield plants served different purposes. The Dodge plant stored nearly 240,000 tons of anthracite during its peak service, so that shipping and distribution could remain constant despite weather or mining-related difficulties. The Schofield plant stored bituminous coal for the same purpose as the Dodge facility but it also "blended" it with hard coal for a variety of railroad, industrial, and residential applications. The Delaware & Hudson Railroad was widely known as a mining, transporter, and user of anthracite coal—hence the wide Wooten fireboxes employed on its engines—so the Dodge facility at Delanson played a key role in distributing anthracite coal to all locomotive servicing facilities along the line of the D&H.

Supporting the operation of the Dodge and Schofield sites were boiler houses, store rooms, foreman's office(s), repair shops, booms and gantries, and washrooms and toilets for the numerous employees that worked there. These, of course, were in addition to a 108-foot-long freight house, an icehouse (that received its supply from Schenevus Lake), and a 65-foot turntable that was married to a six-stall roundhouse. All of these facilities inhabited the area between the passenger station and DJ Tower, standing on the east side of the mainline tracks. Only the depot, roundhouse/turntable, and tower were on the other side of the tracks. Rounding out the yard-master's domain at Delanson were upwards of twenty-two sidings in addition to the double-track mainline. Three tracks each served the Dodge and Schofield storage facilities from which their black diamonds could be loaded into hopper cars or locomotive tenders alike.

As you might imagine, the Delanson yard was a busy and important facility for the railroad, and the wages earned by its employees helped to bring prosperity to the railroad's town at the expense of Quaker Street whose residents remained quite content to appreciate all of the activity from afar. For many years, James L. Cummings was the railroad's man in charge of Delanson's coal storage and blending plants, and his son, James W., assisted him as weighmaster and timekeeper. But, all good things must come to an eventual end, and for the hustle and bustle at Delanson, that end came about during the Depression years. Governmental regulations regarding

At the Cole Road grade crossing of the D&H mainline, DJ Tower controlled the junction of the mainlines to Schenectady and Albany. It was northeast of the depot. In 1930, Howard H. Palmer and John L. Boynton served as assistant signal maintainers, with William L. Foote as their boss. LEN KILIAN COLLECTION.

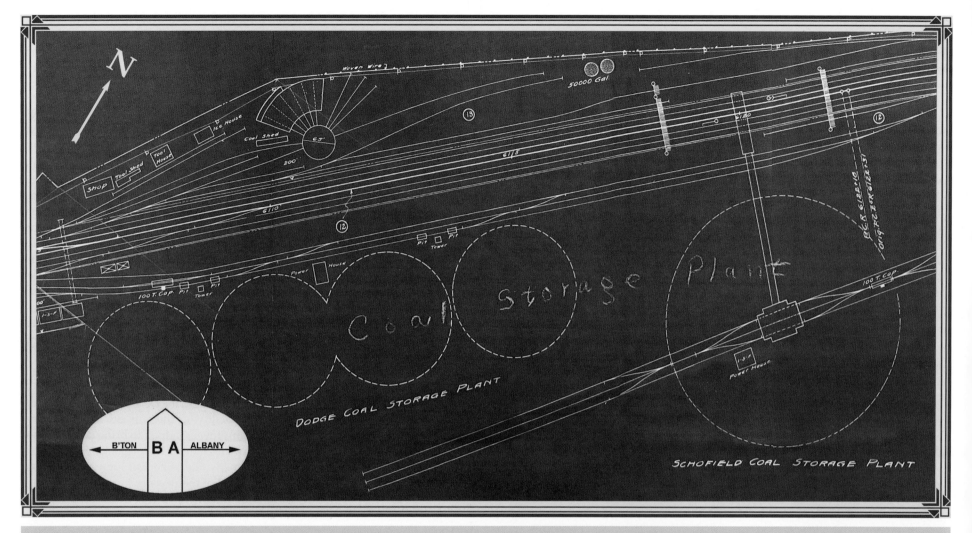

The majority of Delanson's yard was situated on the east side of the mainline tracks, between the depot (out of frame to the left) and DJ Tower (out of frame to the right). The Dodge and Schofield coal storage plants were of equal importance to the fortunes of both the railroad and the community. The storage facilities could store nearly 240,000 tons of anthracite and bituminous for the railroad and distribution to both industrial and residential end-users. James Mapes Dodge was a Cornell and Rutgers-educated mechanical engineer who was always interested in equipment for elevating and conveying coal. He joined William Ewarts who had patented a unique, detachable link-belt system. In 1892 Dodge formed the Dodge Coal Storage Company which was not a coal dealer but a business built around devices to mechanically unload, move, sort, screen, store, convey, and reload coal of different sizes. His system was used at Delanson to handle anthracite coal and was capable of storing up to 120,000 tons alone in 1909. Coal arrived by hopper or gondola and was unloaded by gravity into receiving bins sited under the unloading tracks. The coal passed through a gate onto a trimmer chute. The trimmer was manned and the operator picked up coal and directed it to the ground where he began to build a coal pile. The trimmer machine could move side-to-side so as to build the storage pile uniformly. Each anthracite pile contained as much as 50-60,000 tons. The Schofield facility was able to handle an equal quantity of bituminous coal, albeit in lower, broader mounds necessary to prevent self-ignition. NATIONAL ARCHIVES COLLECTION.

ABOVE: Looking south with the depot's location between the steaming locomotives to the right, cones of anthracite coal have been piled high by the Dodge coal plant's elevators and trimmers in anticipation of another high usage season once summer has gone. Delaware & Hudson locomotives, however, require that fuel year round, so in order to supply them—and load hopper cars—a coal tipple was provided (ABOVE RIGHT) which spanned several of the yard's tracks. The engine facility's water tanks stand just beyond the coaling station with the roundhouse further away and out of view. RIGHT: The Schofield coal storage plant loaded hopper cars via this three-track coaling station; its boiler house is seen at the right. A number of switches provide adequate operational control for switching throughout the facility. This view looks north; all others south.

LEFT: *On August 5, 1909, someone known only by the nickname "Rabbit" mailed this penny postcard to one Hudson E. Winans of Preston Hollow, NY. "Rabbit" enscribed the back with "This is a view of the coal heaps here. The two towers here are used to store water for the engines." Indeed, this image, taken north of Delanson along Cole Road, looks almost due south. Shown, from left to right, are some of the elevated tracks from the coal facility, the coal piles and trimmers from the Dodge plant in the background, the twin water towers, one boiler house, and the roundhouse at the far right.* DEPOT SQUARE PUBLISHING COLLECTION. LOWER LEFT: *DJ Tower guards the junction of the Schenectady Branch and Albany mainline trackage and the Cole Road crossing. Beyond and to its left, the Schofield and Dodge coal storage plants and their tipples can be observed. Everything in this view has either changed or has been removed since this picture was taken. Harvest Homes, a manufacturer of modular housing is situated upon the hallowed ground of the old coal storage plants* LEN KILIAN COLLECTION. BELOW: *This final scene of the coal plants shows the variety of high and low-sided gondolas and hoppers used to bring coal here from Pennsylvania. The trimmers and operator's cabs are clearly visible. Three young lads have decided to pose for the cameraman. Perhaps it is a summer Sunday as the normal flurry of everyday activity has come to a standstill.* DEPOT SQUARE PUBLISHING COLLECTION.

Albany mainline. I suppose you could employ a Global Positioning System (GPS) to guide you along, but I still like to do things the old fashioned way, by orienting with a map. Dad's dash-mounted compass would come in handy, too.

Regardless of the guidance system you use you won't be able to bring back the dead. The right-of-way is devoid of rails and ties all the way from Kenwood Yard to Voorheesville. Lots of ballast remains however. At Elsmere, an ornate iron railing still is in place to assist visitors up concrete steps to a grassy area that was once the site of the depot. Slingerlands' new station is gone, but its original still sits beside the forlorn right-of-way. The old building was moved to its current location to make way for its replacement—which no longer exists.

At Voorheesville, the diamond crossing of the D&H across CSX is gone, of course, as is the union station and the Friar's Grove Hotel which overlooked this spot. The union freight house survives, its boards and battens well-weathered from over one hundred years of exposure to the elements. Beyond the old crossing, one's heart may begin to beat a little faster as the old Albany mainline rails are still in place, though rusty. A little further on, near Meadowdale, the rails turn shiny as that is the eastern end of the old line that SMS uses to access the Northeastern Industrial Park from Delanson.

ABOVE: *Quaker Street's original two-stall wooden enginehouse was replaced by a more traditional six-stall brick roundhouse (RIGHT) a few years before Superintendent C. H. Hammond changed the location's name to Delanson. The new roundhouse, sixty-five-foot turntable, and a few auxiliary tracks were situated on the west side of the yard as shown on the blueprint on Page 22.*

ABOVE, ESPERANCE MUSEUM COLLECTION. RIGHT: STEVE DAVIS COLLECTION.

railroads owning coal companies, taxation, and a general change in usage of anthracite coal hastened the downturn of Delanson's fortunes. Modern locomotive coaling facilities elsewhere on the system, at Binghamton, Oneonta, Colonie, and South Junction (near Plattsburg) did not help Delanson's cause either. Elder Cummings closed and dismantled the coal plants before retiring; his son ended his railroad career in 1972 as Supervisor of Track, D&H System.

There is no easy way to travel by automobile the twenty-six miles from Albany to Delanson as a myriad of intersecting roads have to be employed to do so. It is much easier just to use the Great Western Turnpike (Route 20) and then turn southward onto Route 395 to gain the railroad's gateway to the south at Delanson. But, if a trip down memory lane is what you desire, equip yourself with a contemporary map to guide you along the route of the D&H's old

LEFT: *Built in 1882, this building replaced the original depot which was located across the tracks. In the distance, the small terminal can be seen where a six-stall roundhouse, turntable, water tanks and other auxiliary buildings stood. A water crane is barely visible between the tracks at the right edge of this image. The coal storage area was to the right beyond the cameraman's shutter. In 1910, the station agent was John S. Empie. The following year, General Electric built V-8-powered motor car No. 2000 for the D&H.* LOWER LEFT AND RIGHT: *The only grade crossing in "downtown" was Main Street. Facing the tracks is the Shoudy Hotel, built in 1874 by James Shoudy. He got his start as a hotelier with a tavern in nearby Princetown (Kelley's station) in the 1870s. In the 1880 Federal Census, he was still shown as a "hotel keeper" with his wife, Rose, four sons, and two daughters. The original Shoudy Hotel burned in 1891 and was rebuilt and reopened in October of that year. William Northrup succeeded Shoudy as proprietor shortly after as Shoudy fell ill with Bright's Disease, then a devastating kidney ailment. These two images also show that the D&H used an elevated switchman's tower and a free-standing shanty to guard this busy crossing. Harvey Dunlap was the crossing watchman in 1930.*

ALL, DEPOT SQUARE PUBLISHING COLLECTION.

A bonanza of sorts awaits you at Altamont as the depot survives as does the wooden freight house. The enginehouse is gone from the east side of the track but, on the west side—if you know where to look—evidence of the turntable's concrete ring can still be discerned. The station, by the way, is being remodeled to house the community's library, which may be completed by the time you read this.

SNY trains still cross the Schoharie Turnpike, which connects Route 20 with our Route 7 at Quaker Street. The community sits astride a quiet Route 7 ever since Interstate 88 was put into service, but diesel locomotive horns can still be heard wailing for the Main Street crossing down in Delanson. All of the railroad facilities of yesteryear are gone from Delanson except for the old double-track mainline that now serves as a single-track mainline and long passing siding. All of the railroad structures from the location of the former depot to DJ Tower have been expunged, including the depot and tower, the Dodge and Schofield plants, roundhouse, and turntable—all save one place. A building does reside on the site of the freight house that could indeed be a remodeled incarnation of the old edifice.

Regardless of the fact that all of these facilities have become a part of history, there still is some interesting contemporary railroading that takes place at Delanson, courtesy of CPRail, Norfolk Southern, and SMS or SNY (whichever initials you choose to use). That activity is centered around the fact that Delanson contains one of

LEFT: *The owner of the original depot for Slingerlands added an endwall bay window and replicated the wavy, hole-laden ornate fascia board associated with Albany & Susquehanna depots.* ABOVE: *Will Davis laments the passing of the Delaware & Hudson's Albany mainline crossing of CSX at Voorheesville, the old West Shore. A modern "Trailer-Jet" train scoots by bound for Selkirk Yard, a scant few miles to the right (southeast). The camera lens looks down the old Albany & Susquehanna mainline in the direction of Albany. The union station had once graced the junction just beyond the last UPS trailer. The Friar's Grove Hotel stood at the left, facing the depot. Both are long gone today.*

only four passing sidings to be found between Mohawk Yard and Binghamton; the other three are at Dante (CPRail calls this location Richmondville even though that community lies three miles to the north), Oneonta, and Afton. We will get to these places a little later, via Route 7, of course.

The passing siding at Delanson extends from CPF499 to CPF503 at Esperance. In D&H parlance, that stands for milepost 27 (near DJ Tower at Cole Road) to milepost 31. To the unknowing, the siding and main track here look all the world like a double track mainline but, beyond the siding limits only single track remains. The siding itself occupies the position of the old north-

bound track, while the main track is the former southbound track. (In case you haven't figured it out yet, the D&H was a north-south railroad, so that locations are either north or south of one another. Respecting these railroad directions, then buildings, roadways, or communities lie either east or west of the railroad regardless of compass direction. Therefore, correct terminology dictates that, as an example, Delanson is north of Esperance and west of Quaker Street.

Because of the few places that today's long trains can pass, it is not unusual to find a northbound train waiting south of Delanson's Main Street for a train to come off of the old Schenectady Branch. The northbound trains

When we turn off of Route 7 onto Route 395 this sign (ABOVE) lets us know that we are leaving Quaker Street behind and entering Delanson. At the bottom of the hill is where Main Street crosses the railroad at grade. Although the coal storage plants are long gone, coal still comes to Delanson (ABOVE RIGHT) in Norfolk Southern train 936 with bituminous coal bound for a Bow, NH electric generating facility. NS No. 9250 (GE C40-9W) leads the way. This is the northern limit of the Delanson passing siding; the Dodge and Schofield plants had once stood to the left. RIGHT: On March 27, 2009, CPRail train 250 crosses Cole Road arriving at CPF499 in Delanson. The old Albany mainline, officially referred to as the Voorheesville running track, veers to the right. DJ Tower formerly guarded the location from across the road and to the left of GE model ES44AC No. 8742.

ABOVE LEFT: *The transfer of enclosed tri-level auto rack cars between Norfolk Southern and SMS trains has brought about a renewed interest in railroading at Delanson. Photographers from around the region come here to digitally record the new operation as shown here on February 11, 2010. SMS crewmen are particularly pleased to have all this attention, and are equally tolerant with providing photo opportunities for visiting rail enthusiasts, provided all safety rules and measures are followed. On April 23, 2010, Conductor Jeremy Lisky (LEFT) poses for the author's camera; Engineer Chris Ahlf (ABOVE RIGHT) generously fills the cab window just two months earlier. Thanks fellas!*

ABOVE: *Northbound train 938 with a pair of GE ES40DCs led by No. 7696 are headed for Albany's Kenwood Yard on April 23, 2010. Here they pass the Cole Road crossing and the safety sign that advises crews to "Make Every Move a Safe One." The Voorheesville running track lies in the foreground, the one-time original Albany & Susquehanna mainline to the capital. DJ Tower controlled this point at one time, standing behind the lead locomotive. The grade crossing is for Cole Road with a portion of the village of Delanson in the background.*

On January 22, 2010, a four train "meet" occurred at Delanson involving trains 938, 939, SMS, and a loaded rail train. LEFT: *Norfolk Southern train 939 has picked up cars from SMS , whose motive power for the day lies at right. The NS locomotives are backing these autoracks onto their own consist. It will then pull south (forward) to CPF503 to wait for train 938 to arrive. After 939 has left the immediate vicinity, the SMS engines look on (*ABOVE*) as a Canadian Pacific rail train crosses Cole Road to head north toward Schenectady. SMS will wait for 938's arrival to pick up cars off of that train which it will then take over to the Northeastern Industrial Park.*

Beginning in early 2010, Norfolk Southern and SMS entered into an agreement whereby new Ford vehicles would be distributed from the Northeastern Industrial Park, using CPRail's Voorheesville Secondary, a remnant of the old A&S mainline. Enclosed tri-level autoracks would be set out from NS train 938 at Delanson and spotted on a siding to the west of the old mainline. Then, train 938 would continue to Mohawk Yard; SMS would pick up the autoracks. After permission is received from CPRail's Minneapolis dispatcher, SMS proceeds through the junction trackage onto the Voorheesville Secondary to reach the Northeastern Industrial Park in Guilderland Center. LEFT: From the fireman's cab window of SMS No. 2003, NS train 938 arrives at Delanson on the passing siding where it is about to cross Main Street on a frigid winter day. In charge is C40-9W No. 9124. Eight autoracks are on the drawbar behind the locomotives. BELOW: Not far out of the junction at Delanson at CPF499, the Schoharie Turnpike, connecting Route 7 at Quaker Street with US Route 20 near Duanesburg, was crossed at grade by the SMS. Here, GP-38 No. 2003 proceeds downgrade with twelve cars bound for unloading at NIP. While the right-of-way shows its age, this is the modern version of the line that once handled the Delaware & Hudson's passenger varnish between Albany and Binghamton, as well as some freight trains. BOTH, DEAN SPLITTGERBER PHOTOGRAPHS.

are too long to pull up to CPF499 to wait because they'll foul the Main Street crossing. This activity is enhanced when Norfolk Southern trains 938 and 939 meet at Delanson. It is those two trains that deliver or pick up cars from SMS, which is generally on the scene at the same time as the arrival of the NS trains. It is SMS that has helped to bring about a resurgence in Delanson's railroading fortunes, although the activity and its importance to the railroad are still far inferior to the historic years under Delaware & Hudson ownership.

Regardless of period, historic or contemporary, this area has prospered immensely from the time that it was known as Quaker Street's Toad Hollow. Thank the railroad for that.

No matter what highway route you use from either Schenectady or Albany, there are still two ways to get to Quaker Street; but only one rail route remains. South of Delanson, Route 7 is the primary road used to follow the railroad further south, to Cave Country.

Continuing the tradition that was begun by the Albany & Susquehanna Railroad in 1863, railroading still arrives at old Quaker Street's Delanson many times on a daily basis. The crossing gates go down to protect the Main Street crossing as every train arrives or leaves the community. CPRail train 251 has that crossing blocked as it heads north. Witnessing its passage is that gazebo (at far left) whose locomotive-topped weather vane (INSET) salutes the passage of each and every train. History is important to Delanson, and it will not be until the final train has run that its complete story can be written. Let's hope that won't be for quite some time.

CHAPTER 2
DOWN AND UP TO CAVE COUNTRY

After contemplating the historical significance of Delanson's locomotive weather-vane we leave the community created by the railroad to return to Route 7 via Route 395. Unlike the railroad that is directionally a north-south line, Route 7 is signed east-west so to follow the railroad south we have to turn right to head west on Route 7. In only a few moments we have left Quaker Street/Delanson behind and are now following along the dying northwestern shoulder of the Helderberg Mountains.

The railroad is still far below us, lying off to the north when we turn off Route 7 onto Gage Road. There's something I want to show you before we continue on our journey. Gage Road connects Route 7 with Route 20, but before the Cherry Valley Turnpike is reached we will cross the railroad at grade—both the main track and the Delanson-to-Esperance passing siding. Gage Road, CPF501 on the railroad, is some-

LEFT: *This sign advises auto excursionists to follow Route 7 to get to Howe Caverns. It may have been many years since vacationers went to the Caverns solely by Route 7—of course Interstate 88 will get you there faster—but that is exactly what we are going to do next. This is the only "seasoned" sign that pre-dates Interstate 88. It advertises Howe Caverns which is still situated along the Schohanna Trail, as Route 7 is unofficially named. We will get to see this Howe Caverns sign in person when we travel a little further down Route 7 near Cooperstown Junction.* RIGHT: *Just beyond the Gage Road grade crossing, southbound trains must begin to descend Schoharie Hill. Warning signs for the crews are commonplace on the old Albany & Susquehanna.*

ABOVE: *Norfolk Southern train 938 has just passed the "Begin Heavy Grade" sign signifying that it has reached the top of Schoharie Hill as it cruises towards a rolling meet (*RIGHT*) with train 939 at the Gage Road crossing. The enclosed tri-level auto racks behind 938's engines will be set out for the SMS at Delanson. Similar cars behind 939's locomotives were picked up from SMS and are now returning to the auto factory as empties. CPRail is replacing the old D&H twin-mast double (or triple) target signals with single-mast, double-target signals as shown in this portrayal of contemporary railroading at Gage Road near Delanson on August 29, 2010.* ABOVE RIGHT: *CPRail train 251 rolls northward on the Esperance-Delanson siding as crossing gates for Gage Road protect the passing of this Montreal-bound train on March 12, 2009. The red paint scheme gives life to the otherwise bleak colors of late winter before the vibrant spring hues return to upstate New York.*

what of a strategic point for two reasons. First, it may be where a southbound train will await the arrival of another train before continuing on. If this is the case, the reason is because the train is too long to go all the way to CPF503 at Esperance (station) without blocking Youngs Road, an intermediate local avenue that also connects routes 7 and 20. Northbound trains have to do the same thing at Delanson as previously mentioned in Chapter 1. Second, the other significance of Gage Road is that just to its (railroad) south, train crews are advised by signage that they are about to "Begin Heavy Grade" as shown in the picture on Page 33. Whether the railroaders who negotiate this trackage frequently need to be reminded that they are about to descend Schoharie Hill is questionable, but railroading is a safety-conscious industry where one miscue can cause injury. So, it is better to be forewarned than not, just in case a rookie is working the throttle one day. We will see more of these "grade" signs as we travel along.

We could have reached Gage Road by taking Thousand Acres Road out of Delanson, just as we could travel over hill and dale, employing interconnecting back roads, compasses, and GPS to go all the way to Howe Caverns. There is little benefit in doing so, however, as anything that we need to get to is readily accessible from Route 7. After all, there is a lot more to see—and learn—by taking this historic highway; we are interested in more than just the railroad, you know!

Now that I have pointed out Gage Road's attributes, we will return to Route 7 and continue westward. Not long after we pass Youngs Road, the highway begins to descend as the Helderberg Mountains evaporate into the Schoharie Valley. Many panoramic scenes will present themselves as we travel down to Binghamton but none may surpass the beautiful view that is now before us. You could take a picture of it, but the camera—even with the widest of lenses—could not do this scene justice. It is far too scenic, broad, distant, and simply breathtaking. There should be a rest area here along the side of Route 7 or, at the very least, a picnic area, so that travelers can stop and marvel at the topographic beauty of this Schoharie Valley setting. It took billions of years—along with the help of four glacial cycles—to mold the landscape into this wonderful scene. We are fortunate to be living during this period so that we can fully appreciate the work done "naturally" all those eons ago. In this valley, of course, is where Schoharie Creek flows, being the only sizeable waterway to descend northward from the Catskills all the way to the Mohawk Valley.

I am going to interrupt this scenic experience by turning onto New York State Route 30, for an interlude that will take us to Esperance, station and village. The railroad is still several hundred feet lower in elevation than Route 7. While our highway was descending, so was the railroad: ninety-six feet since it left Gage Road, hence the "Begin Heavy Grade" sign. The village of Esperance—some three miles beyond the railroad—is even several feet lower in altitude. Esperance is a wonderfully attractive village located abreast of Route 20 (which is an ancestral Route 7) with its eastern limits bordering Schoharie Creek. The village, unfortunately, holds the dubious distinction of lying the greatest distance away from the railroad station whose signboard bears its name than any other along the ex-D&H Susquehanna Division. Still, the Town of

Esperance has always lived by being situated along the old Great Western Turnpike (Route 20) that leads to Cherry Valley. That community and by-way are shown above, looking west from a vantage point atop the Schoharie Creek bridge on March 19, 2010. The old Albany & Susquehanna served this town by means of a depot located about three miles due south. The bridge the photographer is standing on carries US 20 over Schoharie Creek, the primary waterway through this region. It also forms the dividing line between Schoharie (ahead) and Schenectady counties.

Esperance was pleased to have its railroad and contributed $30,000 to aid the construction for the Albany & Susquehanna.

Esperance got its start from the Jacob H. Ten Eyck patent of 1769. The village had two previous names: State Bridge and Schoharie Bridge. Both names derived from a bridge built across Schoharie Creek. A toll of one-cent was charged to cross the creek via this bridge and that revenue provided upwards of $700 yearly for the community and town, both eventually named Esperance.

"Hope" is one of two French translations for "Esperance," and hope was what community leaders and residents alike did to further prosperity for the village. Fortunately, Esperance was situated on the Great Western Turnpike (today's Route 20 to Cherry Valley) that was the state's premier east-west thoroughfare right up until the building of the New York State Thruway.

Early on, all forms of travel proceeded unabated by this early road until the completion of the Erie Canal, which especially siphoned off a preponderance of freight shipments. Things eventually began to get back to normal along the turnpike and then the Albany & Susquehanna Railroad was opened. It wasn't until highways and automobiles evolved that the old turnpike rose to fame, only to be dashed once again by the state thruway. Through all of this, Esperance relied on its distant railroad station to assume a *status quo*. The A&S knew that the village relied on it, too, so they put up

a standard board-and-batten depot that carried a 21-foot-wide by 74-foot-long footprint.

The depot was the connection to the outside world for Esperance. Residents could travel the globe — at least the United States — by simply purchasing a ticket and boarding a train bound either north or south. From the furnaces, forges, paper and feed mills built along Schoharie Creek, manufactured and agricultural goods were brought to the depot for shipment to markets. And, from the farms of William Conover and Waldo Collette came bluestone that could be harvested in thicknesses of up to twelve inches. While the harvesting and shipment of this natural stone product was long lasting, the industry's most prolific years were during the 1890 to 1910 period when local legend informs us that over one mil-

lion dollars was made by the business. All that bluestone, by the way, was hauled to market by the railroad.

The improved state highway eventually became a more convenient means to ship Esperance's marketable goods which reversed the fortunes at the railroad's depot. By 1930, the Delaware & Hudson Company determined that revenue produced at Esperance did not even cover the cost of manning the station, which figured to be $2,469.52 that year. After a series of five hearings were held by the state's Public Service Commission — three in Albany and two in Esperance — the PSC ruled (on February 2, 1932) that the railroad was justified in closing the station, which it did on the first day of March. One last-ditch effort was made by Esperance elders to reverse the PSC decision at a meeting held in Albany

on March 21, 1932, but the railroad and the commission stuck to their guns and the station remained closed. Freight coming from or going to Esperance would be handled at Delanson; two passenger trains in each direction, however, continued to call at the closed station. Greyhound Bus Lines, by the way, provided two buses each way between Albany and Syracuse that served Esperance village directly from Route 20. That didn't help the community's efforts to keep the depot open. With its railroad depot three miles distant, the village of Esperance continued to live by the road, at least until the Thruway was built. Within a year, or two, Esperance station was removed by the railroad, becoming just a memory. Wooden railroad depots don't really die; they just become fond memories of railroading's past.

Of course today, the depot is still gone at Esperance. Oak Hill Road doesn't cross the tracks anymore, but there is still life there in the form of a talking detector. This electronic device counts the axles of a passing train, senses the temperature of each roller-bearing journal, and then reports verbally with a (recorded) human voice to the engineer in the lead locomotive cab: "D&H detector, mileage 503, checking southbound train. 324 axles. Temperature 48 degrees. Have a safe trip." (Yes,

LEFT: *Dating from the early 1880s, this photograph records Station Agent John Hunter standing on the Esperance platform with who may be his second wife, Elizabeth Cinderella Gardiner (at left), and his widowed mother, Margaret, at this time a resident of Duanesburg. The two little girls—Maggie and Ella—are his daughters from his first marriage to Princess Ann Baker who died in 1872. The agent here throughout the 1870s and 1880s, Mr. Hunter had retired from the Delaware & Hudson by 1900 to operate a coal business in Duanesburg. Despite the date of this picture, the depot, which was built in 1864, appears somewhat rundown, yet the original station signboard at upper right still proudly denotes that this is the stop for Esperance. Compare that sign with the version (BELOW LEFT) shown above the head of Edward Albert "Monkey" Cromwell whose brother, Raymond, worked as the Esperance telegrapher in 1910. Staying with the railroad, Ray held the position of chief clerk at Delmar by 1930. A native of Quaker Street, Edward Cromwell also secured employment with the D&H—first as a clerk in Esperance and later as chief clerk at the company's Bainbridge and Schenectady freight offices. BELOW RIGHT: During its life, the Esperance depot was divided into rooms that served the needs of the railroad as well as those of an agent and his family. Could this be why Agent Hunter's wife and children are at the station? All, ESPERANCE MUSEUM COLLECTION.*

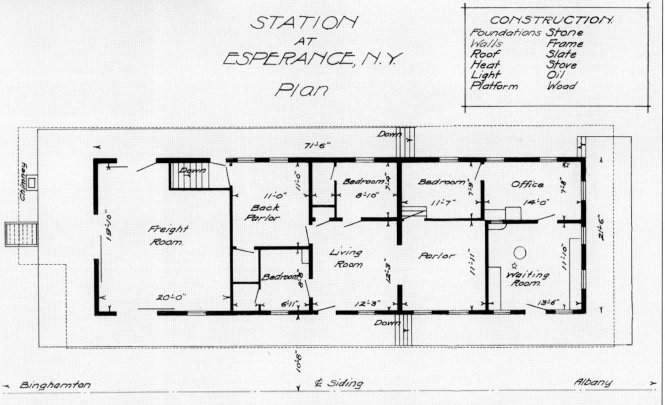

STATION
AT
ESPERANCE, N.Y.
Plan

CONSTRUCTION.
Foundations — Stone
Walls — Frame
Roof — Slate
Heat — Stove
Light — Oil
Platform — Wood

Immediately south of the former site for Esperance's depot, CPRail's single track mainline divides to form a main track and a passing siding that runs four miles to CPF499 in Delanson. At this location, noted by the milepost for CPF503 (LEFT) northbound train 938 meets its southbound counterpart, train 939. While it appears that 938 is taking the siding, in actuality it is going "main-to-main" as noted by the diagram on the side of CB Cabin (CENTER LEFT AND RIGHT). The single tower, double-mast, six-target standard D&H signal was one of only two still in operation when this picture was taken on March 19, 2010. (BELOW) Headed south, CPRail train 250 passes the site where Esperance's depot was located. Oak Hill Road is at right. This image was taken on February 27, 2009.

ROADS, RIVERS, AND RAILS

At Esperance Station, as the railroad depot site was referred to to differentiate it from the village of Esperance, highway building and relocation caused a change in the complexion of the area. Present Oak Hill Road, as noted on the previous page—and by the sign in the picture at right—at one time crossed the railroad at grade immediately north of the depot. But, when new Route 30 and its underpass of the railroad (RIGHT) were put into service, Oak Hill Road was diverted into the new state roadway. Similarly, Esperance Station Road did not exist until the building of new Route 30, and this sign (LOWER RIGHT) has since directed persons to a (still) dirt road that leads to the former station grounds. LOWER LEFT: Norfolk Southern train 938 is going main-to-main at Esperance on March 31, 2009 with Oak Hill Road on the extreme left of the picture. It was just about where the photographer is standing that the roadway had crossed the tracks at grade earlier. RIGHT: NS train 930 with C40-9W No. 9852 in the lead is captured on March 19, 2010.

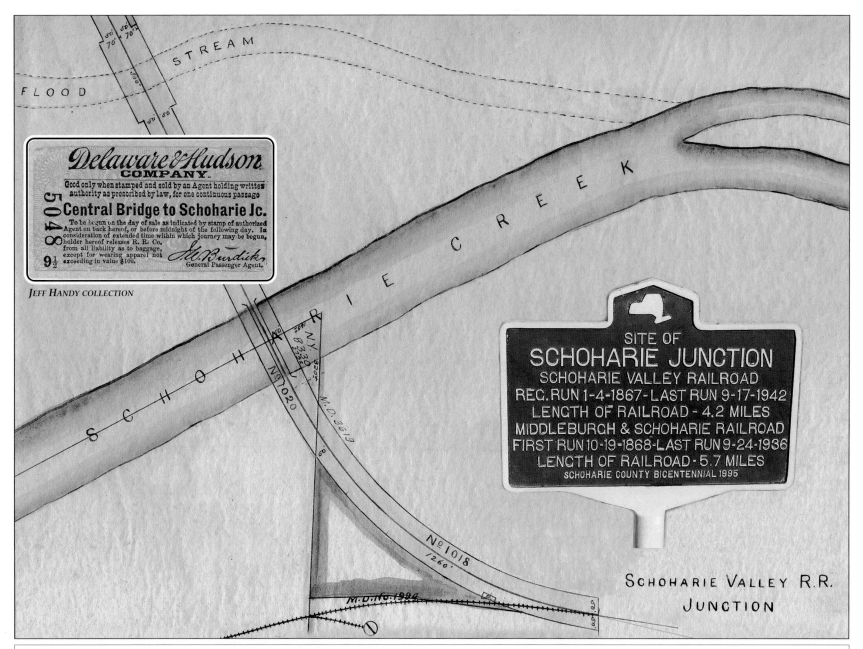

Delaware & Hudson
COMPANY

Good only when stamped and sold by an Agent holding written authority as prescribed by law, for one continuous passage

Central Bridge to Schoharie Jc.

To be begun on the day of sale as indicated by stamp of authorized Agent on back hereof, or before midnight of the following day. In consideration of extended time within which journey may be begun, holder hereof releases R. R. Co. from all liability as to baggage, except for wearing apparel not exceeding in value $100.

$9\frac{1}{2}$

H. Burdick,
General Passenger Agent.

JEFF HANDY COLLECTION

SCHOHARIE CREEK

STREAM

FLOOD

SITE OF
SCHOHARIE JUNCTION
SCHOHARIE VALLEY RAILROAD
REG. RUN 1-4-1867 - LAST RUN 9-17-1942
LENGTH OF RAILROAD - 4.2 MILES
MIDDLEBURGH & SCHOHARIE RAILROAD
FIRST RUN 10-19-1868 - LAST RUN 9-24-1936
LENGTH OF RAILROAD - 5.7 MILES
SCHOHARIE COUNTY BICENTENNIAL 1995

SCHOHARIE VALLEY R.R.
JUNCTION

At Schoharie Junction, the 4.2 mile-long Schoharie Valley Railroad connected with the Delaware & Hudson Company; the SV became a property of the D&H in 1906. Just to the south of the junction the D&H crossed Schoharie Creek and its flood stream and then entered Central Bridge. The humpback bridge (Page 42), and Route 7 are just off this map to the left. Note the Schoharie Valley maintained a turntable at the junction. MAP, WALTER G. RICH COLLECTION.

even in this CPRail era the voice still says "D&H.") The engineer then knows all is well with his train. Station agents and telegraph operators used to give all trains passing their station a "roll by," which was essentially what the detector does. Then, when the caboose passed, a friendly wave, or a thumb to the nose, was given to crewmen therein to let them know that their train was either okay, or had a hotbox. But, in today's railroading world, there are no station agents, telegraph operators, cabooses, or crewman other than an engineer and conductor. Times may have changed on the railroad, but trains still roll past the site of Esperance's station.

Taking Route 30 south, we return to Route 7, turn west, and again marvel at the panoramic view of Schoharie Valley. But, in only a couple of miles we are no longer descending into the valley, we are in it. So is the railroad, but only temporarily. We will join it by turning onto Junction Road, a thoroughfare that has an historical railroad significance. Its name comes from the junction of the Schoharie Valley and Delaware & Hudson railroads. The Schoharie Valley Railroad ran from the junction to Schoharie by following the Schoharie Creek valley. Meanwhile the D&H traversed the valley from the downgrade off Schoharie Hill to the 1.02% grade up Howes Cave Hill. In so doing, Schoharie Creek is crossed by bridge No. 24; its flood stream (overflow), by No. 25. We will cross the creek as well, but not just yet.

The only bridge of note on the SVRR was the old humpback bridge that took Route 7 over the railroad. Both it, and the railroad, were born in 1867, quite possibly making the humpback bridge New York State's earliest grade crossing elimination project. The wooden bridge was constructed to dimensions that were cozy enough for two horse-drawn wagons to pass over it at the same time. It remained that way until 1930 with the only alteration being the raising of the bridge as taller railroad cars began to be used. By that time, automobiles had replaced the horse-drawn wagons, and cars themselves had become bigger and faster. Automobilists had to approach the bridge slowly because of its sharply inclined approach ramps and very short flat section at top. It was difficult for two cars to pass on this structure without "bruising" door handles. Many an unsuspecting motorist, unfamiliar with the bridge's physical characteristics ran onto it too fast and simply bounded across the top in much the same manner as Evil Kneivel used his motorcycle to leap across a line of cars. Some of the bridge's "victims" ended up like Kneivel, too: broken into pieces. The bridge, although a curiosity, was cursed at for years, and that may be why nary a photograph of it was ever taken. When it was replaced by a new span, applause

Like the Old Fashioned 'Whatnot', 'Hump Back' Bridge Goes Its Way

Old "Hump Bridge," one mile north of Central Bridge.

Jacob Vrooman, who purchased the railroad at one time for $25,000.

Schoharie County Land-mark, Mile North of Central Bridge, Now in Limbo of Yesteryear.

LIKE the whatnot that littered the living room of the old-fashioned ohthem, "Hump Back" bridge, a mile north of Central Bridge, is gone. Like the old fashioned horse and buggy which gave way to the automobile this almost ancient bridge has given away to a concrete structure.

For more than sixty years the bride, like a "Thank-You-Man,"

The new concrete bridge replacing it and the railroad.

which in the old days was a level spot on a hill where teams of horses could rest, but nowadays a place where automobiles were sometimes thrown off the road, has been the scene of accident, injury and death, and, in its way, progress. It was built in 1867, spanning the Scho-harie Valley and Middleburg rail-road which was completed in 1863.

It is the last of the historic land-marks of its kind in Schoharie coun-ty, and one of the few remaining in New York State. In June, the Esperance covered bridge over the Schoharie Creek, and five miles from Central Bridge, was taken away, because of its structural weak-ness, and inability to take care of the ever increasing traffic.

When the "Hump Bridge" was built, it was much lower than when torn down recently. Within the past sixty years, it was necessary to raise the bridge to accommodate the height of the railroad cars, and each time it has become more dangerous. About ten years ago, it was raised for the last time, making it much higher than the road.

THE APPROACHES were steep, and the portion above the tracks was flat, not long enough to accommodate the length of a car, and just wide enough to allow two cars to pass, with the danger of falling off. A wooden railing, built to protect traffic in the "buggy age," served only as an ornament in the automobile era.

The road on each side leading to the wooden structure was short and steep. The highway from the south ended at the foot of Oak Hill, a sharp descent. Cars coming down this hill would hit the bridge at a high rate of speed, and their pas-

sengers would have the surprise of a lifetime when the car would leave the top of the bridge and land on the other side.

Mrs. Charles Bensen, who lives on the north side, gave a description of some of the dangers. She said: "I have seen cars come down the hill and when they came off this side, they were actually in the air. It is a wonder there has not been more accidents. I remember only one in-cident in the three years that I have lived here when a car was damaged. Then a car, while its four wheels were off the ground, turned and when it struck the road on this side ran off and hit a telegrahp pole. Most of the accidents I have seen were to persons in the cars. Many injured persons have stopped in front of my house. One woman got out and barely was able to walk, be-cause she had sprained her back. Another person had been thrown in-to the top of the car and suffered a deep cut on the forehead and nose. It will add to public safety when the new bridge is completed."

There was a reason for that old "Hump Bridge." When the rail-road was being constructed, the Schoharie Company, which formed to build it, was asked to lower the road bed, but it refused. As a re-sult, the state was compelled to build high in the air.

About 1860 and for many years after, Schoharie county was a thriv-ing hop center, and the farmers took their crops to Schoharie and Mid-dleburg over almost impassible roads. This was the reason why the rail-road was built. On July 4, 1867, opening day of the railroad, 400 passengers were carried, and in Sep-

tember the same year 3,750 persons used that line.

THE COMPANY sold out Satur-day, April 4, 1874, at public auction to Jacob Vrooman, who paid $25,000, because of a fore-closure of a mortgage. The auction took place in front of the old Scho-harie court house.

His grandson, Colonel Elsworth Vrooman, sixty-nine, was the man-ager and general passenger agent of the eleven mile line. He is living today in Schoharie. Colonel Vroo-man is a bright, kindly, and highly educated man, and has some inter-esting clippings about the old rail-road, including the ninety-five orig-inal passes issued to him forty years ago when he was connected with the company.

"The Dummy" was the first loco-motive to pass over the tracks, and received this name because, as Ly-man S. Homes, president of the Schoharie county board of elections, who remembers it, said, "It received that funny name because it was a dumb looking thing. It looked like a freight car with a cowcatcher on each end, and a homemade engine and boiler standing upright in the car."

The railroad is still in use with two trains a day making the trip from Schoharie to Middleburg, while the "Hump Bridge" although an example of the workmanship of those days, is gone. It was not, as the Esperance bridge, torn down be-cause of its structural weakness, be-cause it was as strong as the day it was built. It was torn down because it has been an increasing menace to public safety.

---

echoed throughout the Schoharie Valley; not a tear was shed. Humpback bridges, like depots it seems, just be-come another thing of the past.

The Schoharie Valley Railroad lasted a little longer than its noteworthy bridge. That may be because the Delaware & Hudson Railroad, which acquired the line during 1906, was able to help it weather the Depression. The D&H desired to gain financial control of the SV to thwart a scheme that would have incorporated the SV route as part of a new line to Schenectady. The D&H never had any desires to do similarly with the Middle-burgh & Schoharie Railroad that connected with the SV to

form a roughly ten mile line between Middleburg and Schoharie Junction. Wisely, the D&H never interfered with the operation of the SV, preferring to just enjoy the line's meager income from hauling quarried stone, SOCONY oil and gas, and a trickle of passengers, all of which ended up at the D&H's Schoharie Junction door-step. The D&H didn't even own the Schoharie Junction depot; that belonged to the SVRR, too.

The SV, and the M&S, ended up like the humpback bridge. The M&S was abandoned first, in 1936, and the SV passed away six years later. Schoharie Junction ceased to be a junction at the same time. Standing there today,

it is hard to imagine that there ever was a junction at all. Time has a way of doing that. It is hard to believe that at one time there was more than today's single track there. The D&H Susquehanna Division was completely double tracked by the end of the 1800s. During the new century, sections of the line were triple-tracked. Schoharie Junction to Delanson became the first of the three-track sections in 1916; Oneonta to Cooperstown Junction got its third track in 1918, and the railroad put a third track between Schenevus and Richmondville Summit (Dante) into service on December 7, 1921. At Schoharie Junction, a new electromechanical interlock-

ABOVE LEFT: *The Schoharie Valley and Middleburgh & Schoharie railroads combined to form a nearly ten mile long railroad to serve the communities of Schoharie and Middleburg, connecting them to the "outside world" via the Delaware & Hudson Railroad at Schoharie Junction. At Schoharie, the SVRR's brick station—which still survives—greets the arrival of a train from the junction with 4-4-0 No. 5 that has been running backwards, a not uncommon occurrence for both the SV and M&S.* A. BRUCE TRACY COLLECTION. ABOVE RIGHT: *At Schoharie Junction, M&SRR engine No. 2 waits with two cars for the arrival of the connecting D&H train while members of the crew and several onlookers pass away the idle moments. One fellow has even found a seat on one of the D&H mainline rails, possibly indicating that the train's arrival is still some moments away.* RIGHT: *The station at Schoharie Junction was the property of the SVRR, but its second floor telegraph operator's bay was used by D&H men to govern the movement of trains on both railroads. Agent Harry Cameron is standing between his station and the D&H mainline tracks; he is probably the man who worked within the operator's bay window. The NYCRR boxcar stands upon the SVRR track on June 16, 1936. In 1923, a new electro-mechanical interlocking tower went into service superceding operation from the depot operator's bay.* LEFT: *Several years earlier, a third track had been added between the junction and Delanson which necessitated the need for a modern tower. Whether new tower, or old operator's bay, the telegraph call was JX.*

OTHER THREE PHOTOGRAPHS, LAMBERT D. COOK.

With the D&H's summer schedule for 1938 (BELOW LEFT), the railroad advised passengers that Schoharie Junction depot would close on June 30th, and that trains would stop at the "former" site of Esperance Station, indicating that the depot had been removed. Binghamton is often misspelled, even in railroad timetables! (RIGHT) On January 15, 1976, D&H RS-3 No. 4082 loafs along behind the caboose of train RW-6 as it rounds the curve through Schoharie Junction. Its 1,500 horsepower will be required to push the train up Howes Cave Hill after Schoharie Creek is crossed. (BELOW RIGHT) Amidst the scenic Schoharie Creek valley farmland, CPRail southbound train 250 with four ES44ACs brings 16,000 hp to bear, rounding the curve into Schoharie Junction on August 27, 2009.

LEFT, LEN KILIAN COLLECTION. BELOW RIGHT, GEORGE HOCKADAY PHOTOGRAPH.

ALBANY, COBLESKILL, ONEONTA AND BINGHAMPTON

308 Daily	302 Except Sun.	Mls.	TABLE 8	305 Except Sun.	309 Except Sun.	313 Sun. Only
READ DOWN					**READ UP**	
PM	AM		Lv. .... Ar.	AM	PM	PM
4 20	7 00	0	.....ALBANY.....	11 35	6 25	1 30
.....	f7 14	5.5	.........Delmar.......	f11 23	p6 12	f1 17
.....	7 25	10.8	.....Voorheesville.....	11 15	p6 03	f1 08
4 48	7 37	17.2	.....Altamont.....	11 05	p5 54	f12 58
5 04	7 56	26.8	.....Delanson.....	10 50	5 40	12 44
5 18	8 11	35.3	.#Schoharie Junction.	10 36	5 25	.....
5 24	8 17	36.2	.....Central Bridge..	10 33	5 20	12 28
v5 31	8 25	39.2	.....Howe's Cave..	10 27	5 14	12 22
5 42	8 41	44.7	.....Cobleskill.....	10 17	5 04	12 12
v5 51	8 52	49.9	.....Richmondville.....	10 08	4 55	12 04
v6 04	9 07	56.9	.....East Worcester..	9 55	f4 43	f11 51
6 11	9 15	61.5	.....Worcester.....	9 46	4 37	11 44
6 19	9 24	66.5	.....Schenevus.....	9 37	4 29	11 36
v6 31	f9 41	76.3	.....Colliers.....	f9 22	f4 15	f11 20
6 40	9 50	81.7	Ar.....Oneonta....Lv.	9 15	4 08	11 12
6 47	10 00	81.7	Lv.....Oneonta.....Ar.	9 07	4 01	11 07
v7 00	10 14	89.6	.....Otego.....Lv.	8 54	3 48	10 54
v7 06	10 21	94.0	.....Wells Bridge.....	8 45	f3 41	10 46
7 13	10 29	98.8	.....Unadilla.....	8 37	3 34	10 38
7 25	10 40	103.3	.....Sidney.....	8 28	3 25	10 30
7 36	10 51	108.4	.....Bainbridge.....	8 14	3 16	10 21
v7 44	11 00	114.3	.....Afton.....	8 03	3 05	10 13
7 54	11 09	118.8	.....Nineveh.....	7 55	2 58	10 05
h7 57	11 13	120.3	.....Harpursville.....	7 51	w2 54	10 01
h8 09	11 25	127.0	.....Tunnel.....	7 39	w2 43	9 49
h8 19	11 34	132.5	.....Sanitaria Springs.	7 28	w2 32	9 39
8 40	11 55	142.5	.....BINGHAMTON...	7 10	2 15	9 20
PM	AM		Ar. .... Lv.	AM	PM	AM

Effective with the close of business June 30, the station at Schoharie Junction, N. Y., will be discontinued and no trains will stop at that point.

Trains 302, 305, 309 and 313 will stop at former site of Esperance Station (located between Delanson and Central Bridge), to pick up and discharge passengers.

PARLOR CAFE CARS ON SUSQUEHANNA DIVISION
★ Indicates air-conditioned cars.

No. 305 (Weekdays)—No. 313 (Sundays)
★Parlor Cafe Car...................................Binghamton to Albany.

No. 308—(Daily)
★ Parlor Cafe Car...................................Albany to Binghamton.

ing plant and tower, named JX, began service in 1923; Schenevus got a new tower, WN, the previous year.

All of the three-track railroading, and even some of the double-tracking, became a thing of the past when a Centralized Traffic Control (CTC) system went into operation between Oneonta and Delanson in 1940. That's why, when standing at Schoharie Junction today, all we see is a single track and a short siding that serves a new CPRail maintenance-of-way facility. The short siding may be all that is left of the former Schoharie Valley Railroad. (More detail about the CTC implementation will be covered in the section on Schenevus.)

Just around the curve that passes through the site of old Schoharie Junction is the place where the railroad crossed the Schoharie Creek and flood stream bridges, and then entered Central Bridge. For us to get to town, we have to go back to Route 7 and turn westward once again. Before we cross the highway bridge over Schoharie Creek we will pass the site of the humpback bridge over the SVRR tracks. Nothing is left of either structure.

Once we cross the creek, we enter "old" Central Bridge. The name for the settlement came about because its bridge over the creek was situated between the Schoharie Creek bridges at Esperance and Schoharie. Thus, it was the middle, or "central," bridge. That's not the only historical claim to fame for "old" Central Bridge. There is a human footnote to history here and that was George Westinghouse who was born there in 1846.

When George was only seven years old he began hanging around in his father's shop where threshing machines were made. As you might suspect, his interest was in making toys, much to the dislike of his father. But, seven years later, his father put him to work in the shop, which pleased George because now he had money to spend on his own projects, one of which was making a violin! Mr. Westinghouse moved his shop to Schenectady where it was easier to obtain raw materials for his threshers, and it was from there that George went off to fight in the Civil War in 1863.

When the War of the Rebellion was over two years later, George returned to Schenectady and resumed working for his father. But, several things happened to change the direction of George's future. He often trav-

elled to Albany by train, most likely the New York Central & Hudson River Railroad. On one trip a derailment occurred. While he was watching the men attempting to get the cars back on the track he realized that what was needed was a device to rerail cars. Thus, the rerailer was born and he was soon making them. Sometime thereafter George learned of a tragic railroad wreck that was caused by one heavy train not being able to stop before colliding with the other.

He could think of nothing else than developing a better means of stopping trains. His thoughts languished until he struck upon the idea of using compressed air to actuate a braking system. The real genius of the idea was to use air not to apply the brakes, but to keep the brakes from being applied. In this manner the loss of air would automatically bring a train to a halt. At age 22, he formed the Westinghouse Air Brake Company, and it was his invention that would revolutionize railroad operations. I suppose the sign of a great invention is that it is long lasting, and if that is the criteria, then the air brake was a great invention. Railroads today still slow and stop their trains with air, and although the system has been improved, railroaders still rely on "Old Man Westinghouse" to bring everything to a halt. On the old D&H, as well as today's CPRail, the automatic air brake comes in mighty handy when descending hills on the old Susquehanna Division. Dynamic brakes come into play, too, but those weren't developed until the diesel locomotive era, which was many years after the death of George Westinghouse in 1914. Railroads still use rerailers.

George Westinghouse wasn't quite finished with railroading. In 1881, he founded Union Switch & Signal Company to develop and implement his ideas on improving railroad signaling. US&S is still in business today. All told, Central Bridge's George Westinghouse received 361 patents. Among these were: a system for making it possible for natural gas to be distributed through piping, telephone line switching,

and promoting the attributes of alternating current electricity (to the dismay of Thomas Edison who favored direct current electricity).

Mr. Westinghouse and his company are the first of many noteworthy persons and businesses we'll visit on our way to Binghamton. We will meet Lester Howe and his cave shortly. First, we have to visit Cobleskill Creek and "new" Central Bridge.

At Route 30A, we turn off of our favorite highway, and almost immediately a bridge takes us over Cobleskill Creek, its outlet into Schoharie Creek — off to the east — not quite visible.

The nearly sixteen mile course of Cobleskill Creek extends from the Chesapeake Bay-Hudson River watershed at Dante to here at Central Bridge. The meager flow of its water is substantially increased with the addition of West Creek at Warnerville. In spring time, winter's melting snow causes rough water as West Creek's rocky bed dives under the railroad and, quite often, water overflows into adjacent farmland before the Cobleskill is reached. Throughout its journey, Cobleskill Creek is bridged only once by Route 7 — at the eastern limits of Cobleskill — while the creek and railroad never get to meet each other. For the initial part

Birthplace of George Westinghouse in "Old" Central Bridge, NY.

BIRTHPLACE OF GEORGE WESTINGHOUSE 1846-1914 INVENTOR OF THE WESTINGHOUSE AIR BRAKE of its trip to the Schoharie, the creek descends more quickly than the railroad, so that when both pass through Richmondville the waterway is far below the railway. At Warnerville the two neighbors are on about equal footing, though some distance apart, but that is also where the railroad begins its northward assault on the grade to Howe's Cave. At this latter location, the railroad, while higher in elevation than the creek, descends almost to water level at Central Bridge.

Considering the more severe profile of the railroad as opposed to the rather steady descent of Cobleskill Creek, you may be wondering why the A&SRR did not locate along its bank. The simple answer—because a lesson in geology is not the bastion of this project—is twofold. Although the waterway's descent is rather steady,

ABOVE: *The Cobles Kill near its eastern extreme at "Old" Central Bridge is heralded by this highway sign.*

it is still a grade inferior to that of the railroad, its downs and ups notwithstanding. In addition, the profile of hills at Richmondville left little room for anything other than the community and the creek. Yet state engineers shoehorned the new four-lane Interstate 88 through Richmondville even though its grade is still more severe than that of the railroad, especially as the watershed area is approached. Regardless of their physical location in relation to one another, the creek, railroad, and our Route 7 form a compatible association throughout the mileage from Dante to Central Bridge.

"New" Central Bridge was where the railroad was located. The village developed there because that is where the Albany & Susquehanna built its depot. Unlike Delanson, the railroad chose to stick with a tried and true name. But, the prosperity of "old" Central Bridge was indeed usurped by the "new" just as Delanson did to Quaker Street.

Similar to Esperance, there were two previous names for the community before "Central Bridge" took hold: Kniskern's Dorf, and Smithville. The original name came from Johann Peter Kniskern, an area landowner of German descent, while Innkeeper Sam Smith provided his name in 1824. By 1837, everything was Central Bridge, including the post office. When the railroad came to town in 1863, hotels, a church, an agricultural works, a feed mill, and residences all came to new Central Bridge. The residences lined Main Street on the west side of the railroad tracks; the business district was on the opposite side. It was the railroad that made it possible for prosperity to gain a foothold in the annexed village. Also arriving in Central Bridge not long after the railroad was Daniel W. Jenkins. He had been station agent at Quaker Street, replacing his father who had ousted Joshua Whitney. Agent Jenkins was a man of long and esteemed tenure, but not as long as

The focal point of the station grounds at Central Bridge was the depot (marked by the letter "P" on the track diagram below; "F" is for the freight station). FACING PAGE: Looking west on July 31, 1918, a fellow casually leans against the door jamb while passing an idle moment at the depot on this very quiet afternoon between trains. RIGHT: This southerly view displays the relationship of the depot to the water tank location. Unlike the other photograph, the agent has spotted express and other items for shipment on the next consist. Station agent Daniel W. Jenkins served here between 1872 and 1900. FACING PAGE AND BELOW, NATIONAL ARCHIVES COLLECTION. RIGHT, A. BRUCE TRACY COLLECTION.

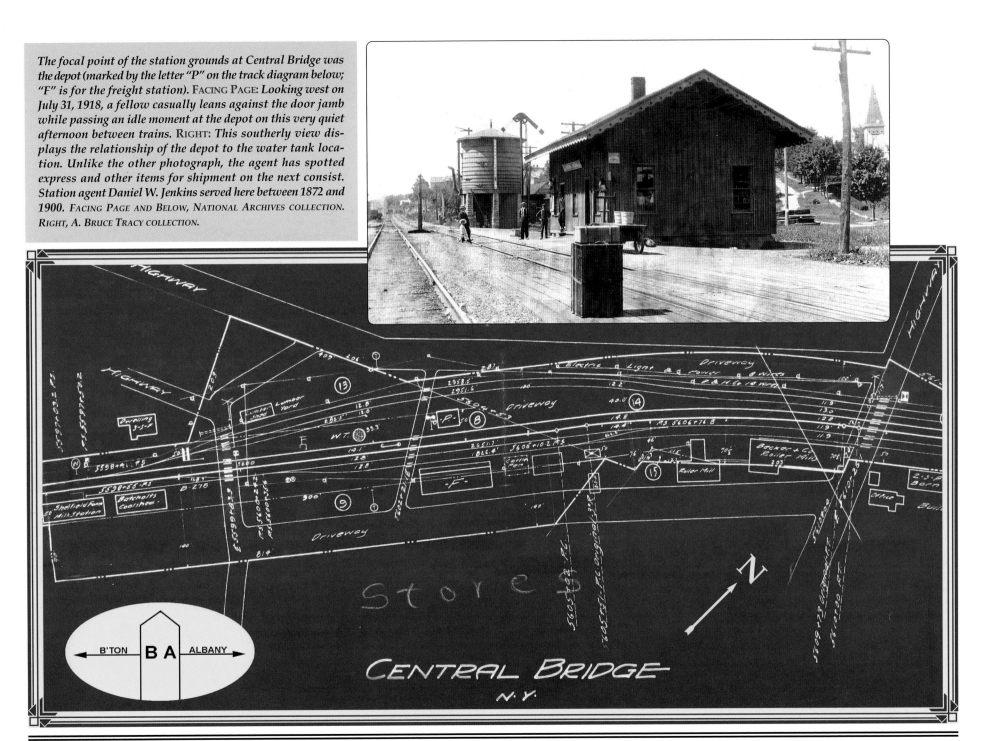

CENTRAL BRIDGE
N.Y.

later Agent Burr W. Newby who was Central Bridge's stationmaster for over fifty years beginning just after the dawn of the Twentieth Century.

The station grounds at Central Bridge had everything a railroad should have within this area. A passenger depot, 24'X36' in size, was on the west side of the main tracks just north of a 37,000 gallon water tank. An additional tank of 100,000 gallons came in 1918. These water tanks, both Type WT1, came in mighty handy for steam locomotives needing to quench their thirst before continuing any further up Howes Cave Hill. Even the Schoharie Valley Railroad came here for water early on. They interchanged passengers here, too, before the SV built their own station at Schoharie Junction. Behind the depot were several team tracks for use by less-than-carload shippers and consignees, one of which also served a lumber yard.

A large (30'X110') wood frame board-and-batten freight house was situated directly across the main tracks from the passenger depot. The railroad made a statement with this large structure: they expected a lively freight business to

THE DELAWARE AND HUDSON RAILROAD CORPORATION

"the D&H"

Greets: _____
BURR W. NEWBY

Upon Completion of

Fifty Years of Faithful Service

In appreciation of loyal and conscientious performance of duties, a GOLD PASS for permanent use is hereby issued and this CERTIFICATE presented with every wish for continued health and happiness.

Vice President
Operation-Maintenance

President

Train comming into Central Bridge

Burr W. Newby (INSET, UPPER LEFT) completed "Fifty Years of Faithful Service" for the Delaware & Hudson Railroad during the early reign of President William White. If Newby were around today, he could best inform us of the days when trains like 302 (UPPER RIGHT) passed his station bound for Binghamton behind engine No. 522 on June 16, 1936, or when the J Class Challengers (4-6-6-4) like No. 1503 arrived in Central Bridge (RIGHT) from the *south on July 1, 1952. Certainly, Agent Newby knew of Blue Cut (LEFT), which was situated south of his station where all northbound trains had to pass through when coming to Central Bridge. Although he is gone, we are very fortunate to have photographic representation of this era from the Robert Holt collection, the photographic artistry of Lambert D. Cook, and the collection of Len Kilian.*

On July 16, 1982, northbound train WR-7 arrived at Central Bridge behind a variety of ALCo diesels. It is passing the 30'X110' ex-freight house built by the A&SRR which now serves the Beacon Feeds business. During the CPRail era, the building became home to maintenance-of-way forces and material. Into its third century of life, the building was replaced by a new facility at Schoharie Junction and the freight house shown here was demolished in 2008 — as seen in the image BELOW RIGHT.

A century's worth of historic notations (LOWER LEFT) were lost in the demolition of the freight house at Central Bridge. As can be seen, thirteen year-old Main Street neighbors, Robert W. Austin and Walter Colyer, left their marks for posterity on June 21-22, 1903. Robert's father, Henry, was the proprietor of The Austin House located on South Main Street. While living in Albany twenty years earlier, Henry had worked as a railroad engineer, but it is not known *if his employer was the Delaware & Hudson. Alexander Colyer, Walter's father, supported his family by wholesaling hay and straw. Both young men survived service in World War I. Although they had grown apart by then and were separated by many miles, Robert and Walter still had something in common. They each filled out their Draft Registration cards on exactly the same day — June 5, 1917. ABOVE, TODD HUMPHREY. BELOW, ROBERT HOLT COLLECTION.*

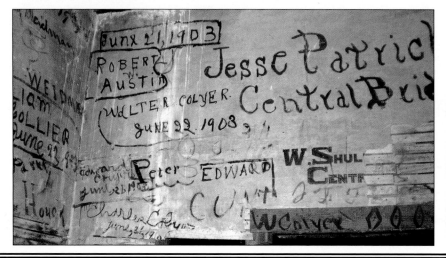

When this picture was taken on March 12, 2009, Central Bridge's Blue Seal Feeds mill was alive and well, its American flag flying high to salute the passing of NS train 939. The mill has since been shuttered leaving the village noticeably quiet, a condition that residents hope does not last too long.

blossom here. Most often, the A&SRR built large combination stations for passenger and freight business, but at Central Bridge separate buildings were erected. Considering all the other Type W103 stations, the only other location to have buildings similar to those here was at Colliers not far north of Oneonta. Just up from the freight house was a cattle pen where, I'm sure, horses came and went. Several team tracks were placed on this side of the mainline.

Because the commercial district was on the east side of the tracks, that was where the Sheffield Farms milk station was. Frank Batcholts' coal and lumber shed and the Becker & Company Roller Mills were there too. Wellington D. Becker was listed in the 1910 federal census as a "miller and farmer." His mill specialized in buckwheat. Born in 1862, Becker was a director of the Central Bridge Water Company. Later, he was both director and president of the Farmers and Merchants Bank of Cobleskill (begun in 1893). Becker died in Cobleskill in 1937.

His mill complex replaced the Peter I. Kniskern hay barns. Becker was supplanted over time by the I. L. Richer Feed Company and Blue Seal Feeds. The humming of the latter mill's machinery resounded throughout the "downtown" area, a comfort certainly for folks whose income was derived there. The mill is unfortunately quiet now, but right up to its closing in 2010 its siding's rails were kept polished by the constant arrival of covered hopper cars bearing grains and feeds to be mixed as a customer saw fit. Such is the business of a feed mill. A hardware and paint store rounded out the small businesses on the east side of the tracks. You can just imagine all of the activity that went on here over the years. If Burr Newby was still around, what stories he could tell us from his years as agent at Central Bridge.

Like most all of the line that CPRail operates today, only a single mainline track exists,

Lester Howe

not including the siding for the temporarily dormant feed mill. The passenger depot? That was knocked down by a derailed train on September 24, 1964. The freight house? It survived into its third century, but the wreckers arrived in 2008. Its last purpose was as a CPRail maintenance-of-way facility. It was replaced by the new building at Schoharie Junction. Everything that the railroad needed to provide and receive economic benefit is gone. That's why the folks at Central Bridge would like to hear the feed mill's machinery once again. It is the only survivor.

Now, it is time to visit Mr. Howe's cave where the railroad also had a depot. In our travels thus far, we have marveled over wonderful sights above ground along the way. Now let me tell you about a marvel that is un-

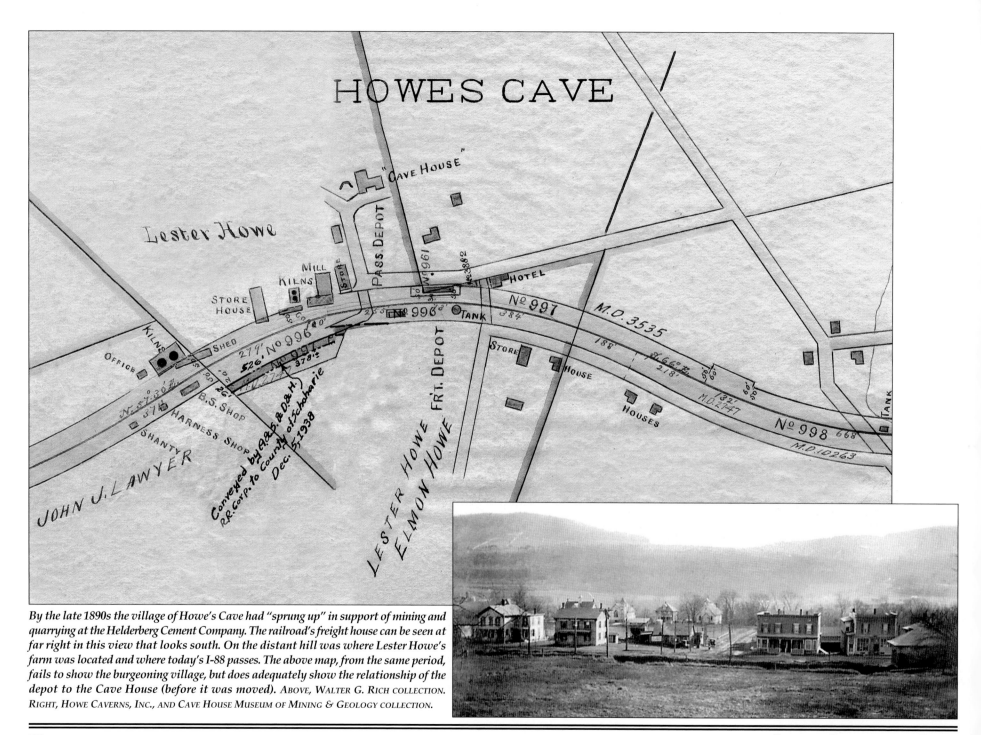

HOWES CAVE

"CAVE HOUSE"

Lester Howe

MILL

KILNS

STORE

STORE
HOUSE

PASS DEPOT

No.3961

No.3882

HOTEL

No.997

M.D. 3535

279' No.996

526, No.991

378'5

No.996

TANK

384

188'

STORE
HOUSE

HARNESS SHOP

LESTER HOWE FRT. DEPOT

M.D.2747

No.998

668

OFFICE

SHED

26'

ELMON HOWE

HOUSES

M.D.10263

KILNS

B.S. SHOP

SHANTY

JOHN J. LAWYER

Conveyed by A&S. & D&H.
RR. corp. to County of Schoharie
Dec. 5, 1938

TANK

By the late 1890s the village of Howe's Cave had "sprung up" in support of mining and quarrying at the Helderberg Cement Company. The railroad's freight house can be seen at far right in this view that looks south. On the distant hill was where Lester Howe's farm was located and where today's I-88 passes. The above map, from the same period, fails to show the burgeoning village, but does adequately show the relationship of the depot to the Cave House (before it was moved). ABOVE, WALTER G. RICH COLLECTION. RIGHT, HOWE CAVERNS, INC., AND CAVE HOUSE MUSEUM OF MINING & GEOLOGY COLLECTION.

ROADS, RIVERS, AND RAILS

This pre-1910 postcard offers a perspective of Howe's Cave, the Delaware & Hudson Railroad, the Helderberg Cement Company, and the surrounding buildings. In the foreground are two stores, including the tiny building at right. The passenger station is perched on a masonry foundation beyond the trees; the considerably larger freight house with a single D&H truss-rod boxcar is in the right foreground. In 1910, the depot would be relocated 200' north just out of sight to the right and a new, smaller freight station would be built next to it (as shown in upcoming images). Over the shoulder of the depot is another commercial enterprise with the owner's quarters on the second floor, a common occurrence in the era. But it is the Helderberg Cement Company and its quarry that dominate the scene. The facility continued out of sight to the left. The mill itself is the large main building with the clerestory roofline. The stacks represent the locations of the cement drying kilns. The head house, where the limestone is collected and crushed is in the right background. While the Howe's Cave House easily established itself as the primary hostelry in town with the capacity for some 300 guests, the Boyce Hotel was located just to the right of this scene. John Boyce ran this emporium, charging $1.50 a day for room and board, a fitting, affordable price for the traveling salesman. In 1900, Howe's Cave supported about 250 residents. Many of the able-bodied worked at the mill, including many Russians and Poles. DEPOT SQUARE PUBLISHING COLLECTION.

ABOVE: *Lester Howe stands at the entrance to his cave, awaiting the next group of spelunkers.* ABOVE RIGHT: *Visitors coming from the railroad depot walked through this underpass to get to the Cave House, shown above the arched tunnel termed the "Barrel Vault," and from there to the cave entrance.* RIGHT: *Handheld lamps illuminate Washington Hall inside of Howe's Cataract Cave. A guide employs a Flambeau lamp whose torch sits at the end of a long handle, its flame provided by a cotton wick soaked in kerosene. These men and ladies seem to be lightly dressed for the 52 degree temperature of the cave.*

derground. While we return to Route 7 and continue west, let me tell you a little about Lester Howe and his cave. Cobleskill Creek and the railroad are on our right.

Lester Howe was born in Decatur, NY near Worcester, on January 7, 1810. He was the second of six kids; his was a farming family. He became a farmer as well, but not at Decatur. His farm spanned the Cobleskill Creek valley inbetween Cobleskill and Central Bridge. Besides being a farmer, he was also a person who noticed things. On hot summer days his cows tended to congregate in the same spot near a rock out-cropping on a slope on the north side of the valley. Actually, where the cows lounged was just inside his neighbor Henry Wetsel's property. Curiosity finally got the best of him. Upon investigation he discovered that behind some brush there was an opening into the hillside from which cool air emanated. Then, he made his first foray inside the "cave" as far as daylight allowed. The date was May 22, 1842 but, even before the cows found the cave, the local Indians knew about it. They called it Otsgaragee, the "Cave of Great Galleries" or "Great Gallery Cave."

Lester must have known a little something about caves, particularly Grand Caverns in Virginia that was discovered in 1806, and Kentucky's Mammoth Cave that had been found in the 1830s. Newspapers of that period devoted prime column space to such nationally-interesting phenomenon. Neighbor Wetsel was in on Lester's discovery, but showed little interest in the cave. Lester, however, knew a good thing when he saw it, so he paid Henry $100 for this piece of his land in 1843 and named the cave "Howe's Cataract Cave." Further investigations, some of which were for prolonged periods, found that the navigable portion of the cave was nearly a mile in length, full of walking passages, large rooms (some measuring 30 feet wide by 60 feet high), pools of water, and a flowing stream. Lester Howe, farmer, had become Lester Howe, spelunker (one who explores and studies caves), entrepreneur, and promoter.

For caves to form, a continuously flowing subterranean waterway must be present, and the underground creek that formed Howe's cave over millions of years is the River Styx. The flowing water must be slightly acidic so that over a long period of time it can dissolve "soft" stone such as limestone. Besides dissolving limestone, the waterway carries the materials away and this action can create sinks, tunnels, passageways, and chambers. All of these ingredients were present for Lester's cave to form: a waterway that flowed south-southeast down to the Cobles Kill, eroding limestone of the Coeymans and Manlius types that are part of the Helderberg group in the Cobleskill Plateau. Time, of course, was needed too and that started long before humans were around to set a clock.

In some manner, Lester Howe got the word out about his cave, so that the curious—as well as more experienced spelaeologists—began to arrive for an examination of his underground attraction. At first, these folks came from nearby. Before too long, ladies and gentlemen travelled from Albany and as far away as New York City to experience first-hand Howe's subterranean marvel. As you may suspect, travelling such a great distance was not an easy thing to do in the early 1840s. Boating up the Hudson and Mohawk rivers coupled with overland stage rides brought these early explorers to the site of Howe's cave.

TOP: *The uniquely styled railroad depot seems to be patterned after the design for Howe's Cave House* (ABOVE), *which at the time of this picture had become abutted by the Pavilion Hotel. At least one depot door, it seems, was always open to improve ventilation during the hot days of summer. Born in July 1880, Verner Crounse Wands was the station agent around 1910-1920. The depot picture was taken on July 30, 1918 for Interstate Commerce Commission valuation purposes.* TOP, NATIONAL ARCHIVES COLLECTION.

The Howes Cave railroad depot (RIGHT) sat snugly between its railroad and the village's Main Street. (The station agent in 1872 was William E. Dante. He went on to become a telegraph operator for the rail-road at Afton, NY.) Just beyond the depot—and on the other side of the tracks—was the Howe Cave Hotel (LOWER RIGHT) that catered to cement industry workers who, as you can imagine, used it to blow off steam and unwind after a hard day's work. Miners and quarry men were a rough and tumble lot, which may be indicated by this hotel's nickname: the Bloody Bucket. But, there was education at Howe's Cave too, provided by a school (BELOW) that sat on the next—and only—street to the south from Main Street. There was religion, too. The church was located just to the right of the school.

RIGHT: NATIONAL ARCHIVES COLLECTION.

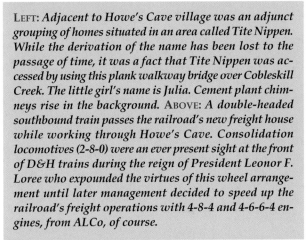

LEFT: *Adjacent to Howe's Cave village was an adjunct grouping of homes situated in an area called Tite Nippen. While the derivation of the name has been lost to the passage of time, it was a fact that Tite Nippen was accessed by using this plank walkway bridge over Cobleskill Creek. The little girl's name is Julia. Cement plant chimneys rise in the background.* ABOVE: *A double-headed southbound train passes the railroad's new freight house while working through Howe's Cave. Consolidation locomotives (2-8-0) were an ever present sight at the front of D&H trains during the reign of President Leonor F. Loree who expounded the virtues of this wheel arrangement until later management decided to speed up the railroad's freight operations with 4-8-4 and 4-6-6-4 engines, from ALCo, of course.*

Main Street crossed the tracks at grade immediately south of the depot (once it had been moved 200' from its original location in 1910), which seemed to be just out of the photographer's frame in both pictures. Freight car switching was done in abundance during cement making's heyday years, as noted by the switcher at the far left. A pair of banjo signals guard the crossing.

Through the Years at Howe's Cave

Main Street in Howe's Cave was lined by residences and stores (Above Left) on the south side of the unimproved thoroughfare while the depot and freight house were on the other side against the tracks. The depot, which appears at the base of one of the cement plants chimneys — but certainly isn't — appears to be painted a light shade of yellow with decorative woodwork around its north end window. A number of years later (Above) the depot's paint has become more drab and the fancy window moldings have been removed. But, at the store, a second story porch has been added. The store became a lunch room and local hangout named Tilison's, where its fortunes withered when activity at the plant greatly diminished. It is now abandoned (Left) and broods over the passing of every train, such as NS 931 on August 17, 2010. Main Street has been only slightly "improved," while the depot and freight house have been "removed."

Realizing that these intrepid excursionists would be a weary lot by the time of their arrival, not to mention them having to withstand the rigors of their underground examination of the cave, Lester built a hotel (in 1845) directly over the cave's entrance. Using his hotel, visitors could rest from their journey, explore the cave — guided by the owner himself — and rest once more so that they could again withstand the physical punishment of travel. Lester named his hotel the "Cave House," and it could have been one of the earliest recreation destinations in all of New York. Niagara Falls came first, but Howe's Cataract cave and Cave House certainly was a close second.

Misfortune first came to Howe in 1847 when his Cave House was destroyed by fire. Just like any enterprising fellow would do, he built a larger, albeit still wooden, Cave House. In this new building, its north wing sat over the cave entrance so that visitors used a staircase from the basement of the hotel to enter the cave.

By this time, Howe's Cave had become the third successful commercial cave behind those previously mentioned in Virginia and Kentucky. Virginia's Luray

To assist in its quarrying operations, the Helderberg Cement Company employed a narrow gauge railroad (ABOVE RIGHT) to move steam shovels (ABOVE) around the property as well as to move stone jennies into position for production purposes. The gathering of limestone for Natural and Portland cements was also pursued underground (RIGHT, in 1888), an operation that may have led directly to the closing of Howe's cave in 1909 after an above ground detonation of dynamite. These fellows above and at right were most likely the men who frequented the "Bloody Bucket."

Caverns did not open until 1875. Carlsbad Caverns in New Mexico was the latecomer, not opening until the Roaring Twenties. In promoting his underground attraction, Lester developed informative, imaginative, and romantic names for locations within his cave: Chinese Pagoda, Fat Man's Misery, Devil's Gangway, Jehosephat's Valley, Giant's Chapel, Congress Hall, and Lecture Room were but a few of the names given by Howe.

All in all, things were going fairly well for Howe's Cataract Cave. You would think that the coming of the railroad could only help tourist business at the attraction. Well, it did, and it didn't. The coming of any railroad could giveth, but it could also taketh away. When the Albany & Susquehanna Railroad arrived at Howe's Cave, beginning on January 2, 1865 (when the railroad opened as far as Cobleskill), it did both. Yes, the railroad made it easier for persons to travel to the cave for a first-hand tour of Howe's wonder. It also made it possible for persons to travel to a significantly greater number of places to either see the sights or visit relatives that heretofore had been at too far a distance for traveling economically, safely, and quickly.

The railroad also brought something else to Howe's Cave, a means to ship—in bulk quantity—the readily available and prolific deposits of limestone. This meant that Howe's Cave was about to become a multi-industry location for both tourism and industrial mining; the latter eventually disrupting the former, temporarily.

There never was much to the railroad's facilities at Howe's Cave besides the small, uniquely-styled depot. A slightly larger freight house came in 1918. There was a Sheffield Farms milk station but that was the extent of the local industry other than a bounty of limestone.

The first person to grasp the business aspect of the railroad and limestone connection may have been Oneontan Harvey Baker. He was the railroad's contractor assigned to build the Cobleskill to Oneonta segment of the A&S. He was also a staunch supporter of the railroad; that is how he became a construction contractor. During 1863, Harvey visited Howe's Cave and it was then that he understood the industrial and financial significance of the Coeymans and Manlius limestone

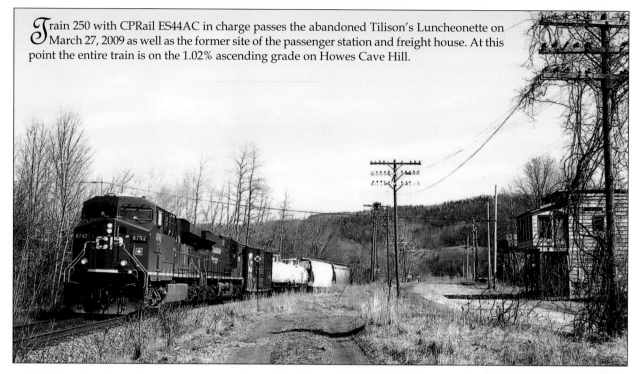

Train 250 with CPRail ES44AC in charge passes the abandoned Tilison's Luncheonette on March 27, 2009 as well as the former site of the passenger station and freight house. At this point the entire train is on the 1.02% ascending grade on Howes Cave Hill.

strata lying in such close proximity to the railroad. The contractors there had to whittle away part of the outcropping so that a shelf could be built for the right-of-way. Baker's men were forced to do the same thing near Richmondville.

It was only a few years later (1868) when Baker, fellow Oneontan E. R. Ford, Jared Goodyear of Colliersville, and—believe it or not—A&SRR President Joseph Ramsey purchased seventy acres of land and formed the Howe's Cave Lime & Cement Company. Within a year or two, the foursome allowed Lester Howe to become involved in the new company. Of all the things that Lester Howe was, he was not a businessman, nor did he realize that his four partners were more interested in lime and cement than they were in cave explorers.

If this lack of business understanding may be considered Howe's second setback, then the destruction of his second Cave House by fire in 1872 was the third. Undeterred, Lester built a third Cave House, and this new one was more impervious to smoke and fire. It was

built with stone in a Gothic-influenced design, and it would stand the test of time since. It still survives more than a century later.

It was just about this period, however, that through some questionable means, whether by bamboozling, flim-flam, or razzle dazzle, Ramsey secured outright control of Howe's cave and Cave House property. Lester was out, and he would forever after complain that he had been forced out through legal contracts and proceedings that he did not understand. Instead, Howe relied on his partners to act in good faith. Before he died in 1888, the embittered Howe proclaimed that he had discovered another cave nearby, one more glorious than his original. But, he passed away with its location remaining a secret.

Meanwhile, the Howe's Cave Lime & Cement Company blossomed and, surprisingly, so did the cave business. Under Ramsey's management, another wood structure was built immediately east of the final Cave House that was even larger than its stone neighbor.

Inside was a restaurant and dining rooms for eating, ballrooms for dancing, a billiards room for shooting pool, and of course additional rooms for relaxing and sleeping. Outside, guests could play tennis and croquet, both then all the rage. Now providing a one-two punch for visitors, the Cave House and new Pavilion Hotel truly made Howe's Cave a multi-purposed tourist destination.

When the railroad first came to Howe's Cave in 1865, it listed the location on its timetables and elsewhere exactly as Mr. Howe desired: Howe's Cave (notice the apostrophe). As the years wore on, however, the railroad dropped the apostrophe so that their location at Howe's Cave became Howes Cave. Howe's Cave came to mean the village and industry, while Howes Cave referred to the railroad. This was an important differentiation between the railroad and the community that developed in support of successors to the Howe's Cave Lime & Cement Company: Helderberg Cement Company (1898) and North American Cement Corporation (1925). Later owners of the mining and quarrying plant here were:

Marquette Cement Company (1961), Penn-Dixie Cement Company (1964), Flintcote Cement Company (1977), and Cobleskill Stone Products, its current owner.

Regardless of community, railroad, or company name, the lime and cement making industry at Howe's Cave flourished and became a major source of revenue for the railroad. A siding from the southbound main ran directly into the plant. Produced here from the Cayugan and Helderbergian limestone formations were Natural and Portland cement, the latter getting its own plant in 1900. Natural (or Rosendale cement) was widely used in major construction projects like the Brooklyn Bridge but its slow curing time caused formulators to look for additives. Once the building boom after World War I arrived, Portland cement became more widely used because of its faster curing time. Rock was crushed; additives mixed in. The mixture was calcined to a powder at about 1500 degrees. In the old days, the powder was shipped in paper boxes or paper-lined barrels.

Meanwhile, Howe's Cave saw the construction of

dwellings, a school, church, post office, hotel (in addition to the Cave House and Pavilion Hotel), and a smattering of stores that catered to local residential needs. While the village and industry prospered, business at the cave went on the decline.

In 1900, a fire destroyed a portion of the Pavilion. Explorer tours were discouraged if not refused. Visitors to Howe's old cave were noticeable by their absence. Quite possibly the reason for this was the cement plant's encroachment to the cave's entrance at the Cave House. Besides the general dust, noise, and confusion associated with this type of industry (tolerated by the village because of its financial importance) dynamite explosions periodically rocked the community and surrounding area so that visitors to the cave may not have felt welcomed or at ease. Their concerns were neither trivial nor unwarranted.

At Howe's Cave, religion and education were present, but the village mostly survived by dynamite, sweat, and liquor. During 1909 a series of dynamite explosions took place to dislodge more limestone for the plant's manufacturing of cement. Not only did the explosions produce the needed material above ground, they unfortunately dislodged the ceiling of the cave, which effectively blocked tourist entry beyond 300 feet from the cave's Cave House entrance. Washington's Hall, Cataract Hall, and the Music Room were destroyed. Howe's cave was closed and it entered a period of dormancy.

Howes Cave depot at milepost A39/B104 on the D&H—CPF511 on today's CPRail—sat near the top of Howes Cave Hill. The summit was situated just to the south, near where the switch for the cement plant's siding was located. After the closing of Howe's cave, the 14'X36' passenger station saw few visitors other than persons who had business to conduct with the cement plant. The passenger station was on the east side of the track where the highway going to and from Central Bridge crossed the tracks. (Today's crossing of the railroad by Howe Cave Road did not exist then.) From the depot, it was only a matter of a short walk for cave visitors to arrive at their destination: Cave House,

*L*ester Howe's legacy lives on at Howe Caverns, where a chalet-style welcome center contains some Cave House architectural elements. Therein, visitors descend within an elevator to Howe's original Cataract Cave.

At Howe's Cave on September 19, 2010, Lester Howe's Cave House (Above, at the right) stands amidst the forlorn property of the old cement plant, but still looks out over the Cobleskill Valley. It witnesses the passage of all today's trains, like 931 at left that appears so small in relation to the now defunct silos and buildings whose purpose are just a memory of years past. At track level (right, on the same day), train 939 passes beneath the watchful gaze of the Cave House. The relative size for both Cave House and train has changed from this photographic perspective.

Employing a telephoto lens to capture this scene, Norfolk Southern train 938 with a string of tri-level autoracks on the head end leans into a reverse curve at Howe's Cave beside the dormant cement works (RIGHT). In the valley beyond can be seen the Cobles Kill, Route 7, and Interstate 88. The Cave House (ABOVE) is being developed by parent Howe Caverns, Inc. as a mining and geology museum as well as a history center for Howe's Cave. From a window within its far side end wall, a view of the original Cataract Cave entrance (LEFT) can be contemplated. At Howe's Cave, history is alive and well.

Howe Caverns, Inc. was formed on October 11, 1927, with the express desire to re-open the cave for tourist visitation. To do this, exploration within the cave had to be undertaken so as to find a suitable place to locate a new entrance. Promoters of this project realized that people would no longer be able to walk right on in to the cave as heretofore; that an elevator would need to be employed to transfer visitors back and forth between the surface and cave interior.

Finding a location for an elevator and excavating for its shaft was not an easy undertaking, but it was eventually accomplished. So was an expansive chalet style building that would serve as a visitor welcome center as well as the location where the elevator could be accessed.

On May 27, 1929, after lying dormant for twenty years, the new Howe Caverns opened for business, making it possible for spelunkers and just plain ordinary folks to again enter Lester Howe's old cave where a year round temperature of 52 degrees would greet them. This subterranean temperature obviously made a visit to the cave more desirable during the heat of a New York summer.

the Pavilion, or both. With the cave closed for visitation, only an occasional curiosity seeker ventured over to the Cave House, which eventually began to be used for office space by whichever cement company was then in operation. The Pavilion, having burned down, was nothing but a memory.

Immediately north of the passenger depot was the 18'X40' freight house, which sufficed for local freight arriving in L-C-L fashion. The main freight here was, of course, cement and lime, and all of that went out in car-load lots via the siding that was connected directly with the railroad's southbound main track.

The years following the closure of Howe's cave quite possibly were the best years for the cement business, so there was little concern for the closed cave. Other folks, however, desired to reopen the cave so its glory years could also be realized. Towards that end,

At Howe's Cave today, the old school house and church (ABOVE) still survive; both being situated on Lester Lane. And, of course, the passage of trains being operated by CPRail (RIGHT) struggles by the old cement plant at the crest of Howes Cave Hill. Dean Splittgerber photographed CPRail No. 8796 on the lead with train 252 on the drawbar during the late fall of 2010.

The new Howe Caverns was located nearly a mile away from the cave's original entrance, which made it somewhat inconvenient for visitors arriving by train at the Howes Cave depot. By the date of its opening, auto touring was becoming more popular so that motorists could simply drive to the Caverns' door. Management of the Caverns still expressed a desire to have the railroad move its passenger depot to a more suitable location, but the D&H would have none of that, and the depot remained where it was. They were doing more business there than they ever would have at a new location where motorists would erode passenger receipts.

Despite this setback, Howe Caverns has prospered just as its promoters envisioned, so that today, Howe's cave is open to visitors year round. As was the case with the Pavilion augmenting the Cave House, a motel has been built adjacent to Howe Caverns main building so that visitors may be provided overnight accommodations should they desire. Just as in the good old days, Howe Caverns is an historically-charged tourist destination where the underground cave of the past can still be contemplated, interpreted, and enjoyed. Caverns management has also recently regained use of the

ABOVE: *Just as we're ready to turn onto Howes Cave Road to return to Route 7, we notice the railroad signal just to the north has blinked to green, revealing that the arrival of a northbound train is imminent. After only a few moments, train 938 with a C40-9W in front quietly makes its appearance as it descends Howes Cave Hill, passing Cobleskill Stone Products in the distance. Considering milepost 511 at right, we still have 104 miles to go before we reach the end of our story at Binghamton.* RIGHT: *Once we have returned to Route 7, we are provided a last look at Cave House and the quarry where mining, railroading, and cave exploration all helped to develop the community of Howe's Cave. Much is gone from the village now, but much still remains of Howe's Cataract Cave, the Helderberg Cement Company, and the old Albany & Susquehanna Railroad.*

surviving Cave House and is in the process of developing it into a museum of mining, mineralogy, and history of the settlement of Howe's Cave. The single track railroad and trains of today pass the Cave House Museum and Howe Caverns, completely oblivious of their one time association. Although the old cement plant is today Cobleskill Stone Company's main location for producing roadway and decorative stone, none of it is shipped via the railroad. The siding still goes into the plant, but it is not used and is completely overgrown. Meanwhile, underground, Howe's cave can be seen as it mostly was in 1842 when Lester Howe discovered, developed, and promoted it, so that it became the third commercially successful working cave exhibit in America. Mr. Howe must be getting the last laugh, at the expense of Joseph Ramsey whose meddling in a successful business caused him to be stricken from participating in the operational control of "his" cave.

Whatever happened to the new cave that Howe discovered and kept a secret until the day he died? That is believed to be Secret Caverns, which is not far from Howe Caverns.

At the Route 7 traffic light at Howe's Cave, Wetsel Hollow Road leads toward the location of Lester Howe's farm. Mainly the road just serves to perpetuate the name of Henry Wetsel who first ventured into the cave with his neighbor Howe. Now we turn to the right, onto Howe Cave Road, cross Cobleskill Creek, and head on up to the former village of Howe's Cave where little remains, other than Cave House, to remind us of the community's former glory. The school house and church survive, and it is a wonderful sound to still hear the church bell being rung to call parishioners to Sunday service. Less than a handful of dwellings remain from the earlier prosperous years, and Tilison's Lunch, which had been a grocery store but later catered to cement plant workers as a luncheonette, still stands though it served its last meal many years ago.

The narrow depot and freight house have been completely removed from the scene, as has the old highway grade crossing over the railroad, its purpose usurped by the new Howe Cave Road/Sagendorf Hill Road crossing. Near this new grade crossing the foundation for the old Sheffield Farms milk station can be viewed, as can a trackside signal to the north that will inform us of the imminent arrival of the next CPRail or Norfolk Southern train. Mr. Wetsel has a road named for him, and so does Mr. Howe. Lester Lane (RIGHT) can be considered Howe's Cave's main street though there is little located upon this main "drag" other than the Schoharie Valley Animal Shelter.

If we had the time, and we really don't as we still have a lot of driving ahead of us, we could go into the Cave House Museum of Mining & Geology where we can look down at Lester Howe's original entrance to his cave through one window. Think about that while I turn us around and return to Route 7 where we will venture over to nearby Howe Caverns via Caverns Road. Along the way, we'll get a last glimpse of Cave House from Route 7. At Howe Caverns, time is again our enemy, and thwarts our desire to see Lester Howe (who returned on February 18, 2011 as an animated figure), ride the elevator down 156 feet into one of America's geologic marvels, see a 500,000 year old stalagmite, view the Bridal Altar where (to date) 619 weddings have taken place, and enjoy the same beautiful stone formations that Mr. Howe first glimpsed in 1842. I suggest, when you have some quality time to spend, that you return to Howe Caverns and treat yourself to the underground scenic beauty that without doubt rivals any

above ground scene. But for now, though, we will leave Cave Country behind and head "Over the Hill" to Dante, with stops at Barnerville, Cobleskill, Warnerville, Richmondville, and West Richmondville where even more wondrous sites, history, personalities, and stories await our arrival.

Underground beauty at Howe Caverns, February 17, 2011

CHAPTER 3
OVER THE HILL TO DANTE

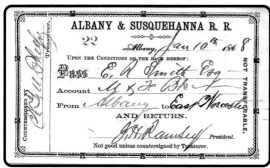

*A*bove-ground beauty is portrayed by Richmondville's hills and the Cobleskill Valley, looking north on June 3, 1936. LAMBERT D. COOK PHOTOGRAPH.

*F*rom the grounds of Howe Caverns, we are treated to a view of the Cobles Kill valley in all its splendor. It is a wonderful scene; one that rivals our previous Schoharie Valley vista, only this one is not quite as expansive. We could enjoy Mother Nature's attractiveness endlessly but, since we have already marveled at the Earth's formations above and below ground, it is time to move along. Besides, in not too many miles we will encounter an equally attractive setting at Richmondville, one where photographic proof reveals the true beauty of Cobles Kill's valley.

Reluctantly, we leave Howe Caverns behind, using Caverns Road to once again duck under the railroad as we did upon our arrival here. Instead of returning to Route 7, we will bear right onto Barnerville Road, which will take us to its namesake hamlet. There a small wooden building, 16'X20' in size, contained only a simple waiting room that once acted as the railroad's connection with the community.

You are probably wondering why we are forsaking Route 7 for Barnerville Road. Well, the simple answer is that I want to take you to that hamlet the most direct way. If we went back to Route 7 and continued west we would have to go all the way into Cobleskill and then turn back to get to Barnerville. In that manner, there is little for us to see as Route 7 hugs the lower south hill of the valley where the railroad lies north of the highway and up on hill. But, the main reason we are using Barnerville Road is that it is likely the ancestral Route 7.

Barnerville Road extends from the eastern limits of Cobleskill (village) to Caverns Road; they jointly form a through route from Cobleskill to Howe's Cave. Along the way, the hamlet of Barnerville is reached. Even with just 111 citizens in 1928 (and not many more today), that would have been sufficient reason for Route 7 to go that way in bygone days. However Route 7 bypasses Barnerville today. A local road, now closed, once gave motorists access to the settlement. In this area, an alternate path affords a more historic and direct connection to the D&H than Route 7. That will be the case at a variety of other points on our journey to Binghamton.

Now that you know that this is an historic portion of Route 7, our arrival at Barnerville may be anticlimactic. The hamlet contains only a handful of residences. One wonders if Barnerville's current appearance might be

The engines of northbound train 938 have just crossed Barnerville Road and are now passing the former site of the hamlet's waiting room. The small wooden building had been situated between the road and the railroad. The highway is an old portion of Route 7. Barnerville's "station" (INSET) was discontinued in 1933.

almost the same as when Joseph Barner founded the community in 1777. Although Barnerville had been in existence for eighty-five years when the railroad opened to Cobleskill on January 2, 1865, the Albany & Susquehanna did not think the tiny community would provide much revenue. It passed Barnerville without erecting any facilities. But, Barnerville folks desired to be placed upon the railroad's map, so they erected a passenger depot and freight station with their own funds and muscle. The two buildings were placed on opposite sides of the track: the passenger station on the east side; freight, on the west.

Looking at a map, however, it is difficult to see how anyone could have reached these buildings; they were on property owned by George Barner where it appears highway access was non-existent. George, a descendent of Joseph Barner, most likely promoted building the railroad structures on the "founder's" property, yet, the railroad was not pleased with the location regardless of the two-structures given to them as a gift. So, they put up a small sized waiting room (mentioned earlier) on the east side of their tracks near the grade crossing for old Route 7. This site, astride the main highway to Cobleskill, was a great improvement for persons desiring to take full advantage of the railroad's services. Regardless of location, however, the railroad suffered operational difficulty in stopping or starting trains at Barnerville. At either location the "stations" were on the ascending grade to Howe's Cave (the western flank of Howes Cave Hill). Until 1933, the railroad provided a modicum of service to the hamlet,

but during that year the waiting room was taken out of service. It was subsequently retired and razed.

The Depression hit small communities the hardest. After 1933, Barnerville residents could only look on as the railroad's passenger and freight trains passed them by. Fortunately, they were also served by an important roadway that connected them to both Howe's Cave and Cobleskill. When the improved present Route 7 was placed into service, a simple sign erected at Barnerville's main—and only—intersection directed motorists off the old highway and toward the new one that was only a short distance away. This road, however, is now closed, which further isolates the hamlet from the hustle and bustle of modern society. Today, commerce bypasses Barnerville on both the highway and the railway, but the community had secured its place in history because at one time it had been connected to the outside world by rail.

Traveling two and a half miles further west on Barnerville Road brings us to the eastern limits of Cobleskill. At the intersection of Route 7 and Barnerville Road, the D&H's bridge over Route 7 and—just beyond—the highway's bridge over Cobleskill Creek can be seen. These bridges are the first for our "Roads, Rivers, and Rails." From here Route 7 will cross over the railroad nine

ABOVE: At CPF516, Norfolk Southern southbound train 939 drifts downgrade into Cobleskill. It is about to cross the railroad's bridge over Route 7. The roadway is seen at lower right leading to the Cobleskill Creek bridge. LEFT: There is a traffic light there today, but back when Henry Sollman took this aerial view of Cobleskill's still rural east end, Barnerville Road merged unobstructed into Route 7 just to the north of the railroad's bridge at lower left. Curving to and fro across the upper part of this view is Cobleskill Creek. A mall and fast food restaurants occupy this area today.

LEFT, COBLESKILL HISTORICAL SOCIETY COLLECTION.

more times between Cobleskill and Binghamton. Except for two cases—including this one—Route 7 crosses over the railroad. The highway bridge over the Cobles Kill is the only time the roadway and waterway get to see each other. As one enters Cobleskill, the railroad runs parallel to our road. Since our tour began at Mohawk Yard, Route 7 and the old A&SRR are finally entering a village together, one that predates the arrival of both.

"Kill" is a Dutch word for a minor river or creek, but German was what Jacob Kobel was. He was one of the original settlers of the area. Indians were here first, of course. They called Cobel's Creek "Otsgaragee" because of hemp that grew along the course of the creek. (Again, I'm no expert on the Indian language, but isn't that the same name they called Howe's cavern?) Re-

ABOVE: *A mantle of deep snow, ice and cold lies over the landscape in central New York on February 14, 1914. This image taken in front of the depot shows a crew working to clean off the station platform and the adjacent rails. In 1872, John Overpaugh and Charles Courter bought the sash and blind mill of Alexander and William McHensh & Co. This complex can be seen just over the head of the employee at the far left in the upper image. From the balcony of the Commercial Hotel behind the depot, the Courter family mill, now run by Stanton Courter (LEFT), was photographed during the railroading era that employed 4-4-0 locomotives and four-wheel bobber cabooses. The mill used a substantial quantity of lumber to produce sash, blinds, doors, and ornamental work. It also handled lumber, paints, oils, glass, hardware and other building supplies, all of which required the railroad's services for switching and distribution. At different times, Peter Feek, James Kennedy, and Thompson Perrine each owned a factory that built "light buggies, carriages, and cutters" which were sold nationally. Inventor David Anthony developed award-winning horse-powered agricultural implements and threshers. His Empire Agricultural Works was taken over by Reuben and Minard Harder. ABOVE: EDWARD P. BAUMGARDNER COLLECTION. LEFT, STEVE DAVIS COLLECTION.*

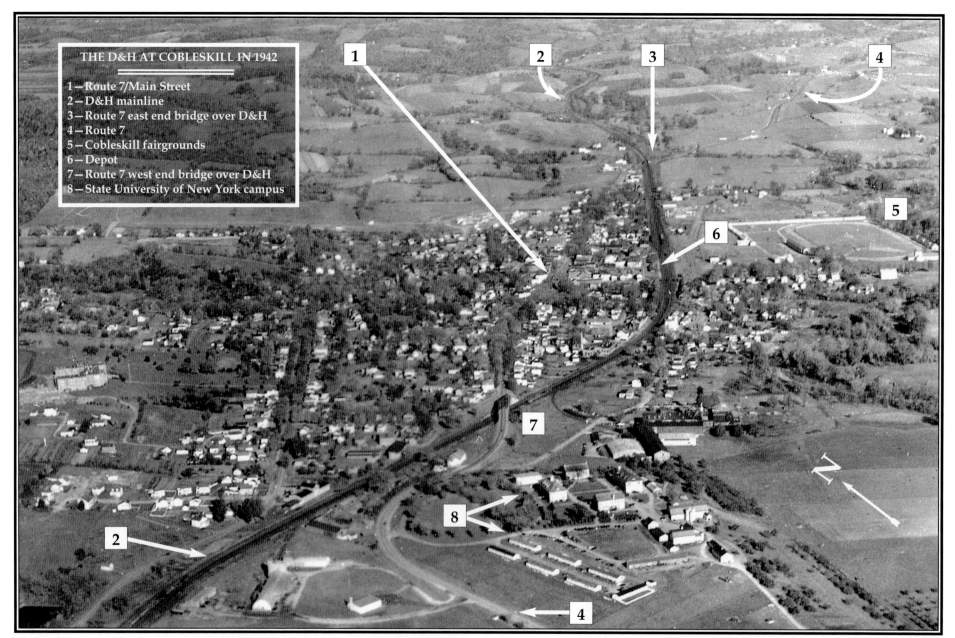

As he did on Page 20, Henry Sollman took this aerial view of Cobleskill, NY in the early 1940s, looking generally north. The D&H mainline is prominently featured as is the path of Route 7 through downtown and the adjacent countryside. While the business district anchors the right middle of this image, the industrial base was just south of the depot and on either side of the college. There were significant rock quarries at one time across the upper left. In 1899, the Weiting Quarry shipped 10-15 carloads per day of crushed rock. By 1905 the Cobleskill Quarry Company was moving 20-30 carloads per day to New York City alone, a steady contributor to the Delaware & Hudson freight revenues.

The D&H AT COBLESKILL IN 1942

1 — Route 7/Main Street
2 — D&H mainline
3 — Route 7 east end bridge over D&H
4 — Route 7
5 — Cobleskill fairgrounds
6 — Depot
7 — Route 7 west end bridge over D&H
8 — State University of New York campus

During the Delaware & Hudson's diesel years, photographers used the new—but now old—station and the Cobleskill Coal Company building as props to help showcase the railroad's passing trains. LEFT: Noted lensman John J. Young, Jr. pictured northbound train BM-3 passing the still-attractive station during November 1968. Two ALCo Century-628 locomotives and a lone General Electric U30C are at the head end of the train bound for Mechanicville. The Cobleskill Coal Company building was just to the south of the station across the Grand Street underpass where—during earlier years—it received black diamonds via the railroad for distribution around the community. BELOW LEFT: August 14, 1971 finds GE and ALCo locomotives rolling train WR-1 upgrade past the coal facility, while two years later, the Susquehanna Valley Special (BELOW RIGHT) arrives at Cobleskill behind three of the railroad's four ALCo PA passenger engines (September 29, 1973). Both the 1966 Volkswagen Beetle and the 1967 Plymouth Fury III were vehicles used by the author to arrive at this location. A 2X3 Century Graphic camera did the photographic work. All of the trackage in these views, except that which the trains are upon, has since been removed. INSET: Blotter advertising Cobleskill Coal. JEFF HANDY COLLECTION.

ABOVE: *A resident of Oneonta for thirty-two years, Perry R. Young was a prolific photographer who at one time maintained studios in Cobleskill, Worcester, Schenevus, Oneonta, and Sidney. He sold out in 1913 and moved with his wife, Maria, to Eugene, OR to live near their son. It is Young who pointed his camera east down what was then called just "Main Street" to record this scene between North Grand and Union streets. The primary business anchor in downtown was the Hotel Augustan—the third and fourth structures from the left flank its recessed entryway. It was built in 1874 on the site of the National Hotel which had been destroyed by fire the year before. Cobleskill also hosted the United States Hotel (visible below and just to the left of the steeple belonging to Zion's Lutheran Church), the Exchange Hotel located on West Main Street, and the Commercial Hotel near the depot.* DEPOT SQUARE PUBLISHING COLLECTION. BELOW: *Route 7 follows "East" Main Street today, and as this image shows, commerce still takes place in the neatly-painted and well-preserved buildings. The trees at center left obscure the structure once occupied by the Hotel Augustan.*

gardless of the names Kobel and Cobel's, the village became Cobleskill in 1752. It became a stop on the railroad one hundred thirteen years later. Two men from here were instrumental in making that happen: Joseph Ramsey and Charles Courter. Ramsey, of course, became president of the Albany & Susquehanna Railroad; Courter was a banker. Both men were directors of the A&S, and both had locomotives named for them: The "J.H. Ramsey" was No. 4; the "Chas. Courter" was No. 5. Of the two men, however, only one was loyal to the railroad.

In 1869, When Jay Gould and Jim Fisk were attempting to gain control of the A&S, Charles Courter aligned himself with them. Fortunately, for Ramsey, the railroad remained under the president's control. If it had not there may never have been a railroad division of the Delaware & Hudson Canal Company and this book would most likely be written about a portion of the Erie

Railway. Another Cobleskill hero of the battle for control of the A&S was the railroad's first station agent, H. T. Dana. As the physical portion of the fight escalated, he received a telegraph directing him, "By orders of the Company you will remain on duty to keep your station in our possession." Agent Dana did just that. He was a loyal employee of the railroad who made Ramsey proud. Ramsey's victory over Gould and Fisk was bittersweet. He whipped the traitor Courter, but then Ramsey leased his railroad to the D&HCCo on February 24, 1870.

Before the fight for the railroad began, the village of Cobleskill received a station made of stone. This substantial structure was most likely provided because of Cobleskill natives Ramsey and Courter delivering the railroad to the community's door. A separate freight house was built across the track (east side) from the station. By 1900, both buildings had become outmoded; they were simply inadequate to handle the volume of business then being done at Cobleskill. Both structures were razed. The stone depot was replaced by an architecturally-pleasing structure that was topped by a cupola upon a roof dormer; the freight house by a brick building 35'X150' in size. The new freight house did not occupy the site of its predecessor, rather, it was located south of the station and on the west side of the tracks. The reason the freight house was built at a new site was so that property on the east side of the tracks could become improved as an interchange and team yard. It was from there that Cherry Valley Branch trains originated and terminated.

Cobleskill has always been, and is today, a prosperous and personable community—as improbable as that may seem with a Walmart store situated nearby. Yet, the downtown business district that straddles Route 7 (which is Main Street) thrives. Early prosperity came to Cobleskill because the village was connected to the surrounding area by a network of roads; some eventually became state highways. The community is the central meeting point for routes 7, 10, and 145 that brought residents from the outlying farms to markets, shops, and mills. Also connecting Cobleskill to the outlying rural area was the Cherry Valley, Sharon, & Albany Railroad. The Delaware & Hudson Canal Company gained control of the CVS&A and operated the line as its Cherry Valley Branch from its opening day of June 15, 1870 until abandonment on August 15, 1956.

Cherry Valley, as you may recall, was an important regional center for business and a crossroads for commerce during the late Eighteenth and early Nineteenth centuries. Turnpikes from all directions made it so. Because it was a local mecca for trade, that may have been the inspiration for the branchline built over rolling hills from Cobleskill to Cherry Valley. Another likely reason was that Cobleskill was attempting to become more prosperous at Cherry Valley's expense, which turned out to be the case. The Cherry Valley Branch certainly helped Cobleskill's cause. Besides terminals at the line's endpoints, depots were built at Hyndsville, Seward, and Sharon Springs. The latter station, along with Cherry Valley, were patterned after the larger wooden station houses put up by the A&S. Hyndsville and Seward were more modest board-and-batten structures. All, however, were combination facilities that adequately served the farming region of Otsego and Schoharie counties.

Operationally, Cherry Valley Branch trains departed from the Cobleskill terminal where a four-track yard, enginehouse, and turntable catered to passenger, freight, and locomotive needs. The yard was located across from the passenger station on the east side of the main tracks where a lack of substantial real estate had caused the freight house to be relocated in 1900. An engine house had also been located on this side of the mainline. A larger building was constructed later on the west side of the main tracks married to a 65-foot turntable. Both were immediately north of the passenger station.

From this modest terminal, Cherry Valley Branch trains proudly marched down the mainline trackage for only a mile and a half. There they reached the switch that directed them onto the lighter rail of the branch. This location was known as Cherry Valley Junction, and was where an Armstrong-operated interlocking tower, "KF," was built so that safe and efficient intermingling of branch and mainline trains could be pursued. Enroute to the junction, the mainline trackage passed under Route 7 on the west side of Cobleskill.

In 1930, and throughout its life, passenger trains made three round trips per day along the 20.9 mile line. Within three years, however, passenger service was discontinued. The last run took place on Saturday, January 28, 1933. On that day, *The Cobleskill*

Yes, Virginia, it does snow in Cobleskill during the winter! This D&H Mogul 2-6-0 locomotive has just returned to Cobleskill from a trip over the Cherry Valley Branch with stops at Sharon Springs, Seward and Hyndsville, apparently none the worse for wearing a mantle of snow and ice. The Commercial Hotel is barely visible through the engine's smoke and steam. STEVE DAVIS COLLECTION.

LEFT: *KF Tower controlled the junction of the D&H mainline with the Cherry Valley Branch. It was located on the east side of the mainline just to the north of the actual junction that is behind the photographer; the view looks north towards Cobleskill. The tower had been closed by the time this September 1, 1939 picture was taken.* BELOW: *Camelback Tenwheeler No. 543 has arrived at Cherry Valley, where its crew casually poses for a picture on the turntable on May 20, 1939. The man in the cab window is Engineer Paul Natske.* BOTH, LAMBERT D. COOK.

FACING PAGE: *This schedule from 1930 lists all of the Susquehanna Division's passenger service. Binghamton, this time, is spelled correctly!* ABOVE, FROM TOP DOWN: *On the Cherry Valley Branch, station stops could be found at Hyndsville, Seward, Sharon Springs, and Cherry Valley. Only Hyndsville does not survive.* ALL, A. BRUCE TRACY COLLECTION.

Times Editor Charles L. Ryder (who acquired the paper in 1919) bought the last ticket for passage to Cobleskill from Cherry Valley Agent Edmund R. Hall. (A Mr. Esmay purchased the last ticket at Seward.) Editor Ryder wrote in a following edition of his newspaper, "The iron horse on the Cherry Valley line has come and gone as far as passenger service is concerned. One resident of Cherry Valley, Harry Giles, was a passenger on the first train and he was likewise a passenger on the last train Saturday afternoon. He was one year of age on the first trip in 1870, and began firing on the branch when he was seventeen years old. In fact, he fired an engine for his father, Thomas, and both are now retired from (D&H) railroad service."

After January 28, 1933, the railroad's service on the branch consisted of a combined freight, milk, and express train that operated from Delanson to Cherry Valley and return on a daily basis. Improved highways and modern motorized vehicles eroded even that service so that the D&H was allowed to abandon the branch in 1956. The Hyndsville depot was closed and removed in 1932; KF Tower was abandoned in 1933. The stations at Seward, Sharon Springs, and Cherry Valley have survived under non-railroad ownership. They may be seen today carrying out their new purposes as a residence and businesses, but they still perpetuate the memory of the rural Cherry Valley Branch of the Delaware & Hudson Railroad.

The complexion of Cobleskill has changed over time from agriculture to agricultural learning. In 1916, the Schoharie State School of Agriculture opened, which eventually grew to become a component of the State University of New York, with its College of Agriculture & Technology. Students are provided dormitories and lecture halls alongside Route 7, but there are no classes on the history of the railroad that runs by within sight.

As you can imagine, the railroad's terminal at Cobleskill has changed over the years as well. Gone are the engine facility, turntable, all the yard sidings, and one of the mainline tracks. CPRail does no business here

SUSQUEHANNA DIVISION—ALBANY, COBLESKILL, ONEONTA AND BINGHAMTON

READ DOWN .... READ UP

316	314	312	322	308	306	318	320	302	Mls	TABLE 15	321	303	305	315	325	309	311	313	317
Sun. Only	Sun. Only	Except Sun.	Except Sun.	Except Sun. (Note)	Except Sun.	Daily	Sat. Only	Except Sun.			Except Sun.	Except Sun.	Except Sun.	Daily	Sat. Only	Except Sun.	Except Sun.	Sun. Only	Sun. Only
P.M.	A.M.	P.M.	P.M.	P.M.	P.M.	P.M.	A.M.	A.M.		Lv. Ar	A.M.	A.M.	NOON	A.M.	P.M.	P.M.	P.M.	NOON	P.M.
§4 05	§8 20	†11 30		†4 20	†3 20		S12 30	†7 15	0	ALBANY	†7 35	†8 35	†12 00	S3 20	†6 35		†11 00	§12 00	§6 50
			5 14				12 34			Madison Avenue	7 31	8 31		3 16					
	f8 36	f5 10	5 27	3 37	3 41		12 46	7 33	4.8	Elsmere	7 19	8 18	f11 43	3 02			f10 44	f11 44	f6 34
	8 39	11 51	5 30	3 41			12 49	7 36	5.6	Delmar	7 16	8 14	11 41	2 59			f10 41	11 42	f6 30
	8 42	11 55	5 34	3 44			12 52	7 39	7.0	Slingerlands	7 12	8 09	11 37	2 55			f10 37	11 38	f6 26
		f5 38					12 56		8.5	Font Grove		8 05							
4 30	8 49	12 02	5 44		3 52		1 04	7 47	10.9	Voorheesville	7 03	7 59	11 31	2 47			10 30	11 32	6 18
		f5 48	5 52		f3 56		1 12	f7 52	13.9	Meadowdale	6 55	7 52						f11 26	f6 12
4 41	9 00	12 14	6 00		4 03		S1 20	7 59	17.2	Altamont	†6 50	7 45	11 21	S2 35			10 21	11 21	6 07
f4 58	f9 28	12 37		4 25	4 25			8 22		Delanson		7 22	11 05				10 05	11 15	5 50
		v12 43		5 19	4 32			8 29	31.0	Esperance		7 12	10 54					10 57	5 43
					4 42			8 37		Schoharie Junction		7 03						10 49	
f5 11	9 37	v12 53			4 48			8 42	36.2	Central Bridge	6 57	6 57	10 44				f9 50	10 47	5 34
	9 45	v1 00			5 01			8 50	39.3	Howe's Cave		6 51	10 38				f9 44	10 41	5 28
					5 12			8 57	42.2	Barnerville		f6 45					5 11		
5 31		1 10	5 39		5 12			9 12	44.8	Cobleskill	6 40	6 40	10 28	4 05	4 55		9 25	10 32	5 19
	10 07	t1 21			5 22			9 24	50.0	Richmondville	f6 29	10 18	10 18				9 13	10 22	5 09
					5 29				52.8	West Richmondville	f6 23								
f5 52	10 22	t1 37		5 38	5 38		9 39		56.9	East Worcester	f6 16	10 06	10 06		4 37		9 13	10 10	4 57
6 00	10 30	t1 44		5 46	5 46		9 48		61.0	Worcester	f6 08	9 57			4 30		9 04	10 00	4 48
6 08	10 38	f1 52		5 56	5 56		9 57		66.6	Schenevus	f6 00	9 49			4 23		8 55	9 51	4 40
	10 44	v1 58			6 03		10 04		70.0	Maryland	f5 53	9 42						9 45	4 34
6 23	10 54			6 25	6 15		10 13	76.4		Colliers	f5 43	9 33			4 18		8 48	f9 34	4 25
6 30		2 15		6 33	6 23		10 20	81.7	Ar. Oneonta Lv	5 35	9 25			4 05		8 30	9 25	4 15
6 40	11 10	2 20		6 40	6 45		10 30	81.7	Lv. Oneonta Lv	5 25		9 18		3 56		9 20	9 20	4 07
6 54	11 25	2 36			7 00		10 46	89.7	Otego	f5 09		9 05		3 43	8 07	9 07	9 07	3 53
7 01	11 32	2 42			7 07		10 53	94.1	Wells Bridge	f5 01		8 58		3 36	8 00	9 00	9 00	3 46
7 08	11 40	2 49			7 15		11 00	98.9	Unadilla	f4 52		8 50		3 28	7 51	8 52	8 52	3 39
7 17	11 47	2 56		7 10	7 26		11 11	103.3	Ar. Sidney Lv	4 44		8 40		3 20	7 42	7 44	8 44	3 30
7 17	11 47	2 56		7 10	7 26		11 11	103.3	Lv. Sidney Ar	4 44		8 40	†11 35	3 20	7 36		8 44	3 30
7 26	11 55	t3 05			7 36		11 21	108.5	Bainbridge	f4 35		8 29	11 25	f2 58	7 19		8 35	3 21
7 34	12 03	3 15			7 45		11 30	114.4	Afton	f4 25		8 20	11 05		7 10		8 26	3 12
7 44	12 12	3 25			8 00		11 40	118.8	Nineveh	f4 18		8 10	10 50		6 54		8 18	3 04
7 48	12 16	f3 29			8 05		11 45	120.3	Harpursville	f4 14		8 07	10 30				8 14	3 01
							f4 23		123.5	Belden			f10 20			f6 49		
t8 04	12 31	t3 43			f8 21		12 02	127.1	Tunnel	f4 04		7 54	10 12		6 42		8 03	2 50
8 13	12 41	t3 52			8 31		12 12	132.5	Sanitaria Springs	f3 52		7 45	9 55		f6 36		7 52	2 40
							f4 55		135.6	Port Crane			f7 36					
§8 35	§1 05	†4 15		†8 15	†8 50		†12 35	142.6	Ar. BINGHAMTON Lv	†3 30		†7 20	§9 30		†2 12	†6 10	§7 30	$2 20
P.M.	P.M.	A.M.	P.M.	P.M.	P.M.		A.M.	P.M.			A.M.	A.M.	P.M.	P.M.	P.M.	P.M.	P.M.		

(Column 318 carries the note "Mixed train subject to delay"; column 320 "Runs Saturdays only"; column 309 "Mixed train subject to delay"; column 325 "Runs Saturdays only".)

FOR ARRANGEMENT OF PARLOR, SLEEPING AND CAFE CARS, SEE PAGE 9.   Trains 321 and 322 will stop at Hilton's Crossing on signal.

MECHANICVILLE—DELANSON

READ DOWN .... READ UP

386	Mls	TABLE 16	381	389
P.M.		Lv. Ar.	A.M.	P.M.
	0	Mechanicville	6†55	
	3.0	Coons	6†47	
	4.5	Ushers	f6 40	
	7.5	Elnora	6 31	
	13.7	Crescent	f6†22	
	15.9	Alplaus	f6†08	
		Mohawk	6 03	
3†25	17.4	Schenectady	5†55	6†45
f3 34	20.8	So. Schenectady		6†34
f4 10	32.0	Delanson		6†00
		Ar. Lv.		

COBLESKILL—CHERRY VALLEY

READ DOWN .... READ UP

342	344	340	Mls	TABLE 17	341	345	343
P.M.	P.M.	A.M.		Lv. Ar.	A.M.	P.M.	P.M.
§5 40	†5 50	†9 20	0	Lv. COBLESKILL Ar.	8†40	†4 50	$2 00
5 55	6 04	9 36	4.7	Hyndsville	8 27	4 38	1 45
6 08	6 14	9 47	8.3	Seward	8 16	4 30	1 25
6 25	6 27	10 00	13.5	Sharon Springs	8 05	4 20	1 00
§6 50	†6 50	†10 30	22.6	Ar. CHERRY VALLEY Lv.	7†45	†4 00	$12 30

Trains 340, 341, 342, 343, 344 and 345 will stop on signal at Janesville, Hansons, Leesville and Prospect.

COOPERSTOWN & CHARLOTTE VALLEY R. R.

READ DOWN .... READ UP

361	Mls	TABLE 19	360
P.M.		Lv. Ar.	P.M.
*6 15	0	Lv. ONEONTA Ar.	*4 20
6 30	5.3	Colliers Lv.	4 10
f6 33	6.2	Cooperstown Jct.	f4 05
		Cliffside	f
6 38	9.3	Portlandville	3 58
6 48	13.9	Milford	
6 53		Clinton Crossing	f3 41
f6 56	17.8	Hartwick Seminary	f3 41
6 58		County Farm	f3 39
*7 10	22.6	Ar. COOPERSTOWN Lv.	*3 30

SCHOHARIE VALLEY RAILROAD

READ DOWN .... READ UP

4	2	TABLE 18	1	3
P.M.	A.M.	Lv. Ar.	A.M.	P.M.
†5 35	†8 45	Lv. Schoharie Junction Ar.	†8 10	†5 05
f5 40	f8 50	Hallenbecks	f8 05	f5 00
f5 45	f8 55	Vromans	f7 55	f4 55
6 00	9 10	Schoharie	7 55	4 50
6 25	9 30	Ar. Middleburgh (M. & S.) Lv.	†7 30	†4 20

Light faced figures denote A. M. time.   Dark faced figures denote P. M. time.
NOTE.—Train 308—Passengers for Pennsylvania Division points change at Oneonta to Train 306, which makes connections at Nineveh.
For Explanation of Reference Marks, see Page 10.

anymore. The three-story J. S. Hutt Company factory, Courter's Mill, Slawson & Decker Company, Cobleskill Coal Company, and the Borst & Robinson Feed Mill that all brought revenue to the D&H are gone now. The Commercial Hotel (and its livery stable) that once catered to railroad travelers is but a ghost. That's the bad news. The good news is that the 1900-era passenger station and freight house both survive. The station is a restaurant and local drinking establishment called "Locomotions Sports Bar."

Leaving Cobleskill, we pass the SUNY campus immediately after crossing Route 7's bridge over the railroad (that is now to our north). Not too far away we turn onto Warnerville Cut-Off Road to get back to the railroad tracks, first crossing Cobleskill Creek. While the name of this road seems to refer to a railroad location and, yes, it does get us to the railroad track, the moniker

is derived because it is a shortcut from Route 7 to Route 10. Just a short distance down Warnerville Cut-Off Road, we arrive at a what appears to be the location of an ordinary grade crossing. Yet much more was, and is, here. First, it is very obvious that the railroad grade is ascending north, which will continue all the way through Cobleskill and on to Howe's Cave. Only a few hundred yards to the north was the location of KF Tower and Cherry Valley Junction. It is nearly impossible to decipher any of this, but if we continue on Warnerville Cut-Off Road to Route 10 we will cross the branch's abandoned right-of-way that is quite visible. Then, if we turned eastward onto Route 10 we would find that an historic marker has been placed to inform us and point to the location of Cherry Valley Junction.

Back at the grade crossing, when we look south, we can see the railroad's bridge across West Creek, which

is a major tributary to Cobleskill Creek. Just beyond the bridge the railroad's grade appears to hit rock bottom, but only temporarily. For, beyond the eastward curve that takes the tracks from our view, lies CPRail's milepost CPF519 and a sign that again advises crews to BEGIN HEAVY GRADE. This is where the southbound ascending grade known as Richmondville Hill gets its start.

Already on our journey from Mohawk Yard we have encountered Kelleys Grade, Schoharie Hill, and Howes Cave Hill but these do not compare with the 1.31% grade that we about to examine. From here, the ascent continues three miles before it reaches its namesake community. While it has climbed upon the side of one of the Tertiary era's uplifts, Cobleskill Creek has snuggled up to that hill's base. From Richmondville it is another four miles until the summit of Richmondville Hill is reached at Dante (pronounced "dan-tee"). While today's high-horsepower diesel locomotives propel their train across Warnerville Cut-Off Road at the allowed forty miles-

C40-9W No. 9230 leads train 939 as it speeds downgrade across Warnerville Cut-Off Road, an appropriate place for a depot at one time. Cherry Valley Junction was eight car-lengths back in the distance. RIGHT: This scene looks north from the railroad's bridge across West Creek.

per-hour, by the time Dante is reached the speed has dropped to just 10-13mph, barely that of an accomplished bicyclist.

Pardon me. In all the excitement of telling you about Richmondville Hill's operational nightmares I forgot to tell you one thing about Warnerville: it never had a railroad depot to call its own. The grade crossing of Warnerville Cut-Off Road would have been a good place for one if it had. It did, however, have a road house

on the north side of Route 7 where the present Post Office is and so Warnerville, much like the villages of Quaker Street, Esperance, and "old" Central Bridge lived by the roadside. And it was that highway (Route 7) that Warnerville residents used to gain the railroad facilities at either Cobleskill or Richmondville.

Back on Route 7 we pass through Warnerville, which was named for George Warner an early settler, and then we get to the new Cobleskill-Richmondville High

School where we will pull onto the shoulder of the road for a moment. Yes, it is a nice modern school house but what is interesting is above it: the railroad grade. When constructed, Harvey Baker's workers blasted away part of the shoulder of the hill to form a shelf for the A&SRR's single track, six-foot gauge, right-of-way. Later, the D&HCCo fitted a pair of standard gauge tracks onto that shelf, but today there is only one track again. Still, the open face of the hill towers above even today's double stack container trains. Years ago, railroad sectionmen regularly rappelled down this limestone rock face in winter time to break away ice formations that might endanger passing trains. That type of work hasn't been done in recent years although it still snows

and gets cold during the winter. I've come to call this man-made cliff "Big Bluff," and just around the curve to the south is a smaller version of Big Bluff that I call—what else—"Little Bluff."

Just before the railroad's right-of-way enters Big Bluff from the north is a spot the railroaders called Hungry Hollow. There is a defile that had to be bridged and then filled to allow the tracks to cross, but where the "hungry" part comes from has been lost to the passage of time. Regardless of its ancestry, Hungry Hollow's unfortunate claim to fame happened on July 15, 1941. That was the day the last explosion of a steam locomotive occurred on the Delaware & Hudson Railroad. It was not the explosion of just any old 2-8-0 Consolidation-type engine either. Instead one of its new 4-6-6-4 Challenger-type engines was involved: number 1510, that had been built by the American Locomotive Company at Schenectady the previous year.

On that fateful Tuesday morning, D&H train MB-2 departed Mechanicville bound for Binghamton at 2:08 AM. At the head end of this forty-five-car train was one of the railroad's new J-class engines. Its Engineer was Charles K. Smith; its Fireman, Elbert J. Price. Also riding in the locomotive cab was Head Trainman James M. "Red" Cleary; the train was in charge of Conductor Albert J. Griffin who rode in the caboose along with another trainman and a flagman.

Sixty-eight year old Engineer Smith guided his train through Mohawk Yard non-stop and then proceeded without incident up and down Kelleys, Schoharie, and Howes Cave hills where daylight announced the start of what seemed to be another ordinary day. Just before 6:00 AM, MB-2 proceeded through Cobleskill, then quickly passed Cherry Valley Junction, and Warnerville Cut-Off Road and began its ascent of Richmondville Hill. After proceeding one-half mile beyond milepost 47 (today's CPF520)—and within sight of Big Bluff—the boiler of No. 1510 exploded with a deafening roar.

When the boiler of Challenger-type No. 1510 exploded, it tore away from the engine's chassis, somersaulting through the air. It landed on the track ahead of the now dead engine, which pushed it along for nearly 200 feet before coming to rest.

ABOVE: *Close up views of the boiler and engine chassis carcasses reveal the devastating damage that can be unleashed by an exploding steam locomotive boiler. Unfortunately, the loss of human life is also a by-product of this cataclysmic event. Engineer Charles K. Smith, Fireman Elbert J. Price, and Head Trainman James M. "Red" Cleary were killed when the exploding boiler ripped the locomotive cab away and tossed it effortlessly into the air. It fell to the ground (LEFT) several hundred feet away from the now shattered engine, Cleary's mangled body still inside. Smith and Price—already dead—fell out of the cab while it was in flight and landed nearby within several feet of each other.*

LEFT AND ABOVE: LAMBERT D. COOK. TOP: ESPERANCE MUSEUM COLLECTION.

It was 6:05 AM, the last morning of life for Charles Smith, Elbert Price, and Red Cleary.

When the boiler exploded, the blast tore the cab containing the three crewmen off of the engine. At the same time the explosion tore the boiler from its mountings on the locomotive's frame. The boiler somersaulted through the air, coming to rest on the mainline ahead of the now boiler-less engine. It was facing the opposite direction to which it had been traveling. The skeletal chassis, still moving on inertia alone, then collided with the remains of the boiler, pushing it nearly 200 feet further up the track. After finally coming to a halt, the train had travelled a little over 500 feet from the time of the explosion. Eleven cars derailed behind the lifeless locomotive. The cab containing the engine crew was blown to the east side of the track, crashing to the ground some 200 feet away from the mainline. Cleary's mangled body was still within the cab's wreckage. The bodies of Engineer Smith and Fireman Price had fallen out of the cab while it was still in flight. Their horribly mutilated bodies were found almost side-by-side an additional hundred feet from the cab wreckage.

The cab and other debris from the locomotive landed in a field owned by Ray Dauley. Jesse Linster, farmhand, had been leading twenty-eight cows out of the pasture when he heard the roar of the explosion. "I looked up quickly," he said, "and saw the iron flying through the air for what I think to be 150 or 200 feet. The smoke and steam was so thick that I couldn't see the cars." Oscar Hendrickson felt a terrific concussion pass through his bedroom as he was dressing; his home was one-half mile from the site of the wreck. Other folks thought there had been an earthquake (H. Strobel), an accident involving a large truck (David Hayes), that the Germans were making a raid, or that a large bird had flown into their screen door. Ray Dauley thought that the roof of his barn was going to fall in. But, word quickly spread around the communities of Cobleskill, Warnerville, and Richmondville that there had been a boiler explosion up "on the hill."

Officials from the railroad explained to news reporters that the explosion could have occurred in two ways. "When the boiler becomes empty of water, due

The first concern for wreck crews is to clear the mainline so that operation of trains can begin anew. Behind Challenger No. 1510 are its tender and eleven derailed cars, some having overturned. This view looks south at Big Bluff. The locomotive chassis can still be discerned on the southbound track. LAMBERT D. COOK PHOTOGRAPH.

The boiler was pushed off the track into the adjacent grass and weeds and left to be recovered at a later date by the D&H. LAMBERT D. COOK PHOTOGRAPH.

to the terrific heat of the firebox, the crownsheet is drawn downward and an immediate explosion follows. Or, the blast could also have been caused when the crownsheet became heated, and cold water was turned into the boiler by the injector. The resultant force created by the cold water against the red hot metal would cause the blast."

It was a common practice of engineers to run their engines with only a small amount of water constantly covering the firebox's crownsheet. In doing this they felt that the steam was hotter and provided more power from which their engine could operate more efficiently. Of course, the trick was to keep the crownsheet covered with water at all times. When traversing undulating terrain it was an experienced, careful engineer and fireman that always kept an eye glued to the water glasses located on the backhead of the boiler on their respective sides of the cab to make sure there was sufficient water in the boiler. Whether Engineer Smith was one of these practitioners or not we do not know. Regardless, he would have certainly monitored the water level in his engine's boiler. He did not know, however, that the piping to the cab water gauges had become partially blocked so that the levels he and his fireman saw in their water glasses were not accurate. They thought they had water when, in actuality, they did not. Investigators ruled that clogged water pipes were the direct cause of the explosion of No. 1510 that resulted in the deaths of Smith, Price, and Cleary. Since July 15, 1941, the countryside surrounding Big Bluff has remained quiet, except for the normal sounds of diesel locomotives straining to drag their trains upgrade against gravity to conquer the summit of Richmondville Hill.

As we continue on our tour along Route 7, I'll let you continue to gaze up at Big Bluff and contemplate the events of July 15, 1941. But, I'll interrupt your thoughts momentarily to draw your attention to the roadside sign that informs us of our arrival at Richmondville, a village that is "Focused on the Future." Yet, within an oval inset into the sign a northbound steam train is shown rounding a curve near the location of the depot. Focusing on the future, but remembering the past, gives you a good indication that Richmondville is a hearty and progres-

sive community. Although the village was incorporated in 1845, and the Town of Richmondville was formed four years later, there is still a degree of ambiguity surrounding the origin of the village and town name.

There are three theories regarding the derivation of the name Richmondville. First, Thomas Fairbanks, an early settler, was married to a woman from Livingston Manor, NY whose name was Jane Richmond. Because he desired to perpetuate her family's name he persuaded other residents to call the village Richmondville. Next, George Warner, the namesake for Warnerville, was also an early settler who had immigrated from Richmond, England. He is said to have named Richmondville in memory of his native town. Finally, an early postmaster was named John Richmond. It is thought he named the village after himself rather than in memory of any person or place. There are supporters and objectors to all three theories. Take your pick, you can't be wrong.

Regardless of name derivation, Richmondville has withstood the test of time. It has always been, and still is, the quintessential rural village: spire-topped churches, post office, school, hotel, bank, hardware and dry goods stores, grocery markets, and small dwellings most of which line Route 7, which is the community's Main Street. There is but one four-corners where some commercialism extends south up Summit Street, or north down Depot Street. Richmondville fortunately had one other thing: it had a benefactor. His name was John Drew Holmes.

John was born on May 11, 1870. When he graduated from Cobleskill High School he immediately began working for the private banking firm of Westover and Foster, whose company was the forerunner of The Bank of Richmondville. Mr. Holmes worked at the Richmondville bank for seventy-eight years, the final forty as its president. The Guinness Book of Records list him as having worked the most continuous years at the same bank. That would be good enough for plenty of people, but not for the generous John Holmes. He donated $100,000 to the Community Hospital of Schoharie County at Cobleskill, followed later by two additional bequests of $175,000 each. For Oneonta's Hartwick College, he made it possible for a women's

While Richmondville is "Focused on the Future" it still remembered to inset an oval containing a northbound train that is rounding the curve to its depot.

dormitory to be built, it being named for his late wife Edith Frasier Holmes. When the Village of Richmondville needed a new pumper engine for its fire department, John Holmes bought it for them, and when the community desired a swimming pool he came forward with the funds to have it built. But, his most generous gift to Richmondville was supplying the funds to retire the village debt. Richmondville is a prosperous and attractive community today because of the financial gifts he made. After he died at his home on Depot Street, at the age of 96, the village renamed the street Holmes Street. By 1966, not many people were using the street to get to the depot anyway.

For many years, Depot Street turned north off of Route 7 and then descended the hill to cross Cobleskill Creek where an early grist mill and water supply pond had once been situated. From the creek, the street almost bent over backward to climb the hill. At the top the railroad and depot were located. From the rear windows of the depot could be gained a wonderful bird's-eye view of the village down below. The railroad was nearly one hundred feet higher in elevation than Route 7.

By the time I first came to Richmondville, Depot Street had already been renamed to honor John Holmes

ROADS, RIVERS, AND RAILS

THIS PAGE, LEFT AND BELOW: Traveling photographer, John H. Dearstyne, captured this circa-1910 portrait of the Commercial Hotel which fronted Main Street (later, Route 7). A livery stable was positioned directly behind the inn. On this day, the two men sitting on the porch at left are of the age and are wearing clothing that suggests they could be veterans of the Civil War. In 1862, at least twenty-six men from Richmondville signed up for military service. The volunteers were assigned to Company G of the 134th New York Infantry Regiment —recruited from the communities of Cobleskill, Gilboa, Richmondville, Seward, and Sharon in Schoharie County. By the time this photograph was taken, only two of the local volunteers were still living: David Palmatier and David H. Zeh. After all these years, we can only guess at the names of the men pictured here and wonder about their connection to the Civil War. Maybe some descendants will recognize the faces.

BOTH, DEPOT SQUARE PUBLISHING COLLECTION.

PREVIOUS PAGE, UPPER LEFT: One of Richmondville's three rooming establishments, the Commercial Hotel is seen at the extreme left of this 1908 photograph. Main Street (Route 7) glides by its impressive, columned entrance. Guests could enjoy a leisurely shave and hair cut at the barber shop just two doors up. On the same "block" and rounding the corner to Summit Street, awnings protect the window displays of a drug store, the jewelry shop run by Reuben Barringer, and Arthur C. Borst's dry goods business. PREVIOUS PAGE, UPPER RIGHT: A look up a tree-lined Summit Street provides another glimpse of the Borst store. To the right are the front steps of the Westover House—THE place to stay while in Richmondville. Rounding out the town's accommodations was a small wooden hotel that stood up on the hill near the depot. PREVIOUS PAGE, LOWER LEFT: A very proud Phillip H. Keyser and his wife, Ora, pose in front of the store they opened in 1898. While her husband kept the inventory stocked and the displays in order, Ora took an active role in their livelihood by waiting on the customers. The shop catered to the everyday needs of Richmondville households until it closed in 1951. A sign in the window advises passersby that the store was a "Post Card Station" and that the Keysers "Have all up-to-date novelties in this line." Possibly they sold this post card, too. PREVIOUS PAGE, LOWER RIGHT: Opened in 1864, the brick Westover House occupied the corner of Summit and Main streets and was built by John Westover—a contemporary of Joseph Ramsey and a director of the Albany & Susquehanna Railroad. The hotel's popularity rose to the point where a third floor had to be added in 1866. Located at this busy intersection, the Westover House was the centerpiece of downtown Richmondville until fire destroyed the building in May 1959. The village Post Office now occupies the site.

but you could still use the street to scoot up the hill to get a picture of a train. You cannot do that anymore. When Interstate 88 was built, it severed old Depot Street immediately south of Cobleskill Creek, leaving the bridge over the creek and the road-to-nowhere intact. An historical sign still advises motorists whizzing by on Interstate 88 that this was where the grist mill had been located.

To get to Richmondville's railroad today—and that is where we are heading—we will pass the traffic light at the intersection of Route 7 and Summit/Holmes streets, then turn right onto Mill Street. Cross over I-88 to Winter Street which runs directly into old Depot Street. The latter will take us where we want to go. The site where the two-story depot and its nearby 30'X80' freight house had once been located is now just a grassy area. In her 2001 book entitled "Tri Valley," author Marilyn Dufresne tells us that the depot "had been torn down several years earlier." Judging by the remnants left at the site, it was much earlier than that.

Upon arriving at the old station grounds, we note CPRail's milepost CPF522, which corresponds to the old Delaware & Hudson milepost 50 (from Albany) that once stood at the southwest corner of their old depot. That two-story station, by the way, was the only multi-story building erected along the Susquehanna Division. A few feet past CPRail's milepost lies the single mainline track that has come up Richmondville Hill three miles from the BEGIN HEAVY GRADE sign at Warnerville. There are still four miles of the hill to go before Dante is reached. In traversing Richmondville's hills, the railroad (built by Harvey Baker's men) curves to and fro not just to remain along the hillside, but to gain a little distance to minimize gradient. All those curves cause wheel flange friction against the rail, so that friction probably offsets the greater distance factor. Facing us is an uplifted hill around which the tracks curve in a manner that would make the Pennsylvania Railroad's famous Horseshoe Curve (near Altoona, PA) proud. Both north and south of this location, reverse curves lead into the Albany &

Susquehanna's own "horseshoe curve" in the same manner that the Pennsy's approaches transitioned into their curve. It is exhilarating to watch a train of any era negotiate this serpentine right-of-way. Locomotives strain. Wheel flanges squeal. Cars pitch and yaw. A slow but steady speed of 12 mph makes a train look like a drag freight. If we stay here long enough maybe we'll see a train. We haven't seen one since Howes Cave.

Besides the undulating contour of both land and railroad, we notice one other thing: it is noisy—and not from trains. All those sounds now come from vehicles using Interstate 88.

This interstate highway runs along the base of the hill that holds the railroad. Because we are directly above this roadway, the sound of speeding vehicles, cars and gear-shifting, engine-braking, tire-humming eighteen-wheelers rises directly to our elevation, obliterating any semblance of the former pastoral setting. Of course, the automobile traffic contributes its share of the road noise, but it is the trucks that generate the most decibels even

ABOVE: *Looking west at Richmondville along Route 7 on August 7, 2010. At the changing traffic light, Summit Street goes left while Holmes Street (previously Depot Street) turns right. The latter once led to the railroad and station. The shadow at left is made by the Bank of Richmondville building.*

LEFT: *Judge John Westover established the Bank of Richmondville in 1881. John D. Holmes worked there for seventy-eight years.*

when the road is not that crowded! Our height catches the sounds from farther away as vehicles approach Richmondville, pass through it, and leave town in a rush.

Fortunately, down in the village, all is peaceful. Up on the hill it is nearly impossible to hear much of anything, like a train approaching or a bird chirping. While the highway noise is certainly annoying, the number of trucks on the interstate reminds us that if the new road was not in operation, those same trucks would have to utilize the much slower Route 7 or the New York State Thruway with its high tolls.

I realize my opinion on this noise pollution is rather strong but, you see, I was here before Interstate 88 came along. I

ABOVE LEFT: *Richmondville's Depot Street crossed Cobleskill Creek, then climbed the hill to trackside. The freight house shows in the upper right of this circa 1910 view; the station stands behind the two buildings at center. Cobleskill Creek (ABOVE) is just a mere trickle, but beyond the Depot Street bridge lies a pond, thanks to the dam under the bridge. Looking south down the hill from the station (BELOW LEFT) a wonderful panorama of Richmondville village is displayed. The Westover House tower rises near the middle of the scene. St. Paul's Lutheran Church is the large structure on the right.*
ALL, RICHMONDVILLE HISTORICAL SOCIETY COLLECTION.

remember how quiet it was in Richmondville, Cobleskill, and Worcester. The local folk liked it that way. Back in the late '60s, when the only thoroughfare was Route 7, an approaching train working up Richmondville Hill could be heard long before it made an appearance. The mere anticipation of the train's eventual arrival made the actual moment almost anticlimactic. Yet, it was exhilarating to listen to the sounds of the working locomotives echoing off rock ledges such as Big and Little bluffs. There the pitch of the sound waves varied as curves and hillsides shifted the direction in which it traveled. Today, you cannot even see or hear an approaching train until it is staring right at you. On Richmondville Hill — considering the tree and brush growth of today — that distance is rather short.

But, I'm not going to place all the blame on Interstate 88 for this lack of train-approaching-enjoyment; locomotive builders have done their share, too. The General Electric and Electro-Motive high horse-

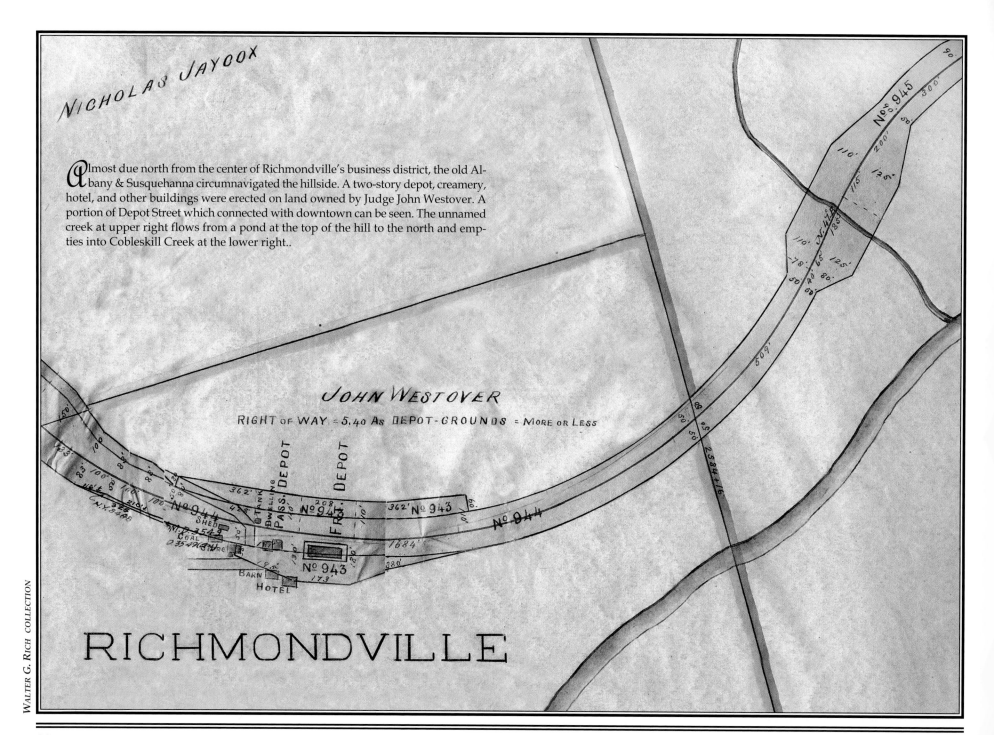

NICHOLAS JAYCOX

Almost due north from the center of Richmondville's business district, the old Albany & Susquehanna circumnavigated the hillside. A two-story depot, creamery, hotel, and other buildings were erected on land owned by Judge John Westover. A portion of Depot Street which connected with downtown can be seen. The unnamed creek at upper right flows from a pond at the top of the hill to the north and empties into Cobleskill Creek at the lower right..

No 945

JOHN WESTOVER

RIGHT OF WAY = 5,40 As DEPOT-GROUNDS = MORE OR LESS

PASS. DEPOT

FRT. DEPOT

DWELLING

No 944

No 943

362' No 943

362'

No 944

208.

1684'

380'

No 943

173'

SHED

COAL

BARN

HOTEL

2584+16

509'

RICHMONDVILLE

ROADS, RIVERS, AND RAILS

ABOVE: *Richmondville's depot was the only two-story stationhouse erected by the A&SRR. (The two-story station at Schoharie Junction was built by the Schoharie Valley Railroad and jointly used by the D&H.) Its footprint was 28'X30' and by the time this March 7, 1918 portrait was taken, an equally-sized one-story extension had been added. The building sat on the outside of a horseshoe curve, its complimenting freight house nearby (to the left).* **RIGHT:** *Inside the depot's bay window Agent/operator John Ferris Lyon seems to be "dressed to the nines" for his picture. Born in Kortright, NY in 1879, Lyon started his railroad career before World War I as a telegrapher in Oneonta. By 1930, he had made his way up to the position of Oneonta "ticket agent." It is not clear exactly when he was assigned to Richmondville, but judging from his age in this photograph, he could be performing his daily duties for one of the last times before retirement.*

LEFT: *A northbound Delaware & Hudson passenger train brakes to a stop at Richmondville's depot that is high up on the hill above the community. Omnibuses from the village hotels, the Westover House and the Commercial Hotel, have delivered a dozen persons to the railroad's door so that they may travel to Cobleskill, Albany, or beyond. At the time this picture was produced, there were several storage sheds for coal and agricultural products to the depot's right. A creamery was behind the photographer. The D&H boxcar is spotted on the freight house siding. James A. Dunning was the "railroad agent" in the early 1870s. David L. Rose started work at the depot in 1880; by 1910, he was the station agent. Melvin W. Harroway handled that role in the 1890s. It is known that Louis C. Hayden worked as the agent here but the dates are unknown; he filled a similar role at Sidney in 1920.*
RICHMONDVILLE HISTORICAL SOCIETY COLLECTION.

RIGHT: *A southbound high-drivered D&H camelback with a string of varnish has paused at the Richmondville station to engage in the usual exchange of passengers, mail, and express. As customers exit the train in the distance, the express agent takes two bags of mail and small parcels toward the depot while another man lifts cans of milk into the head-end car. At right beyond the depot, the freight station is in full swing with a couple of boxcars parked on its siding. Quite soon, the engineer will whistle, open the throttle, and continue on the journey to Binghamton.*
RICHMONDVILLE HISTORICAL SOCIETY COLLECTION.

RIGHT: *On August 16, 1938, Delaware & Hudson's northbound milk train with steel reefers in tow is shown about to pass Richmondville depot's platform and a Railway Express Agency baggage cart as it slows for a stop at the Sheffield Farms milk station just to the north and on the other side of the track. The D&H's milk had originally been shipped to New York City via the Erie Railroad at Binghamton, but was changed to the New York Central Railroad for forwarding the milk to Gotham via Albany. The REA wagon is stenciled "Safety First" to remind employees and travelers alike to be careful while around the station's grounds. That same admonishment should be taken into consideration when visiting the site of Richmondville's station grounds today even though everything in this picture is gone except for the track nearest the hill.* LAMBERT D. COOK PHOTOGRAPH.

LEFT: At some point during its life, Richmondville's depot was manned by (left to right) Agent Joel C. Waldorf, Operator Leroy Hill, and Baggageman/Helper Orson D. Myers. Waldorf was employed as the freight handler and express agent here in 1892. By 1920, he was the station agent—serving in that position well into the 1930s. Orson Myers led a diversified life. In 1905, he had been the postmaster for the small community of Eminence, Schoharie County; worked as a carpenter in Blenheim, NY in 1910; and was listed as a "laborer in the [Richmondville] Express Office" in 1920. Ten years later, he resided in Oneonta and was making a living as a machinist at the Delaware & Hudson's car shops there. Not much more is known of Leroy Hill, but however their lives may have changed in the future, at this particular moment in time, these three men were united in providing exemplary service to the local clientele as well as to those just passing through.

RICHMONDVILLE HISTORICAL SOCIETY COLLECTION.

Throughout the glory years of steam era railroading at Richmondville, the arrival of passenger, milk, and freight trains occurred with such regularity that all the hustle and bustle of the D&H operations became commonplace and was considered to be the ordinary environment of the area. The scenes on this page depict the everyday life of the railroad at Richmondville's station grounds. LEFT: Hotel omnibuses have arrived from downtown and their passengers are now making their way to the southbound train that has just arrived on track No. 1. It appears the locomotive at the head of this train is "popping off," an indication that the fireman has sufficient steam for the engineer to use in starting his train that is now stopped on Richmondville Hill. The arrival of trains at the depot also meant that the community's mail had arrived, too. Mail bags (BELOW) are in the process of being transferred from the RPO car to the downtown Post Office. At communities where trains did not ordinarily stop, their mail was picked up "on the fly" via the catcher arm (which is not deployed) that is above the mailman. A D&H milk train (LOWER LEFT) has arrived at Richmondville's Sheffield Farm's facility where trainmen and milk station employees have turned out to "spin" all of those cans into the milk car. That's Schoharie County milk bound for the metropolis of New York. LOWER RIGHT: LAMBERT D. COOK. OTHERS: RICHMONDVILLE HISTORICAL SOCIETY COLLECTION.

ABOVE: *The harsh reality of a New York winter has brought out a crew to shovel the station platform. The freight house is beyond the depot while the creamery sits around the bend.* BELOW: *Richmondville's new creamery is still in need of its first coat of paint. The sign says: "This roof is covered with Paroid roofing sold by H. F. Benton Lumber Co." of Cortland, NY.*

power diesels of today are substantially muffled. They are so powerful (4,000 hp or more) that it seems a pair of units can drag a mile-and-a-half long train up the slope effortlessly. Richmondville Hill's gradient, however, still serves to humble them in speed. When it comes to the pure enjoyment of an approaching train, the high-tech noise mufflers, the brute strength of the modern motive power, and the competing noise from I-88 literally spoil the thrill of witnessing an approaching train. It just isn't the same as a Challenger belching a plume of smoke and cinders or a lash-up of early ALCos grinding their way up to the summit with tonnage on the drawbar. The same is true at Horseshoe Curve, too.

Nevertheless, here we are now, halfway up one of America's premier railroad grades, at the very spot where Richmondville's depot once sat, hoping for a train to appear. And, appear they have since the Albany & Susquehanna Railroad began service to Richmondville on June 1, 1865. The evidence of this surrounds us, especially on the rocky hillsides where eighty-eight years worth of cinders (1865-1953) have been deposited after being exhausted skyward from hard-working, straining, steam locomotives. The cinders are surviving antiques from the steam locomotion era of the A&S, D&HCCo, and D&H that are our connection to the past.

The Delaware & Hudson Railroad fully dieselized during 1953, but the early American Locomotive Company RS-2 and RS-3 engines that made the D&H a "modern" railroad were somewhat a throwback to the steam age. They were smoky and noisy. Their labored exhaust was unmuffled. It did not contribute to nor contaminate the cinders deposited here during the steam epoch. The transition to quiet diesel locomotives was slow, just the opposite of diesel trucks that quickly erased any semblance of solitude and tranquility up here on Richmondville Hill. If we linger here, however, a southbound train will eventually arrive and, despite not seeing it or hearing it until the last moment, we will still be stirred and excited by its powerful presence. So, whether steam or diesel engine, peacefulness or noise pollution from Interstate 88, Richmondville Hill provides an exhilarating train watching experience. There are, however, few places on the seven-mile hill to be so thrilled.

Richmondville's station grounds of old are today weed covered. Little trace remains of the line's only two-story depot or typically large wooden freight house. One mainline track has been removed, too, but the foundation for the Sheffield Farms milk station can still be seen just to the north. Passenger trains, milk trains, and merchandise trains made up solely of forty-foot boxcars have all become a thing of railroading's past. But, gravity and gradient remain the same, so that every intermodal, ethanol, or coal train of today still has to bow to those forces.

Give me a moment to put my soapbox back in the trunk of my car and we'll be on our way. This would be a great place to pass the time waiting for a train, but I-88's noise—a proclamation that it is the king of this transportation corridor—is too prominent. We're secure in knowing that I-88 will never be the personable and accommodating roadway that Route 7 has always been. Despite its persistent noise distractions, Richmondville's old station grounds is only one of two "platforms" from which train watching may be safely undertaken on "the Hill." We're going to

ABOVE LEFT: *The horseshoe curve around the hill opposite Richmondville's depot is entered from reverse curves from both the south and north. On April Fool's Day 2010, NS train 938 rolls downgrade approaching the horseshoe curve, where CPRail (ABOVE RIGHT) train 251 is just passing CPF522 (former location of Richmondville station). The street sign tells us that this is the end of Depot Street and where Neary Road begins before it crosses the railroad at grade. BELOW LEFT: NS train 939 is working upgrade on January 21, 2010 and is about to cross Neary Road, passing the old depot site in the process. BELOW RIGHT: CPRail train 250 labors uphill from the north as it negotiates the reverse curve leading into Richmondville's horseshoe curve. Combined, these four pictures provide adequate evidence of the sinuous nature of the mainline near and at Richmondville's station grounds.*

ROADS, RIVERS, AND RAILS

the other one next at West Richmondville. From there on out, our road will strike the village limits of all the remaining communities that the railroad serves between here and Binghamton.

Depot, Winter, and Mill streets take us back to Route 7 where we will be on Cobleskill Creek's south hill; the railroad is on the north hill in plain sight. If a train comes along, we'll see it. At this point, the creek is ever narrowing as we near its source where it, along with the roadway and railway, will be situated side-by-side. Route 7, much like the railroad and Interstate 88, is climbing towards an eventual rendezvous with the divide between Hudson River and Chesapeake Bay watersheds. Before we get there, we will turn onto Schoharie County Route 33, which will take us to the railroad crossing at West Richmondville.

For its entire seven mile length, there are only two level grade crossings from which train watching may be undertaken, and now we have been at both; here at West Richmondville and at Richmondville's depot site where Neary Road (an extension of Depot Street) crossed the railroad at grade. There are several roadway underpasses of the railroad, Podpadic Road, Mill Street, and Winegard Road, but from these there is no direct access to the railroad. For all of its operational difficulties and scenic beauty, the railroad on Richmondville Hill is not easily accessible for viewing, contemplation, interpretation, or enjoyment.

Immediately south of the Route 33 grade crossing is an open area where it is possible to await the arrival of a train more comfortably. That's because we are somewhat below the level of I-88; all of its noise is above us (unlike at Richmondville's station grounds). Since we haven't seen a train in awhile, let us turn off the engine and sit here for a moment to listen for the sound of railroading that often interrupts the country quietude. While we are waiting, this will be a good time for me to tell you about Leonard Caryl, Dante, and Lambert D. Cook, the photographer.

Mr. Caryl was an early settler in this area. He became a storekeeper and a leading businessman, not that there ever much of a village here (although there was a schoolhouse and church). Because of its leading citizen, the tiny settlement became known as Carylville. Due to Caryl's familiarity with the area, in 1835 he began to espouse the need for a railroad that would follow the courses of Schenevus Creek and the Susquehanna River into Pennsylvania. Presumably this was to connect with the anthracite coal mining operations being pursued by the Wurts brothers who were founders of the Delaware & Hudson Canal Company. Mr. Caryl's suggestion of a railroad precedes by six years a similar proposal by a Mr. Keyes, of Bainbridge, for a railroad to run down along the Susquehanna River. Keyes' emphasis, however, was directing the railroad towards Binghamton.

When the Albany & Susquehanna Railroad was opened through Carylville to Worcester on July 17, 1865, a depot of sorts may have been placed here; the location was listed on the road's earliest timetables. If a depot had in fact been constructed, it would have been at the urging of Caryl who had become an associate of President Ramsey and a vigorous promoter of the A&SRR. Little is known of the railroad at Carylville during the A&S's early years. It is certain that when the Interstate Commerce Commission was undertaking its valuation of railroads during the period 1916-1921 the D&H's map for this location showed a platform from which passenger trains could be flagged by persons desiring to take advantage of the railroad's transportation. By that time, however the name Carylville had given way to West Richmondville—where we are right now.

Some evidence of the railroad having facilities here persisted in the early Depression years as West Richmondville was listed as a non-agency station, meaning there were no services being provided by an agent. There was a siding (team track) located here where carload and less-than-carload lots could be shipped or received by local customers. The agent at Richmondville, three miles away to the north, was likely the person that handled waybills for freight destined to and from the village of West Richmondville.

Dante is not a location you'll find on a highway map. As a matter of fact, you wouldn't even find it on a Delaware & Hudson Railroad map until 1921. But, if you perused a D&H Listing of Agents, you would find the name of James E. Dante as agent for the railroad at East

At Richmondville, we are these distances from some of the D&H communities we have already visited and some that we will be seeing shortly. RICHMONDVILLE HISTORICAL SOCIETY COLLECTION.

COBLESKILL →5
ALBANY →45
33 ←ONEONTA
93 ←BINGHAMTON
N. Y. STATE HIGHWAY

BELOW: *From the top of Little Bluff, Norfolk Southern northbound train 938 rolls downgrade around Richmondville's serpentine hills and curves on March 5, 2010. From this vantage point a good appreciation of Cobleskill Creek's upper valley can be gained. This view looks south towards the village of Richmondville that is nestled at the base of the distant hills.*

During the late 1930s, D&H 2-8-0 Consolidation locomotives still reigned supreme on Richmondville Hill where — operating in tandem — they supplied the muscle to drag southbound freight trains over the grade. We are fortunate that Lambert D. Cook, then a resident of Richmondville, was on hand to photograph this era of rugged railroading. Above and below, doubleheaders work upgrade with Little Bluff in the distance.

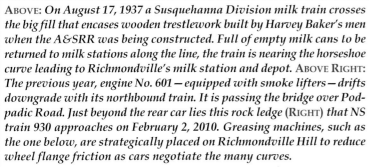

ABOVE: *On August 17, 1937 a Susquehanna Division milk train crosses the big fill that encases wooden trestlework built by Harvey Baker's men when the A&SRR was being constructed. Full of empty milk cans to be returned to milk stations along the line, the train is nearing the horseshoe curve leading to Richmondville's milk station and depot.* ABOVE RIGHT: *The previous year, engine No. 601 — equipped with smoke lifters — drifts downgrade with its northbound train. It is passing the bridge over Podpadic Road. Just beyond the rear car lies this rock ledge (*RIGHT*) that NS train 930 approaches on February 2, 2010. Greasing machines, such as the one below, are strategically placed on Richmondville Hill to reduce wheel flange friction as cars negotiate the many curves.*

BOTH ABOVE, LAMBERT D. COOK PHOTOGRAPHS.

The D&H used Consolidation (2-8-0) steam engines for the overwhelming majority of its freight train assignments. That became a thing of the past when the railroad began to receive Challenger (4-6-64) engines in 1940 and Northern (4-8-4) engines in 1943. Eventually, forty Class J Challengers and fifteen dual service Class K Northerns would be built by ALCo for use on the D&H. Having just rounded Richmondville's horseshoe curve, Challenger No. 1507 (ABOVE) wheels its train downgrade on July 15, 1941 where a beautiful view of Cobles Kill's valley can be enjoyed. Route 7 can be seen at the middle left portion of this panoramic picture. The Class J engines were far from small, yet Richmondville's hills overwhelmed their immense size, as shown by No. 1505 amongst the hills on May 11, 1941 (INSET). On that same day in May 1941, Challenger No. 1500 had pushed a train to the summit at Dante with the caboose behind the engine. After stopping at Dante, the caboose was "flown" by the engine, and then Engineer Sparky Higgins coupled to it to put it back on the train. In so doing, he misjudged the distance to the train and telescoped the caboose with the result shown at right. Engineers, it seems, had not yet become used to that long boiler in front of them. ALL, LAMBERT D. COOK PHOTOGRAPHS.

ROADS, RIVERS, AND RAILS

No. 1   View looking North around curve at
Block Signal # 49.1 on Richmondville Hill.

5/7/36   Richmondville
Neg. by Cook.   N.Y.

"The Doff"

LEFT: *Photographer Lambert D. Cook's first picture taken on Richmondville Hill was this study of track and scenery not quite one mile north of Richmondville station. The inset is the inscription from his index of pictures. Seventy-five years later (ABOVE), train 938's marker passes the same location that has gone from double tracks to double stacks within that three quarters of a century. At Big Bluff (BELOW), train 938 descends the formidable slope (BELOW LEFT) while train 939 climbs the hill on March 17, 2010 (BELOW RIGHT).*

CP Rail train 252 at West Richmondville. February 24, 2009.

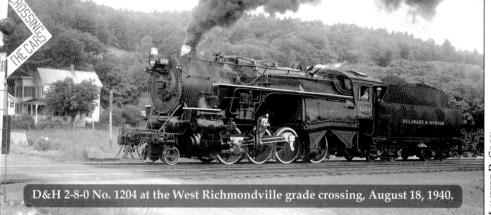

D&H 2-8-0 No. 1204 at the West Richmondville grade crossing, August 18, 1940.

LAMBERT D. COOK

Worcester, a community that is four miles further to the south from West Richmondville. We will be going there in the following chapter.

In 1908, Agent Dante, along with brothers Louis and William, opened the East Worcester National Bank with $25,000 of capital in a wooden storefront building along the village's Main Street (Route 7). The bank did not fare too well. Only eight years later in 1916 it was forced into liquidation. That, however, was just about the same year that the Dante family sold land to the D&H for use by a new "low-grade" line the railroad wanted to build from Schenevus to Richmondville Hill's summit. The following year, the railroad contracted for the building of the new line but, during 1918—even though fifty percent of the grading, and eighty percent of the masonry was completed—the United States Railroad Administration (which had taken over the operation of American railroads for the duration of World War I) put a stop to the work.

For the remainder of the war, the plan for construction of the new low-grade line languished. As soon as the USRA relinquished control of the D&H, on March 1,

1920, the railroad renewed the line's construction. On December 7, 1921, the new line, designated "Track 4"—was put into operation. The total cost for construction of the low-grade line was $1,500,573.90. At the Schenevus end of the line, a new electro-mechanical interlocking tower was erected, designated "WN Tower." Its purpose was to control the interaction of switches and signals used for the operation of trains on tracks 1 (southbound) and 2 (northbound) as well as new northbound track 4. At the northern end of the line at Richmondville Summit, a simple one-story train order cabin was placed at milepost 54 (today's CPF526) whose purpose was similar to that of two-story WN. This cabin was named "Dante," in honor of the East Worcester family. Both WN Tower and Dante Cabin went into operation during 1922.

While WN Tower controlled the northbound double-track expansion into triple-track territory, Dante controlled southbound double-track entry into quadruple-track. In addition to receiving northward freight trains off of track 4 (passenger trains did not ordinarily operate on the low-grade line as no stations were provided), the operator at Dante Cabin could direct southward trains

ALBANY AND SUSQUEHANNA R. R.

TIME TABLE No. 9.

Takes Effect Monday, Aug. 28th, 1865.

TRAINS WESTWARD.			Miles.	STATIONS.	Miles.	TRAINS EASTWARD.		
No. 1. PASSENGER.	No. 2. FREIGHT.	No. 3. PASSENGER.				No. 1. PASSENGER.	No. 2. PASSENGER.	No. 3. FREIGHT.
A. M.	A. M.	P. M.				A. M.	P. M.	P. M.
7.45	9.10	5.00		Albany		11.15	4.30	9.05
† 8.03	* 9.34	† 5.18	6	Adamsville	6	†10.58	† 4.13	* 8.39
8.08	9.38	5.23	1	Slingerlands.......	7	10.53	4.08	8.35
8.17	9.50	5.32	3	New Scotland	10	10.44	3.59	8.26
8.29	10.06	5.44	4	Guilderland	14	10.32	3.47	8.14
8.38	*10.23*	5.53	3	Knowersville	17	*10.23*	3.38	8.02
† 8.53	*10.43	† 6.08	5	Knox............	22	†10.08	† 3.23	* 7.42
8.59	10.51	6.14	2	Duanesburgh	24	10.02	3.17	7.34
9.08	11.03	6.23	3	Quaker Street.....	27	9.53	3.08	7.22
9.16	11.19	6.31	4	Esperance.........	31	9.45	3.00	7.06
9.30	11.39	6.46	5	Schoharie	36	9.30	2.45	6.46
† 9.40	*11.53	† 6.55	3	Howe's Cave	39	† 9.21	† 2.36	* 6.32
9.56	12.19	7.11	6	Cobleskill........	45	9.05	2.20	6.08
10.11	12.41	7.26	5	Richmondville	50	8.50	2.05	5.48
10.20	*12.53	† 7.35	3	Carylville........	53	† 8.41	† 1.56	* 5.36
10.32	1.09	7.47	4	East Worcester....	57	8.29	1.44	5.20
10.45	*1.30*	8.00	5	Worcester.........	62	8.15	*1.30*	5.00
11.00	1.50	8.15	5	Schenevus........	67	8.00	1.15	4.40
11.09	*2.02	† 8.24	3	Maryland.........	70	† 7.51	† 1.06	* 4.28
11.27	2.26	8.42	6	Colliers	76	7.33	12.48	4.04
11.36	* 2.38	† 8.51	3	Emmons	79	† 7.24	†12.39	* 3.52
11.45	2.47	9.00	3	Oneonta..........	82	7.15	12.30	3.40

☞ Observe Rules: important change.　　The Heavy Figures denote Meetings.　　* Trains do not Stop.
† Stop on Signal only.

Albany, Aug. 28th, 1865.

GEO. SKINNER, Sup't.

This timetable was issued upon opening the Albany & Susquehanna Railroad to Oneonta. Listed are some village names you may not recognize: Adamsville (Delmar), New Scotland (Voorheesville), Guilderland (Meadowdale), Knowersville (Altamont), Knox (Duane), Schoharie (Central Bridge), and Carylville (West Richmondville).

EDWARD P. BAUMGARDNER COLLECTION.

ABOVE: *Looking south along the railroad, a D&H freight train has just crossed Winegard Road in West Richmondville and is laboring the final mile of Richmondville Hill before reaching the summit. Pine Mountain (right), and an unnamed mountain to the left, form the "narrows" that separates the Hudson River and Chesapeake Bay watersheds. In 1922, the Dante train order office was located near the base of Pine Mountain.*

RICHMONDVILLE HISTORICAL SOCIETY COLLECTION.

into a 345-car passing siding that extended nearly all the way to East Worcester. Along the way, this four-track section of the D&H's line passed under a Route 7 bridge that pre-dated the current bridge we will be crossing soon. This new bridge, along with the railroad's implementation of Centralized Traffic Control, brought about a reduction of tracks at that location to only two, and at the same time the operator position at "old" Dante was abolished. I say "old" because the junction of track 4 with track 2 was changed to immediately south of the new Route 7 bridge, and that junction of the two tracks became "new" Dante. A train order cabin was not needed at new Dante since—with the CTC operation in effect—the junction was remotely controlled from Oneonta.

Back at West Richmondville, I think I can begin to discern the distant sounds made by an approaching train, so I'll quickly tell you about Richmondville's Lambert Cook. Get your camera ready if you'd like to take a picture of the train.

Although the everyday details of his life are sketchy, I can relate some basic information taken from various sources. Lambert David Cook was born in Richmondville on January 6, 1894. His parents, Myron and Ella, appear to have separated when Lambert was a teenager. Ella, her son, and daughter, Marguerite, resided on Summit Street and then on Railroad Avenue in Richmondville from about 1900 through the 1920s. The young Mr. Cook earned a living during these years as a glove cutter at the local glove factory

RIGHT: *In a wonderful backlit portrait of railroading within the "Narrows," Class G 4-6-0 No. 505 wheels northbound train 209 past Dante Cabin under the watchful eyes of Operator Vincent Martell. The descending grade to Warnerville begins here, as does the 345-car siding to East Worcester whose switch can be seen on track 1. Track 4 from Schenevus joins track 2 (the track occupied by train 209) just on the other side of the locomotive. At least it did when this picture was taken on September 3, 1936. Four years later, the site of Dante would be relocated nearly one mile south, just beyond the new Route 7 highway overpass. Inside the Cabin was a small lever machine that was used to manipulate the switch and signal on track 1 so that the operator did not have to cross the tracks.* LOWER LEFT: *On a subsequent visit to Dante, Lambert Cook used the same hillside to photograph the Dante Cabin grounds, which included a privy that the operator would have had to cross the tracks to use. Safety, it seems, was only a matter for railroad procedures and not for human comfort! The switch that allowed track 4 to enter track 2 is noticeable in this picture. Route 7 can be seen above and to the left of the Cabin.* BOTH, LAMBERT D. COOK.

BELOW: *Welcome signage at CPF526 advises enginemen that they have reached the end of Richmondville's heavy grade. Or, have they? See Page 104. This picture was taken from the same hillside that Mr. Cook used to photograph the scene above some seventy-four years earlier.*

Noticeable by its height, Dante's upper quadrant train order board is set to advise any trains approaching in either direction that they will not be receiving any orders. If either paddle is lowered ninety degrees, then the crew of the signaled train should be prepared to pick up an order, most likely via a high speed delivery fork. Vincent Martell poses for his portrait at Dante. August 3, 1939. LAMBERT D. COOK PHOTOGRAPH.

and as a day laborer for the D&H. His World War I draft registration card (filled out in 1917) also states that he worked for the railroad, but this time, his job was given as "sectionhand." That form included a brief description of the future photographer: he was tall, slender, had blue eyes, and light colored hair. By 1930, Lambert was living on London Avenue in Oneonta—a street just south of the Delaware & Hudson's two roundhouses located below Table Rocks—and was still employed by the railroad. He apparently returned to Richmondville in the mid-1930s where he developed an interest in railroad photography which later led to painting railroad scenes. His artwork, from what I have seen, was similar to folk-art in style. But it is his photographs of railroading on Richmondville Hill that are downright unparalleled in their depiction of operations amid the geographic grandeur of this portion of the Cobles Kill valley. You have probably already noticed the byline of Lambert D. Cook along with pictures used in this story thus far, and you'll see more. Mr. Cook died in Hamilton, NY in 1980.

From his photograph index, Lambert's first image was taken on May 7, 1936. For the next five years with camera in hand he roamed the Richmondville hills and D&H railroad trackage between Tunnel and Delanson. His emphasis, however, was the railroad's section between Dante and Warnerville. Because of his physical efforts traipsing up and down Richmondville Hill, and his superior photographic craftsmanship, we can better understand today what an exciting and scenic stage the Delaware & Hudson Railroad once operated upon while conquering Schoharie County's undulating terrain.

Unfortunately, there is not a happy ending to the story of Lambert D. Cook. For some now unknown reason, he relocated to a home on an island in Leland Pond, near Hamilton, in Madison County, NY. While there, he became ill, made his way to a Veteran's Hospital in Syracuse where

he passed away. At some point, either before or after he left Richmondville, his Main Street home burned to the ground, the flames consuming the vast majority of his photographic negatives. Some of his work, however, was able to be salvaged. Surviving are 204 black and white photograph negatives taken of the D&H (and Schoharie Valley Railroad that was at that time a property of the D&H), eight negatives of the Middleburgh & Schoharie Railroad, as well as twenty-two negatives of New York Central's old Ulster & Delaware Railroad and thirty negatives of the defunct Delaware Northern Railroad. Each negative is contained in a plain (yellowed) envelope (see next page for example) is numbered and has written upon it in an artist's hand information about the enclosed negative. Surviving are negative No. 1, while the highest numbered negative is No. 1061. Whether this was his final photograph, or just the highest number that was saved is unknown.

Also salvaged were thirty-four pages of his photograph index that was meticulously written in a form of calligraphy; the notations refer to negative number, date, subject, and other pertinent information relative to a particular picture. From this index, we find that Lambert also took several photographs of the New York, Ontario & Western Railway, as well as a number of freight and passenger car photographs of a wide variety of railroads and car types. Because Lambert apparently changed negative numbers it is difficult to explain why some negative envelope numbers and their corresponding index number conflict.

Regardless of this admittedly incomplete archive, it is fair to say that Lambert D. Cook was the most prolific photographer of the D&HRR in the Richmondville area. He loved the village of Richmondville and its surrounding hills. Above all, he was a photographer whose composition and technique were far above average. The entire surviving archive of Lambert D. Cook's photographic material is currently being maintained by author/historian Len Kilian. Len, by the way,

ABOVE: *Bow coal train 936 with C40-9W No. 9694 in charge has just crested the actual summit of the grade as it begins to descend the Hill.* CENTER: *Although train 939 has reached "old" Dante where CPRail signs designate the location as the beginning or end of Richmondville Hill, the grade persists for another one-half mile to near the Route 7 bridge. This time, GE ES40DC No. 7698, with an unidentified Union Pacific unit handles the chores.*

got to know D&H section foreman Frank Vodapic who opined that "he (Cook) was always hanging around us taking pictures." Thanks Lambert; we're glad you did.

Wow, did I time all of this storytelling perfectly; the droning of hard working locomotives informs us that we are about to see a train. And, just as it comes into view, a car pulls up to the crossing, its occupants "bailing out" with only seconds to spare to take their pictures. It is a long train 939 consisting of tri-level auto racks (from SMS) and container platform cars. Its speed is not much more than ten miles-per-hour. Six miles of climbing Richmondville Hill's grade has taken its toll on the train's forward progress, but the two high-horsepower locomotives will have little difficulty in continuing on for another mile before the summit at Dante is reached. Even these "quiet" engines seem to be balking at the work the engineer is asking them to do.

During D&H ownership of this railroad grade, head end helpers and rear end pushers were used in getting trains over the hill. Even in the diesel years, pusher engines were sometimes called upon to assist heavy trains up Richmondville Hill. Today, the hill has ceased to be helper territory so long as one of those two engines up front does not fail. If that happens—and it occasionally does—then locomotives from an opposing train will be called upon to aid their fallen brother. Normally, though, everything works out quite well so that both engineer and the Minneapolis train dispatcher can have an uneventful day.

As train 939 labors by us, we engage the camera-toting family in conversation. They are from New Jersey, parents giving their kids a lesson in the fourth R: Railroading. As train 939's marker passes, both we and the family depart, and in a few moments country solitude will return to West Richmondville. If we hurry, which is something that makes traveling on Route 7 less enjoyable, we can see this train once again as it proceeds under the roadway bridge at Dante. From there, with but a few bumps along the way, it is all downhill railroading along the Schenevus Creek and Susquehanna River until the river and railroad diverge at Nineveh. From there, there is another big hill for the railroad to climb; Route 7, too. We'll be there soon.

For now, let's go take a look at the spot where both the Cobleskill and Schenevus creeks get their start. The sources for both are not much more than water filled ditches alongside the railroad's right-of-way; the water being bubbled out of the ground. We can straddle both as they are separated by only a few feet. Yet, Cobleskill's water is already heading for the Hudson River; Schenevus' water is Chesapeake Bay bound. Along their respective courses, both will see a lot of railroading and be admired by motorists who are wise to still enjoy driving along the "old" road that is today's Route 7.

ABOVE LEFT: Foreman Frank Vodapic's section crewmen were, left to right, Tony Gercich, Frank Mossello, Phil Buffo, John Davis, Barney Brown, Clayton Brown, and Charles Ray. Frank is the fellow whose face is barely noticeable beyond Mossello and Buffo. Lambert D. Cook photographed them on 9/20/37.
ABOVE RIGHT: A New Jersey family arrived at the West Richmondville crossing just in time to photograph train 939 on July 24, 2010. That concrete pedestal (lower right) once supported a cantilevered signal mast that is shown in the picture at the right depicting Delaware & Hudson train RW-6 being led up Richmondville Hill's last few miles by a trio of General Electric-built U30C locomotives.

RIGHT, JOHN V. WEBER PHOTOGRAPH.

From the West Richmondville crossing of Route 33 to the new – and current – Route 7 overpass of the railroad is only a few miles, but we were easily able to overtake train 939 whose speed was down to the normal 10-15mph. ABOVE LEFT: From the highway bridge, NS train 939 is pictured as it crests the top of Richmondville Hill and negotiates CPRail's Richmondville passing siding track. On the other (south) side of this bridge was where "new" Dante was located after the 1940 Centralized Traffic Control system was put into operation. ABOVE CENTER: Many years earlier, four D&H ALCo RS units are shown at the same location with airborne sand signifying that the engineer is still applying sand (for adhesion) in order to get his train over the peak of Richmondville's grade. This picture was the inspiration for the contemporary one to its left. Pine Mountain, of course, is prominent in both views. LEN KILIAN COLLECTION. ABOVE RIGHT: On October 20, 1941, one year after CTC was implemented, evidence of the previous track arrangements at Dante could still be found. Taken from the "new" Route 7 bridge, 4-6-6-4 No. 1502 proceeds south on track 1 with its train draped across the summit of Richmondville Hill—head end descending, rear end still on the upgrade. Track 2 is in place, as always, but what's missing is the 345-car siding that had been to the left of the Challenger. Ties for track 4 are still in place at right, albeit with the rails removed. The reason the siding and track 4 have been deleted is due to the new highway bridge which was built to cross over just two tracks, a design feature that was matched by the D&H plan to reduce tracks here with its CTC installation. The telegraph poles at right have been placed since track 4 was taken out of service. By this time, track 4 joined track 2 on the other (south side) of the highway bridge. ROBERT F. COLLINS PHOTOGRAPH. RIGHT: Nearly seventy years after the above photograph was taken, the landscape at the same location looks like there had always been only two tracks. Although the fall foliage is already gone from Pine Mountain, Union Pacific GE C45AC-CTE No. 5476 leading southbound train 939 brightens the scene with its own yellow, blue, and red hues. DEAN SPLITTGERBER PHOTOGRAPH.

CHAPTER 4
CHIEF SCHENEVUS AND HIS CREEK

Dante (pronounced *dan-tee*) is where CPRail's "Richmondville" passing siding is located even though that community is four miles away. Possibly the CPRail folks never heard of Dante. This passing siding is the shortest of all four sidings of similar purpose between Mohawk Yard and Binghamton. It is a little less than two miles in length, which isn't that long for today's trains of 300-400 axles. One train will fit in nicely; two may fit snuggly. Occasionally trains will have to "saw" by each other. Operationally, however, this double-track oasis within mostly single-track territory comes in handy to keep trains moving and dispatchers happy. The north end of this passing siding is where Richmondville Hill ends and Schenevus Creek gets its start. The pronunciation of Schenevus is *ske-ne'-vus*, which is exactly how the Indians spelled the name they gave to the creek. It means "river of speckled fish."

Long before the railroad was even envisioned, but long after the ice age's advances and retreats scoured the valley Schenevus Creek claims today, there was an Indian "Tribe of the Speckled Fish," and its leader was Chief Schenevus. His tribe occupied the area where Schenevus Creek empties into the Susquehanna River. He was all-

RICH KIRALY

ABOVE: Chief Schenevus (pronounced *ske-ne'-vus*) , leader of the "Tribe of the Speckled Fish." LEFT: On May 1, 2009, Norfolk Southern northbound train 938 led by C40-9W No. 9653 has passed underneath Route 7's new plate girder bridge with an intermodal train, proceeding through Dante on CPRail's main track. With the passing siding in the foreground the train has just started its descent of Richmondville Hill although official signage of this fact will not be encountered until CPF526 which is nearly a mile distant.

At Manaho Gorge, near Chaseville, the daughter of Chief Schenevus and Manatee will always be together. This F. E. Bolles view shows the upper falls that cut through the forest.

powerful and feared throughout the watershed. Chief Schenevus had four sons, but only one daughter to pass along the family bloodline. (When considering Indian lineage, only a daughter can pass on the family bloodline to her child.)

The daughter's name was Manaho and regardless of all of his chieftain powers over many warriors, Chief Schenevus loved his daughter deeply and melted when in her presence. While the chief loved his daughter—and she him—Manaho eventually fell in love with a brave named Manatee. Together they would go to their "private" retreat, a waterfall whose effluent cascaded down the hills to make its way to Schenevus Creek. One evening while they were together by the pool at the bottom of the falls, they both looked into the water and saw their mirrored faces reflected on the surface of the pond. "Look," said Manaho, "we are there together." "It is a sign from the Great Spirit," replied Manatee, "that where I am, you will always be." But, alas, that was not to be.

During one summer morning spent hunting, Manatee stopped to rest by the top of the waterfall, gazing at the pool below, obviously entertaining loving thoughts of his Manaho. It was then that another brave, Ghangu—who was jealous of Manaho's love for only Manatee—silently approached Manatee from behind and pushed him over the falls, his body broken by the rock face as he tumbled forth before he landed lifeless in the previously mirror-surfaced pond. Ghangu, realizing what he had done, left the region never to be seen or heard from again.

Later that day, when all the other braves had returned from the hunt, Manaho did not see Manatee and she thought that he may be waiting for her at "their" waterfall. Upon arrival at the top of the falls, and not finding her lover as she had expected, she looked down into the clear water of the pond and was shocked to see the face of Manatee staring up at her from beneath the surface. She pulled her gaze away in horror, and when she had the strength to look once again, she saw their two faces mirrored side-by-side on the pond's surface. Remembering what Manatee had said "that where I am, you will always be," Manaho took this as a sign that the Great Spirit was calling her to be with Manatee. Without a further thought, she cast herself off of the ledge at the top of the falls, and died to be with her love, Manatee.

When the brave and the daughter were found, it caused profound distress for Chief Schenevus, who began to age rapidly; partial blindness followed. On

Because of Schenevus Creek's serpentine course it gets to Colliers after the highway and railway. Near Maryland, the creek cozies up to Route 7 where a man and his best friend enjoy a bit of fishing. The creek enjoys being kept company by man, animal, and roadway alike.

LEFT: *Now updated into Norfolk Southern's numbering system, an ex-Conrail SD60 leads southbound train 930 across Schenevus Creek's ninety-foot plate girder bridge No. 43 and into Schenevus on September 5, 2009. The surviving Schenevus station is less than a quarter mile ahead.* ABOVE: *Travelers on Route 7 can enjoy viewing beautiful farmlands as they traverse the roadway between Schenevus and Maryland. The railroad and creek lie off to the right. Central New York has a ubiquitous architectural style to many of its farmsteads.*

a subsequent hunt, he was unable to keep pace with his braves. Ashamed, he called his sons to his side. "My sons," he said, "I am very old and weary and I can no longer take part in hunting or leading war councils. Therefore, my sons, I command that your last act of obedience be the slaying of your own father." The sons, not daring to disobey their father and chief, followed him into the woods where they helped him mount his horse. "Each of you secure your bows and arrows," the chief said, "and each of you will fit an arrow to your bow and aim as a great hunter would towards a deer. I will fall as a slain deer and none of you will bear the shame of my death."

The sons obeyed their father's command; his last wish was carried out. When the other tribesmen learned of the death of their leader they briefly mourned, and then named the main stream passing through their region "Schenevus," in honor of the fallen, grief-stricken chief.

The Legend of Chief Schenevus has been passed down through the following generations, so that a village near the site of the death of the great chief and his daughter was also named in his honor. When the railroad came to the Schenevus valley in 1865, a station was built in this village near the creek. That depot was also named Schenevus.

From Dante, the railroad, the creek, and Route 7 travel harmoniously together for twenty-two miles until Colliers and the Susquehanna River are reached. In leaving Dante, we also leave the hills of Schoharie County behind and head for the rolling terrain and rich pasture land of Otsego County. Schenevus Creek takes a little longer in getting to Colliers because of a sometimes serpentine course; the railroad has only one restrictive curve: Whitehouse Crossing. So, you could say, Route 7 gets there first, even if you drive leisurely. Along the way from Dante to Colliers, both the railway and roadway call at East Worcester,

Worcester, Schenevus, Maryland, and Cooperstown Junction. Our Route 7 passes through all the village business districts. Worcester has held onto its vitality more than its neighbors to the north and south; Maryland and Cooperstown Junction never had much of a business district in the first place. The railroad had depots in each of the villages, a block or two south off Main Street (Route 7). Only Schenevus's depot remains intact. Maryland's depot is barely holding on. We will learn more about these two places when we get there.

Through all of this, Schenevus Creek flows merrily on its way to oblivion at Colliers (Colliersville today). The creek comes close to the village limits of East Worcester and Worcester, but in the end it's a near miss at both. At Schenevus it allows the railroad to cross via bridge No. 43, which is a ninety-foot-long plate girder affair. It then gets between the business district and the station grounds and takes a circuitous path around Schenevus Lake. At Maryland it almost makes

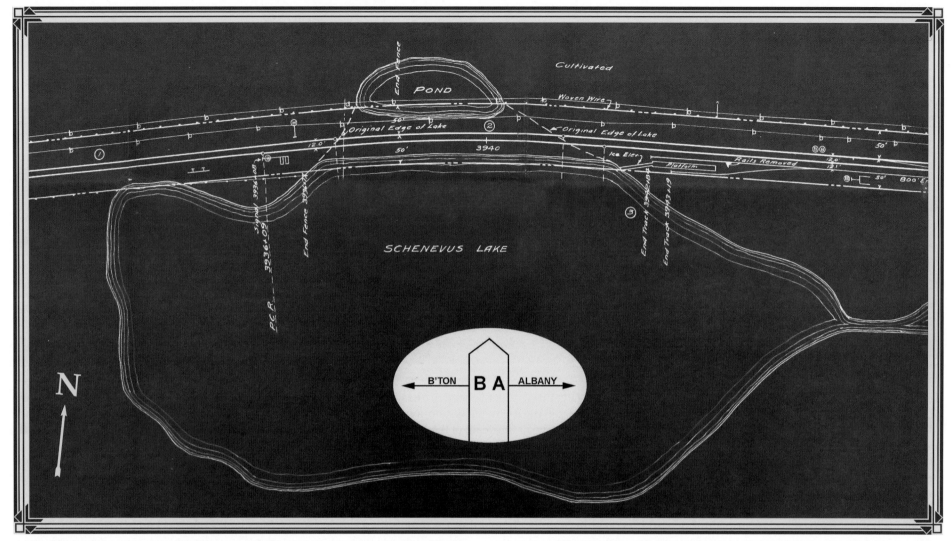

Above: *About one mile south of Schenevus the Albany & Susquehanna Railroad built a trestle across the northern tip of Schenevus Lake. The Delaware & Hudson improved upon this by filling in the trestle so that a long "embankment" separated the bulk of the lake from its most northerly point. The railroad undertook ice harvesting here and to facilitate that undertaking they constructed the necessary inclined ice conveyor, loading platform, and sidings on the northeastern shoreline of the lake. When construction for the low-grade line's track 4 was being pursued, the embankment across the lake was widened using cinders (mostly from Oneonta) and the ice facilities were removed. New track 4 then passed through the site of the ice loading platform; its switch off track 2 was located out on the embankment on the other side of the lake. WN Tower was placed across from the platform site on the west side of track 1.* Facing Page: *Track 4 passed by its own body of water near Worcester. It was named Hudson Lake by John A. Hudson who claimed to be a descendent of Henry Hudson who also had some waterways, bays, and lakes named after him. In this scene, a northbound freight train on track 4 is just pulling up to the water tank to have its locomotive tender replenished. Hudson Lake water did its part in keeping the railroad on the move.*

Above, National Archives collection.
Facing Page, Worcester Historical Society collection.

bisects open farmland where nicely maintained farms, barns, and white-washed homesteads blend perfectly with the lovely rolling hills. To this dairy farming wonderland Schenevus Creek adds its meandering course, as if it was attempting to touch each and every one of the beautiful spots along its way.

Dante was not so much a specific place as a small regional area, considering the original cabin had been placed at milepost 55 (today's CPF526) and then moved to the south side of the new Route 7 bridge—1.1 miles distant—when Centralized Traffic Control went into service at 8 AM on August 27, 1940. (Note: All D&H-era milepost numbers mentioned date from the Interstate Commerce Commission valuation of railroads during 1916-1921.) With CTC came a reduction in the number of mainline tracks. After all, that is the purpose of CTC: to more efficiently use less infrastructure.

The 1940 CTC implementation changed the railroad's trackage between WN Tower (Schenevus) and Dante, and from JX Tower (Schoharie Junction) to DJ Tower (Delanson), 22.5 miles in all. Trackage between Dante and Schoharie Junction over Richmondville, Howes Cave, and Schoharie hills was not a part of the new CTC system and remained unchanged. Within these new Centralized Traffic Controlled sections, 23.67 miles of mainline track was able to be removed. Despite this reduction in track availability, the railroad's train operations were able to be more efficiently handled by the Oneonta train dispatcher.

When our friend, Lambert D. Cook, was pursuing his interest in railroad photography, four tracks had passed under the earlier Route 7 bridge. These tracks were (west to east) a 345-car siding that ran nearly all the way to East Worcester and also passed under the Brooker Hollow Road bridge; track 1, southbound; track 2, northbound; and track 4, which was the "low-grade" line from WN Tower at Schenevus Lake used primarily, if not exclusively, as a northbound track.

The reason the D&H constructed the low-grade line was because of the ascending grade on the double track mainline between WN and Dante, a change in elevation of nearly 300 feet within 13.3 miles. Worcester Hill, as it was known, was nothing like Richmondville

a direct hit on downtown before abruptly curving to the south on the village doorstep. From there it meanders inland away from Route 7, as does the railroad. Within this territory the railroad crosses the creek at a variety of locations. Both end up side-by-side at Cooperstown Junction where the creek is almost licking at the railroad's ties. Then, it is only eight-tenths of a mile to Colliersville where the railroad continues on, but the creek does not.

It was near Schenevus Lake (now known as Seward Lake), at Chaseville, that Manaho and Manatee met their fate; both the railroad and creek pass by. When the Albany & Susquehanna Railroad was being constructed, it built a lengthy wooden trestle across the northern tip of Schenevus Lake, which the D&HCCo improved upon by filling in the trestle so that a huge embankment

was formed. Later, the D&H further improved the area during one of its early Twentieth Century grade reduction programs. Still later, it widened the embankment using cinders so that room could be made for the low-grade line's track 4 to diverge from track 2. The switch for this was on the northern end of Schenevus Lake's embankment, while WN Tower, which controlled the trackwork, was located just to the north on terra firma.

From Dante to Colliersville the road, river, and rails remained in close proximity. Unlike their association north of Dante, all three essentially flow down the same gentle grade, the railroad not having to climb one hill after the other. The further south you travel down the Schenevus Creek valley the more picturesque it becomes, especially between Schenevus and Cooperstown Junction. Along this stretch of Route 7 the road

ABOVE: *Before the new Route 7 bridge was constructed, four tracks passed under the previous one. Just to the south of the old bridge, J Class engine No. 1502 arrives at Dante on track 4 while making its maiden voyage north from Oneonta on July 7, 1940. Route 7 is on the hillside just beyond the dual-masted semaphore signal.* LEFT: *From the same vantage point, a northbound train with perishable freight on the head end makes its way up track 2 behind a pair of Consolidations. Until the arrival of the Js, the 2-8-0 had been the supreme ruler of the railroad's motive power roster. When CTC was put into operation, this portion of track 2 was abandoned.* BOTH, LAMBERT D. COOK PHOTOGRAPHS.

RIGHT: *Photographer George C. Corey stood along the shoulder of Route 7 when he took this picture of a train headed north, arriving at Dante behind a trio of ALCo RS-3s in their original paint scheme with nose chevrons added. Not too many years earlier the low-grade line they are on was designated track 4; now the line is track 2. The new Route 7 bridge (which crosses over only two tracks) is just to the left of this scene. The other tracks are the Dante-East Worcester passing siding nearest Route 7's embankment and track 1. Corey had been standing where the nearest utility pole is in the picture at lower right. BELOW: Also at Dante during its "heritage years" was the Summit pusher siding where men and machines awaited their next assignment. This was a particularly favorite spot for Lambert Cook. On June 10, 1940 he photographed the "Four Aces" with (left-to-right) Flagman Jim McGillian, Engineer Frank Root, and Fireman Ken Hettinger. No. 1111 was the first 2-8-0 (of Class E-5a) that was built by the D&H at its Colonie Shops in 1926 using a boiler supplied by ALCo. It was retired in the summer of 1953.*

ABOVE: *Looking south from Dante's Route 7 bridge today it is difficult to envision that this was at one time four-track territory. Track 4 once joined the original double track mainline here and pusher crews passed the time of day at this location while awaiting their next assignment. On December 7, 2009, train 938 had three engines, which was not uncommon during the winter season. Interstate 88 is just out of the scene at left, just the way I like it.*

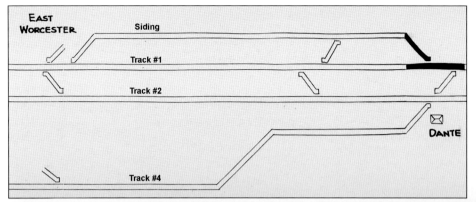

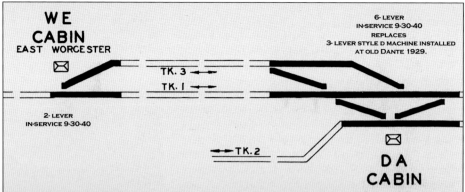

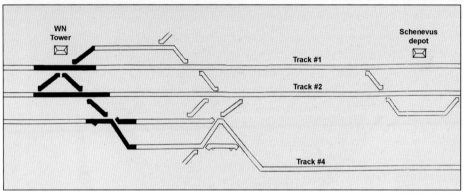

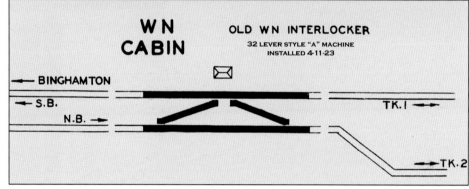

Hill, but the former's grade did tend to slow freight trains at the expense of passenger train scheduling. With the low-grade line in operation, slower freight trains could run via track 4, while the speedier passenger trains remained on track 2 which is where the stations were located. Freight trains, except local and milk consists did not ordinarily require the services of a station agent.

It is interesting to note, however, that the railroad's designation of the new track as the "low-grade" line did not live up to the definition the name implies. At Worcester for example, the low-grade line was nearly eighty feet higher in elevation than the original main-

line right-of-way. It would have been more correct for the railroad to have referred to track 4 as the "by-pass." That is what it did; it allowed freight trains headed north to bypass the stations at Worcester and East Worcester so that their interference with passenger service was nil.

With the implementation of CTC between Schenevus and Dante, track 4 became a two-way route and its designation was changed to track 2. At the same time, the railroad continued to utilize track 1 between Dante and East Worcester but, south of East Worcester, track 1 ceased to exist as it was connected to old track 2 (the latter was now designated track 1). Additionally,

"new" track 1 was also signaled for two-way operation. In other words, all passenger trains utilized track 1 between Schenevus and Dante although a portion of that track had earlier been "old" track 2. I know what you're thinking: how did the passenger trains pass each other on this newly-designated single track 1. For them to still call at the stations they would have to utilize the same remaining track. As we all know, two trains cannot operate on the same track at the same time, so what the D&H did was to keep portions of old track 1 south of East Worcester in place to use as passing sidings. These surviving portions of old track 1

RIGHT: *Two years after Centralized Traffic Control went into operation between WN Tower and Dante, D&H Vice-president and General Manager Glenn H. Caley invited members of the Eastern Signal Engineers to inspect the new system and its signaling. On Tuesday, May 5, 1942, seventeen men met at Albany. From left to right in the front row, they were: A. H. Rice, F. W. Bender, A. H. Rudd, G. H. Caley, W. H. Elliott, G. H. Dryden, R. B. Elsworth, A. Reilly, and A. Vallee. In the back row appears H. L. Stanton, W. N. Hartman, W. J. Eck, W. J. Kocher, W. S. Storms, L. C. Walters, J. E. Saunders, and W. Wallace. This group of men proceeded to Delanson aboard a special three-car train (*BELOW RIGHT*) that was put at their disposal. While the special train waited for a clear signal at DJ interlocking, a southbound freight train off the Schenectady Branch was permitted to pass (*BELOW*). Challenger No. 1508 is abreast of DJ Cabin and in a moment will cross Delanson's Cole Road to continue on its Oneonta-bound trip. In concert with the implementation of CTC, the D&H modernized its signaling from double-masted semaphores to a double-masted, six-target position light system. These signals—which sat upon a single tower—would become an iconic feature of the Delaware & Hudson Railroad. As of this writing (2011) only two of these hallmarks of D&H engineering remain in service (Esperance and Oneonta) while other out-of-service examples have yet to be removed by CPRail. In the photo at upper right, Glenn H. Caley (who came from the New York, Ontario & Western Railway with President Joseph H. Nuelle) is fourth from left in the front row while Susquehanna Division Superintendent W. Wallace is at far right in the back row. Fedoras were all the rage in 1942, and everyone is proud to show theirs off except Mr. Elsworth who is also the only man donning an overcoat.*

ALL, LEN KILIAN COLLECTION.

were given the new designation of track 3. Similarly, the old 345-car long siding that had originally run from old Dante to East Worcester was abandoned north of the Route 7 bridge, but retained south of the bridge from "new" Dante to East Worcester. It, too, was renamed track 3.

In considering all of this, the D&H had become a two track railroad once again although the two main tracks (1 and 2) were separated. Employing a degree of Monday morning quarterbacking, the question has to be asked, "Why didn't the railroad just abandon track 4 and install the CTC equipment on the original tracks 1 and 2 and leave them in place?" Of course, now that sixty years have passed, we are no longer privy to the railroad's considerations and intentions, as illogical as they may seem to us today. All of this, however, became a mute point after passenger service on the Susquehanna Division ended on January 24, 1963, and track 2—old track 4—was taken out of service and abandoned the following year. The right-of-way for this track has mostly been obliterated by the construction of Interstate 88. That is another reason to dislike the new four-lane super-highway. If you know where to look when the leaves are off the trees, however, snippets of old track 4 can still be discerned at Schenevus and Worcester.

The reduction of trackage between Schenevus and Dante seems to have created a degree of operating difficulties, but that was the beauty of CTC operation. So long as you had proper passenger train scheduling, and a dispatcher who had nerve enough to run trains against each other knowing that one could get "in the clear" to allow an opposing train to pass, everything was fine. This Schenevus-Dante section wasn't the only portion of the railroad to be affected by the implementation of Centralized Traffic Control. At Schoharie Junction's JX Tower interlocking, as well as at Delanson's DJ Tower interlocking, tracks and signals were changed so that after all was said and done the mainline tracks were reduced from three to two and these towers could be closed. On September 6, 1940, ten days after the CTC system was placed into service, Dante Cabin, JX Tower, and DJ Tower were closed and the

operator's jobs were abolished. One man (the dispatcher sitting at his Oneonta console) was now in remote control of the line.

On the Oneonta CTC control panel, the dispatcher could now control switches and signals at the former locations of WN, JX, and DJ towers as well as at Dante (DA) Cabin. On his console, four electric levers replaced the thirty-two levers at WN Tower that had been installed on April 11, 1923. At DA the cabin's three-lever

machine was replaced by six levers in Oneonta. The reason for this increase in levers is because the operator at old Dante only used his three lever "Armstrong" machine for the switch and signal governing entrance into the 345-car siding. The switch that allowed track 4 to enter track 2 was thrown manually by the operator. JX Tower's twenty-eight lever machine (installed on March 21, 1922) was replaced by four CTC levers, and at DJ Tower, its forty-eight lever machine (installed

Susquehanna Division passenger service came to an end on January 24, 1963. On that day, a final Binghamton-to-Albany round trip was made by trains 205-208 that stopped in Worcester to pick up Helen Kramer's kindergarten class from the Worcester Central School who would ride all the way to Albany. Principal Arthur Doig stands just beyond Mrs. Kramer, and at right is mailman George Clark. I hope the kindergartners understood the significance of the day's outing. That's the kind of field trip I wish we could take today!

WORCESTER HISTORICAL SOCIETY COLLECTION.

on May 21, 1910) was replaced with five CTC levers. Considering the reduction of levers needed now at WN, JX, and DJ will give you some idea of the extensive track alterations that took place at those locations.

We are going to get back onto Route 7 again in just a moment, but there is one final piece of apparatus that came along with the CTC installation, and that was the "cabin." No, not a wooden, manned cabin such as had been at old Dante, but a new, modern steel box structure that contained the electrical connections and relays that made the system work. After all, when the dispatcher in Oneonta threw a particular lever, it was not "mechanically" connected to a switch/signal; rather, it was electrical. By his turning one lever on the console a multiple number of switches and signals could be changed at the same time.

These aluminum painted electrical cabins were placed not only at the WN, DA, JX, and DJ locations, but also at the beginning and end of all the track 3 passing sidings. All had two-letter designations: the ones between Dante (DA) and Schenevus were: WE (East Worcester), NW and WS (at north and south ends of Worcester's track 3), and WN (just north of Schenevus Lake near Schenevus).

Finally, to wrap up this explanation of the D&H's 1940 CTC installation—and to prove its effectiveness—prior to 1940 the railroad averaged thirty-three trains per day on the Oneonta-Delanson portion of the Susquehanna Division. By the time the United States entered World War II, train movements had increased 91% to an average of sixty-three trains per day, and still railroad operations remained fluid.

Looking south from the Route 7 overpass of the railroad at "new Dante," there are still two tracks in place: the mainline and the Richmondville passing siding. The latter will end just north of CPF528, which can be seen from the Brooker Hollow Road bridge. That'll be our first stop as we continue westward on Route 7.

Brooker Hollow Road gets its name from a small settlement made up of Brooker family members whose dwellings were located east of the railroad. The road named for them ran from Route 7 to Richmondville's

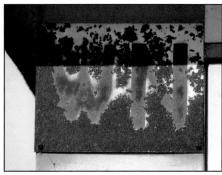

Summit Street via a path over a hill and through a hollow. The bridge, which has been a gathering place for railroad picture-takers for decades, was erected in 1924, replacing a grade crossing over the Dante-to-East Worcester siding and tracks 1 and 2. Brooker Hollow Road passed under the low-grade line that was approximately one-eighth of a mile eastward from the bridge. That's where Interstate 88 now crosses over the road.

Looking to the north from the bridge, Pine Mountain still dominates the distant horizon. Nearly in the shadow of the bridge is a cabin where the Richmondville detector is housed. Axle count, temperature, and dragging equipment: it is all monitored here as has already been seen at Esperance. All northbound trains traversing the single track mainline, and all southbound trains leaving the Richmondville passing siding territory will encounter this detector that is situated at CPF528.2. Also similar to the detector at Esperance, its "voice" still announces that it is a "D&H" detector. Until the installation of CTC here, the three tracks crossed under the through-truss span of the bridge. After CTC was implemented only two tracks remained, and when the Dante–East Worcester siding was removed the bridge spanned only one track. That is what is there today, but the old bridge is now only a pleasant memory. It was razed in late 2010, replaced by a modern deck span that railroad photographers will continue to use to take their pictures of

Norfolk Southern and CPRail trains. Sometimes I wonder just how many pictures have been taken from the Brooker Hollow Road bridge. We'll never know, but if we had a ten-dollar bill for every one of those pictures I'm certain we'd be much more financially secure.

Returning to Route 7, it will take us only a moment to arrive at East Worcester. That is where the Dante family called home. If one looks to the left you will see Dante Street. That is named for them too. After passing Maple, we come to Depot Street which will take us down to Railroad Avenue. Running parallel to the mainline, this is where the 21'X108' A&SRR standard-style combination depot was located. James E. Dante was the station agent here from at least 1880 (succeeding George McGregory) until his retirement on August 10, 1930 at the age of seventy-seven. A life-long bachelor, he is credited with serving the Delaware & Hudson for

Brooker Hollow Road Bridge Project

During the course of our drive along the old D&H railroad on Route 7, we will meet two intersecting roads that have noteworthy bridges spanning the railroad's track. Later on we will meet up with the Pony Farm Road bridge that is situated on the southern outskirts of Oneonta. Here, on the northern fringe of East Worcester just south of Richmondville Summit, we encounter Brooker Hollow Road and its bridge across the railroad that is just several stone throws distant from Route 7. The five-span bridge was completed in October 1924, being a joint effort between New York State and the Delaware & Hudson Company to eliminate the road's grade crossing of three railroad tracks. On April 29, 1924, work on the project was just beginning. The unimproved Brooker Hollow Road in the foreground crossed first the 345 car-long Dante-East Worcester siding, and then mainline tracks 1 and 2. (The short siding the Grand Trunk boxcar sits upon has been installed solely for bringing materials to the work site.) While the grade crossing appears to be adequately protected by both an old fashioned diamond sign and electrically operated Hall banjo signals there appears to be a very limited line of sight for roadsters approaching the railroad from Route 7. Immediately north of the boxcar a temporary road and crossing is in the process of being constructed since the new overpass will replace the position of the current Brooker Hollow roadway. This view looks (railroad) north with the three-year-old Low-grade Line (track 4) passing just beyond this work site. Both it and the foreground trackage will pull abreast of each other near Pine Mountain (far left) and then merge at Dante not far beyond. Today, Interstate 88 occupies the precise location of the Low-grade Line in this area.

ALL PICTURES ON PAGES 118-121, CHARLES A. BILBY COLLECTION.

One month later, on May 29, the D&H photographer has returned to photograph the temporary Brooker Hollow Road crossing where—it appears—the diamond crossing sign has been moved from the original crossing to the temporary road. The underpass in the distance allows the road to pierce the Low-grade Line in order to enter the tiny settlement of Brooker Hollow and continue on to Richmondville village. Route 7 is behind the lensman. At right, a Ford Model T dump truck is dropping off a load of stone, while at the crossingman's shanty a trail of smoke from the stovepipe lets us know that this is a chilly spring morning regardless of the open-air vehicles present and in use.

By the end of June (the 25th) work on the footings, foundations, and abutments for the new Brooker Hollow Road bridge is nearing completion and raising the grade of the roadway to the height of the bridge appears to be well under way. In this view, Richmondville Summit is to the right; East Worcester to the left. Route 7 is just beyond the white farmhouse that still survives as a comfortable residence. To record this scene, the railroad's official photographer is standing upon the right-of-way for the Low-grade Line's track 4. A steam derrick (at right) has the temporary road crossing blocked, and a steam excavator (middle left) is most likely performing ditch digging for drainage along the Delaware & Hudson's mainline trackage.

On August 22, 1924, the photographer paid a fourth visit to the East Worcester grade crossing elimination site. What he found, and recorded on film is this northward view of the completed five-span Brooker Hollow Road bridge with its approach from Route 7 at left graded to the roadway level. The grade work at the Brooker Hollow end (right) is yet to be raised to its proper level. This may be the bridge's first portrait. The two spans at each end of the bridge are all twenty-two feet in length, while the main steel truss span of 127 feet easily spans the three D&H tracks and leaves room for additional trackage should the need arise, which never occurred. You may wish to compare this scene with similar views on the following pages. For eighty-five years this Brooker Hollow Road bridge not only provided safe passage for vehicles from Route 7 going to both Brooker Hollow and Richmondville but allowed railroad enthusiasts and railroad environmentalists to watch, photograph, and interpret the railroad's operation through this wonderfully scenic geologically-formed region. By the way, we are members of the latter group, and as railroad environmentalists we more fully appreciate and understand the railroad's interaction with its surroundings. It is our seeking out this association of the railroad with its neighboring hills, valleys, waterways, highways, villages, and noteworthy personages that sets us apart from ordinary "railfans" who only see the railroad as a one dimensional entity. Nine years later, the Pony Farm Road bridge would be built to provide similar service to motorists and railroad environmentalists. Both of these bridges, that many persons felt had become lifelong friends, were replaced by modern spans during 2010-11. Time marches on for steel and concrete just as it does for human life.

ABOVE LEFT: *The Brooker Hollow Road bridge was built in 1924 to elim-inate a three-track grade crossing: the Dante-to-East Worcester siding, and main tracks 1 and 2. By 2010, it had become too old and weary to soldier on. The picture above may be its last portrait. Railroad photog-raphers took many pictures from the bridge, but few of it. This view looks north with Route 7 just barely visible to the right center of the single through-truss span.* ABOVE RIGHT: *The previous summer the bridge was photographed from track level looking (railroad) north.* RIGHT: *CPRail train 250 with an AC4400CW on point (No. 9564) heads south in a view taken from the bridge. It is just passing the CPF528.2 detector, and at far right is an orange truck that is rolling by on Inter-state 88, which is where the low-grade line had been located until 1964. The new bridge was in the process of being built during the winter of 2010-11.*

The old Brooker Hollow Road bridge was a wonderful platform from which to enjoy trains. Whether watching or photographing, heavy freight consists with many different types of modern diesel locomotive power could be witnessed. ABOVE LEFT: CPRail train 251 approaches the bridge's steelwork from the south while (BELOW LEFT) train 939 is leaving Richmondville Hill's summit and passing siding and now nears the bridge from the north. The pure azure-blue skies that day attest to the deep chill of that winter afternoon. One can only wonder at what the same scene must have looked like with a D&H Challenger towing a freight over the summit of Richmondville Hill with the exhaust on full display. RIGHT: The old Brooker Hollow Road bridge forms a backdrop for northbound CPRail train 253 on July 10, 2009. The detector has just started its song: "D&H detector, mileage 528.2, checking northward train." The cinder path along the railroad here is where the old siding had been located and it is now used as an access road for maintenance purposes. CPRail's No. 8846 and a sister unit have things well in hand on this fine summer day.

Station Agent James E. Dante is buried in the family's East Worcester Cemetery plot. A sign along Main Street (Route 7) locates the street where he lived and helps to perpetuate the family name.

The folks at the Worcester Historical Society believe this may be Agent James E. Dante (left, in picture at left) standing under the signboard for his station conversing with a fellow railroader. While the D&H had its signature signals, forerunner A&S had its own signature fascia board, as noted by the ornate millwork.

of the old Sheffield Farms milk station that Mother Nature is slowly claiming as her own. During the milk station's more prosperous years, a siding from track 1 ran southward to service the facility where carloads of milk cans full of white gold started their trip to New York City. Farmers relied on the milk station and railroad services then; trucks take it away today. At least the milk starts its journey on Route 7, the community's Main Street.

The Main Street of East Worcester has not been treated kindly with the passage of time. Empty storefronts and dwellings in need of repair line the asphalt. The old closed school is home to a heating and plumbing contractor who appears to never throw anything away. The two-room Post Office is situated on Main Street. Its front window facing Route 7 tells everyone what's inside. Gold leaf lettering on the main window proves that there is still some degree of luxury in East Worcester. The postmaster will tell you, if you engage her in conversation, that she enjoys hearing the coal trains go by at night. She told me that. I had to ask, "How do you know they are coal trains?" She replied, "Because the engines are working so much harder to get up (Worcester) grade." Her husband, she admitted, used to work for the railroad. If you ever need postage stamps, and the East Worcester Post Office is a convenient place for you to get to, please buy them there. It sure was nice to see that Dante Street sign.

From East Worcester to Worcester it is nearly five miles by rail, and probably the same distance by road since the two transportation systems parallel each other. Schenevus Creek is to the south but not as far as track 4. Midway between the Worcesters there had been a water tank for use by thirsty track 4 locomotives. That tank got its water from Hudson Lake, which

was fed by Schenevus Creek. Hudson Lake, by the way, was so named because of the nearby property of farmer John A. Hudson. He owned two hundred acres of farm land. His ancestry goes back much more than two hundred years. Mr. Hudson, it seems, was proud to tell anyone who listened that he was a descendent of a more famous Hudson: Henry. You know, the fella that the river and bay are named after. I suppose it was only natural, then, that John A. desired to have a body of water named after himself just like his ancestor. It is a good thing Schenevus Creek already had a name assigned to it!

Upon arrival at Worcester we are greeted by a modern sign that not only tells us where we are, but that the village once had a railroad depot. Within an oval inset the Worcester station is depicted. This is the kind of place we like to visit, one that remembers its past—especially its railroads. This sign, and the one at Richmondville, will be the only village signs we will see on our entire 143 mile tour that display a railroad icon. Thank you Richmondville and Worcester. At least Delanson had a locomotive weathervane on its cupola-topped gazebo.

Driving down Worcester's Main Street (Route 7) we can immediately tell that this village has retained a degree of prosperity. Noticeable are nicely painted residences and well maintained churches, the large brick school still teaches kids the three Rs—four if

sixty-years; most of which were spent at East Worcester. His brothers also worked for the railroad. Augustus was a telegraph operator at East Worcester, while William served as the station agent at Howes Cave and as a telegrapher at Afton.

Everything that Agent James Dante was familiar with at the East Worcester station grounds—which in the early days had included a two-stall engine house and a turntable—is long gone. Except for the remains

ABOVE: *In this bird's-eye-view of East Worcester, the railroad's lengthy combination station stands beyond the hop field in the foreground while the residential portion of the village lies off to the railroad's west side. Depot Street crosses the tracks. It is reported that the first Albany & Susquehanna passenger train—made up of cars painted bright yellow—arrived here from Albany on July 17, 1865. At right, the water tank pokes its head above the small hill from which train 938 (RIGHT) was photographed many years later. Just behind the water tank is the bluestone yard established by James and William Dante. Part of the Sheffield Farms milk station is visible at the extreme left. The flat-roofed, two-story building above and to the left of the water tank is the Central Hotel located at Main and Maple streets. ABOVE, WORCESTER HISTORICAL SOCIETY COLLECTION.*

LEFT: *Track 4 ran along the base of South Hill at East Worcester where a section or maintenance shed was located. A pump car, trailer and velocipede repose at the left. The old humpback bridge in the background carried South Hill Road over the track. This and the next photograph on this page were made by Lambert D. Cook on July 11, 1938, which explains why a semaphore signal rather than a color target is still in use.*

RIGHT: *The water tank shown here is the same one that appeared in the previous page's "bird's-eye-view." Placed on a stone base, this tank was situated on the east side of track 2, just north of the depot that was found on the same side of the track as the distant semaphore. At left is the team track that ran behind the station, serving the local creamery as well as local merchants. Note the flanger sign in the left foreground. This occupies the approximate site of the bluestone yard operated by Delaware & Hudson East Worcester Station Agent James E. Dante and his brother, William.*

LEFT: When Interstate 88 was built where track 4 had been, it cut off South Hill Road so that it dead-ended at this farm. I-88 is immediately behind the photographer. Looking down old South Hill Road, we see train 938 about to cross the road in its non-stop passage through East Worcester. Man's best friend, the border collie at lower left, has undoubtedly watched this event replayed countless times, becoming a rail afficionado in the process.

CENTRAL HOTEL

EAST WORCESTER N.Y.

U.S. POST OFFICE
EAST WORCESTER
12064

ABOVE LEFT: Local photographer Frank Edson Bolles (1876-1913) recorded this view of the Central Hotel—erected after the "Big Fire of March 1893" wiped out all the buildings on Main Street between Depot and Maple (seen at left). Its prime location at the southwest corner of Main (Route 7) and Maple streets allowed it to cater to railroad travelers as well as to early motorists. Riley H. Pitcher, a former school teacher in town, served as the hotel's first proprietor. A long block east, Maple Street brings us to trackside where the thoroughfare becomes Railroad Avenue and leads west to the depot (ABOVE RIGHT). Built in 1867, this station was of standard A&S design and measured 21'X108' in size. Both the old Central Hotel and the depot are gone now, but the post office (LEFT) still tells residents and passersby exactly what it is by using gold leaf lettering on the window facing Route 7. Its neighbor—currently home to a consignment shop—was once the grocery and drug store owned and operated by Millard F. Boorn and his pharmacist son, Leroy (who lived on the top floor with his wife, Ella). The brick building was put up after Boorn's wooden store burned in 1914. Across Maple Street to the right is where the Central Hotel stood. In a nutshell, this is East Worcester's business district today. ABOVE LEFT, WORCESTER HISTORICAL SOCIETY. ABOVE RIGHT, EDWARD P. BAUMGARDNER COLLECTION.

you count the railroad that can be seen from its rear windows. It is the home of Worcester Central School District, whose buses travel up and down Route 7 every morning and afternoon to bring students to school and then take them back home. There is an old opera house, the Wieting, that was built in 1910 and given to the community by Helen Wieting. She named it after her late husband's family. There hasn't been any work performed there recently by Puccini, Rossini, Verdi, or Gilbert & Sullivan for that matter, but the latest Hollywood movies are shown every weekend in one part of the building. The Worcester Free Library occupies another portion of the structure. A local Daughters of the American Revolution chapter has a room within the Wieting, too.

Just up the street is the Worcester-Whitehouse Inn, a three-story hotel and restaurant. It started life in the late Nineteenth Century as the Central Hotel and became the Worcester Inn during the 1940s, always catering to travelers on Route 7 and the D&H alike. If you would like to have a good meal—and I'm getting hungrier by the minute—then the dining room of the Worcester-Whitehouse Inn is for you. They have a less formal snack room with counter service as well. (What's that? You're getting hungry, too? Hold on, we'll get lunch in Schenevus.) Upstairs, on floors two and three, are the guest rooms; I've stayed in them twice. They are modern, comfortable, and during the night you can hear a train or two go by, its horn blaring for the South Hill Road crossing. Late at night, Worcester is quiet; little traffic

utilizes Route 7 after midnight and you can't hear cars and trucks going by on Interstate 88 either. The sound of a train passing (possibly a coal train?) is reassuring that some connection to the past still touches Worcester after dark. My two stays were pleasant and restful; I

BELOW: *Entering Worcester, one is greeted by this colorful sign with a railroad vignette depicting the village's classic depot which no longer exists.* ABOVE RIGHT: *The Worcester Central School District is the next prominent building to greet us.* BELOW RIGHT: *The Wieting Opera House was built in 1910 as a gift to the community by Helen Wieting.*

ABOVE LEFT: *The finest example of Worcester's desire to maintain an attractive face and display its continued prosperity is the Worcester-Whitehouse Inn. It started life in the Nineteenth Century as the Central Hotel, became the Worcester Inn in the Twentieth, and today you will find no better place along Route 7 to dine, rest, and socialize. It is not the only establishment, however, to remain vibrant along Worcester's stretch of Route 7. Just take an eastward look along the village Main Street* (ABOVE RIGHT). *The mansard-roofed building visible in both views is the former home of the Griggs & Bell grocery store. For a comparison with its historic past, please turn the page.*

didn't learn of the third floor "ghost" until later. But, I'll be staying there again sometime soon, to see the Wieting lit up at dusk, to sit on the porch of the hotel after dinner and converse with Worcester's friendly residents, and to hear the call of railroading at night when everything else is quiet. Railroad sounds, regardless of the time of day, transcend era.

There is an historical society in Worcester. It is the perfect place to find out about what used to go on in town and who the noteworthy people were. One can learn that Worcester is named after Worcester, Massachusetts where early settlers came from in 1788. An early prominent citizen, Solomon Garfield owned a farm at the east end of town. His son, Thomas, an historical sign along Route 7 informs us, was the father of United States President James A. Garfield. Seth Flint, a haberdasher in town was a Civil War veteran. He ran away to Albany to "join up" when he was 15 years old in 1862. Three years later, now a man—and a bugler for Ulysses S. Grant's cavalry—he sounded "Taps" at Appomattox to signal the end of the rebellion on April 9, 1865.

Another noteworthy Town of Worcester resident was Lewis Edson Waterman (1837-1901). He came from the nearby hamlet of Decatur; that's where Lester Howe came from, too. But, Lewis' avocation wasn't underground, it was on paper. He developed the "practical fountain pen" that used capillary action to bring ink to the pen tip. The Lewis E. Waterman Company was formed, and for many years it was a successful enterprise—so long as people used fountain pens. I used one when I was in elementary school during the Fabulous '50s, but by the time the Soaring '60s came around ball points were the rage. By the way, the Bic Company now owns the Waterman rights.

All of these fellows, Garfield—but maybe not President Garfield—Flint, and Waterman all would have ridden the railroad during the years of operation by the Albany & Susquehanna Railroad or Delaware & Hudson Canal Company's Northern Railroad Division. They probably bought their tickets from Agent Adelbert L. Emmons. He was employed at Worcester's station as a telegraph operator and later as station agent from 1876 through 1916. I was told by Larry DeLong at the historical society that Emmons hadn't been Worcester's first station agent. He ought to know since his great-grandfather, Dewitt DeLong, was Worcester's first telegraph operator. As early as 1870, DeLong was engaged at this job. For a time, he lived at Elijah F. Knapp's hotel which over the years went through a series of name changes: Knapp's Hotel, Worcester House, Central Hotel, and finally, The Worcester Inn.

In similar views to those displayed on the previous page, Worcester's Main Street (LEFT) is shown when Route 7 was an unimproved thoroughfare, and its esteemed three-story inn, the Central Hotel (BELOW RIGHT), reposes in a dignified fashion along a then snow covered Main Street. (This is the same building shown today in the photograph at the upper left of Page 129 now known as the Worcester Inn.) At the depot, the two-story American Hotel (BELOW LEFT) displayed signs of Victorian elegance with its decorative bargeboards, but its accommodations could in no way compare to those at the Central Hotel. ABOVE AND LOWER LEFT, WORCESTER HISTORICAL SOCIETY COLLECTION. BELOW RIGHT, DEPOT SQUARE PUBLISHING COLLECTION.

ROADS, RIVERS, AND RAILS

DeLong worked for the first Station Agent, Hamilton Waterman (1809-1887), another native of Decatur, and who, it turns out, was Lewis E. Waterman's uncle. As for Agent Emmons, his forty-year hitch at one depot was comparable to that of East Worcester's James

Dante. But, whereas Dante's depot was of a standard A&S design, Emmons' place of employment definitely was not.

Worcester's depot was unique to the railroad. It started life as a 21'X22' board-and-batten combination

According to his March 22, 1929 obituary in **The Otsego Farmer,** *Adelbert L. "Del" Emmons was born in Otego, NY in 1853 and received his primary education at Gilbertville Academy. After graduating from Oberlin Telegraph College at Oberlin, OH, he joined the D&H sometime around 1870, serving as a telegraph operator at several stations along the line. In 1876, Emmons became the telegrapher at Worcester—a position he would hold for six or seven years before being appointed the station agent there. He retired from the railroad in 1916 after forty years of continuous service at Worcester. Living on Depot Street, Emmons then ran a retail coal dealership. While working as the agent, Emmons reportedly owned a "Nyberg" automobile. These vehicles were produced in Anderson, IN between 1910 and 1914. Del Emmons died on March 19, 1929 after a ten year battle with what was described as "shaking palsy"—called Parkinson's Disease today.*

Worcester's grand Gothic Revival-inspired station was of a design that was unique to the railroad. Elements such as the steeply-pitched roof, gable dormers, ornamental trusses and pendants, finials, and curved bay window sashes could not be found on any other A&S-built stationhouse. BOTH, WORCESTER HISTORICAL SOCIETY COLLECTION.

On an everyday basis, during the early decades of the Twentieth Century, travelers arrived and departed from Worcester's station using the timely and efficient services offered by D&H train scheduling. With a southbound train's caboose having just passed the depot, a northward passenger train brakes for its stop to pick up mail and a few passengers that obviously came from "downtown" in the parked omnibus. As D&H ironhorse No. 555, a double-cab Tenwheeler of Class D-3b, rolls to a stop, it seems to be drawing the attention of only one portly fellow; all the remaining pairs of human and animal eyes are more interested in what the photographer is doing. And, what he did is record on film a glorious scene that could be considered the finest photograph of steam-era railroading along the Susquehanna Division. Besides Del Emmons who served as agent for forty years, some of the other men who served here were: John A. Hudson, Express Agent; John E. Champion, Freight Agent; and Orlando Merrill and Martin Stapleton, crossing flagmen.

ABOVE RIGHT: *During the summer of 1909, a large group of Worcester citizens gather at their station to await a train that will take them to Cobleskill so that they can watch their boys play baseball against the local team. Their train may be the one pictured (*ABOVE LEFT*) that also shows the rear of the station facing the American Hotel, out of frame to the right. At the far end of the eighty-two-foot-long freight house, a roof covers scales for weighing coal deliveries. A 40,000-gallon water tank lies just beyond.* LEFT: *Three years later, Omer M. Sloat— manager and owner of the Central Hotel—drove his new Buick touring car down to the depot where it is being admired by (left to right) Fred Cannistra, Everet Galer, Ben Horst, Herman Judd, Anthony Cannistra, Jennie Campbell, and Herman's wife, Inez. Owning a car such as this implies that improvements were being made to Route 7 so that a Sunday drive could be more enjoyable. Sloat, a former New York City policeman, moved to Worcester around 1905. Among the industries in town were a milk station, a lumber yard, cheese factory, and a glove factory.* ALL, WORCESTER HISTORICAL SOCIETY.

Despite Mr. Sloat's optimism in his Buick's ability to negotiate an unimproved Route 7, it was not until the mid-1930s before paving—and highway realignment to straighten curves and lessen grades—were undertaken by the state. Before that time, a dirt roadway prevailed (ABOVE) so that wherever motorists ventured a cloud of dust followed them. UPPER RIGHT: By the end of the Roarin' Twenties, road gangs undertook what must have seemed like a monumental task then of relocating, grading, adding drainage, and eventually paving Route 7 so that it could be an enjoyable roadway to drive upon. When the roadwork was done, the Schohanna Trail mostly paralleled the D&H double-track mainline (LOWER RIGHT) that must not have been looked upon with much favor by the railroad's officials. A good idea of the relationship between tracks 1, 2, and 4 can be had in this view that shows the railroad's water tank at Nugent at the extreme right hand side of the picture.

ALL, WORCESTER HISTORICAL SOCIETY COLLECTION.

ROADS, RIVERS, AND RAILS

station—the smallest on the line. Its real uniqueness was that the office and waiting room were covered by a steeply-pitched gable roof that contained an equally-sloped gable dormer on either side. Just those elements alone would have qualified the depot as especially eye-catching. But there were two other architectural components that classed this building as singular. It boasted decorative trusses within the peaks of its main roofline (harmoniously repeated in its dormers) as well as finials at each end of the roof crest. How it came to pass that these Gothic Revival design elements were incorporated into only this one station will have to remain a mystery. Too many years have passed since it was built when the railroad began service to Worcester on July 17, 1865. Del Emmons could tell us if he were still around—and maybe Harvey Baker could, too.

At some early point a 21'X82' freight room was wedded to Worcester's depot, bringing its total length to 103 feet, an average length for standard A&S combination stations. And, just as we've seen at previous station grounds, the community's industry clustered around the all-important railroad, which was king of transportation back in 1916. On the west side of the tracks, the side where the depot was situated, was a Standard Oil Company of New York facility (SOCONY), a milk station that became a Borden's creamery in 1907, a stock yard, and the two-story American Hotel that was nothing like the Worcester Inn. On the other side of the double-track mainline, were the Palmer Feed Mill, Goodell Potato Storehouse, D. W. Shultz store, and an ever present coal shed. But, we have to remember, that at one time virtually all of the community necessities arrived by rail and ended up in businesses located along Route 7 that was only one block to the north. Pencils, medicines, hats, dresses, linens, food stuffs, and more all came to Worcester—and every other village we're

UPPER: *An unidentified camelback has brought the milk train to the milk station in Worcester. Given the harshness of an upstate New York winter, it was not unusual during the colder months for farmers to deliver their milk via sleigh out of necessity. One such sleigh driver nears the end of his journey as he approaches the receiving station under the canopy.* LOWER: *The facility would later be improved upon and expanded, becoming a property of Borden's. The sharp peak of the station roof is barely visible to the right in the upper view.*
BOTH, WORCESTER HISTORICAL SOCIETY COLLECTION.

visiting—in a railroad boxcar. Today, nothing arrives by train. Whether day or night the trains just cruise right on by. That may be good for Route 7, because communities still need necessities. Although trucks now deliver the goods, their tires will still have to tread on the pavement of the Schohanna Trail as Route 7 is unofficially referred to. The "Scho" is for Schoharie Creek; "hanna" is for the Susquehanna River. But what about Schenevus Creek? I suppose folks in this neck o' the woods figure the Legend of Chief Schenevus is enough for the creek.

The old station grounds at Worcester are barely recognizable today. Only the old Borden's building remains. It became a Grange League Federation warehouse when milk went to trucks. Milk trucks still come and go, however, since the Worcester Creameries-Elmhurst Dairy is located across the single track from where the depot had been. Yes, the unique depot is a "has been." The railroad started the process of its removal with a derailment that knocked off a corner wall of the waiting room. By then, of course, the finials, bargeboard, and agent were already gone. The rest of the building came down in 1999, according to the folks at the historical society. Despite the depot's loss and CPRail's non-stop passage of trains through Worcester, the village is well preserved. Its downtown is not as large as that at Cobleskill, but it is just as vibrant. Thank the friendly village residents for that.

We will be having lunch in just a few moments after driving a short stretch on Route 7; we just have to make a quick stop at Whitehouse Crossing first. We will pass Tuscan Road—an ancestral part of Route 7—that fell from the good graces of Route 7 signage when the roadway's twists and turns were being straightened during the 1930s. Just beyond Tuscan Road's re-entering Route 7 is

Local photographer Frank E. Bolles produced these two "real photo" postcard scenes of Worcester prior to 1912. BELOW: The bird's-eye-view looks almost due north at the railroad and the rear walls of the buildings facing Route 7. One can easily see (from left to right) the D&H water tank sitting on a circular stone base; the combination station; the American Hotel; the creamery; Palmer & Smith's flour, feed, and hay business; and Julius T. Hadsell's lumber mill and yard. The village also contained cider and grist mills, and a wagon shop. RIGHT: Located on the southwest corner of Main Street and South Hill Road, the Worcester House—managed in 1908 by Charles E. Bell—included the community's first opera house. The large sign propped up against the front wall announces the presence of Edwin J. Hadley and his exhibition of "first class moving pictures." Before small towns had movie theaters, Hadley was one of several exhibitors who travelled throughout rural areas offering programs that included early motion pictures, stereopticon viewings set to music, magicians, orators, and comedians. His shows were extremely popular, but with the building of movie theaters, Edwin J. Hadley was essentially out of business by 1920.

BOTH, DEPOT SQUARE PUBLISHING COLLECTION.

The only milk that is shipped from Worcester today is by the above company whose facility is across the track from what remains of the old Borden's Creamery. In the two views at right, train 251 led by AC4400CW No. 8646 passes the old creamery building while working up Worcester Hill (ABOVE RIGHT). Its counterpart, train 250—with oodles of extra horsepower in the form of four ES44ACs—rolls downgrade over Worcester's South Hill Road grade crossing (East Worcester also has a similarly-named grade crossing) and also passes the ex-creamery. Today, the building is used for storage; it is no longer served by the railroad. CPRail likes it that way; they can cruise through town uninterrupted. When staying at the Worcester-Whitehouse Inn, the trains you hear blowing their horns at night are doing so for this crossing of South Hill Road.

Whitehouse Crossing where a left turn will take us down to the tracks, just a few feet away. Route 7 and the railroad run neck-and-neck here. Maybe the white house just on the other side of the track is what inspired the proprietors of the Worcester Inn to make it the Worcester-Whitehouse Inn, but that dwelling obviously gave Whitehouse Crossing its name. The lane only goes to the house and a farm beyond, but still, it must cross the track to do so. The railroad curves across the road in such a sharp arc (for railroads anyway) that a speed restriction is imposed here. No one wants to have some of the double stack containers flying away due to centrifugal force. Well, the curve isn't that sharp; just sharp enough so that engineers have to bleed a few pounds of air from old man Westinghouse's airbrake system to round the bend safely.

That's all there is to Whitehouse Crossing so, with our appetite whet for dining at the Chief Schenevus Restaurant & Bakery, we get back on Route 7; the latter also has its sights set on Schenevus. We'll pass Muehl Road not far from Whitehouse Crossing; it was another piece of the earlier Route 7 path whose curve was too tight to be a part of modern highway. As we arrive at Schenevus, a sign bearing the likeness of Chief Schenevus greets us. I don't have to tell you how Schenevus got its name, do I? Then we'll pass the art deco styled Andrew S. Draper School built in 1941, it being named for New York State's first superintendent of education. He called Schenevus home, too. Unlike children being educated at Richmondville and Worcester, at Draper they cannot see or hear the railroad. The chief reason for this, pardon the pun, is that Schenevus

RIGHT: *The "Kiraly" Block, home of the Chief Schenevus Restaurant & Bakery in Schenevus.*
ABOVE: *Owner, chef, and baker Rich Kiraly poses with Jean Marie Marullo and an assortment of their tasty home-made baked goods. The scones are at upper left on the countertop.*
BELOW: *The Andrew S. Draper School along Route 7 in Schenevus.*

ing them in the face. (The image on the wall was used as the first picture in this chapter.) A previous owner had covered up the Chief for some reason. The Kiraly's embraced the portrait of the (then) elderly and nearly blind Chief, and knew they had found a proper name for their new establishment. The food served here may not be on a par with the fancy chops, roasts, seafood, and steaks served at the Worcester-Whitehouse Inn, but here breakfast, lunch, and dinners are bona fide country-quality fare that will satisfy the hunger pangs of any mortal being and keep them licking their lips for hours afterward. That, however, is not what endeared me to the Chief Schenevus Restaurant & Bakery. It was the pastries, breads, and the tea biscuits that tickled my taste buds. Rich doesn't call them "tea biscuits," he calls them scones. Well, I'm from Long Island, as you know, and on the Island we call them tea biscuits. I don't care what Rich calls them, as long as he keeps making them. And that he does in the wee hours of the morning long before anyone stumbles in still half asleep to get a cup of Joe. I don't know what you would like to have for lunch, and Rich will be happy to make it for you, but as for me, I'll have coffee and a raisin scone. That'll hold me till we get to Oneonta and have dinner at the Neptune Diner.

I enjoy everything about the Chief Schenevus Restaurant & Bakery; its meals, its pastries, talking to Rich, and talking to all the mostly local folks who are proud

ABOVE: *The surviving Schenevus depot looks on as Norfolk Southern train 939 passes by on the now single track mainline with an ES40DC on point. There had been three mainline tracks and two sidings here at one time, with the low-grade line track 4 located just to the right of the telephone pole line. Modern roofing and siding disguise the as-built exterior of one of the A&SRR's largest depots.*

Creek has flowed between the railroad and roadway. Thus the railroad depot has the unenviable distinction of being situated further away from its community than any other discussed in this chapter, but not nearly as distant as Esperance's station. Still, it's a great depot, and we'll be there after lunch, but I first want to introduce you to Rich Kiraly. He is the owner, baker, and "chief cook and bottle washer" of the Chief Schenevus Restaurant & Bakery.

When the Kiraly family came to town in 1989, they acquired a "block" containing several buildings, picking one out to house the restaurant. They then began the process of converting the building, which had more than one previous purpose, for use as a dining room, lunch counter, and kitchen. During the prosecution of that work, they removed a "false" wall and found a painting of Chief Schenevus staring

In years past, the village of Schenevus benefitted from a "self-sustaining" business district along Route 7. The community's residents and outlying farmers need not go elsewhere for food, clothing, banking, or gasoline for the auto. BELOW LEFT: The "Kiraly" Block is shown along the north side of Route 7; the Chief Schenevus Restaurant & Bakery occupies the last tall building. RIGHT: The Kiraly edifice is also shown in the scene at right, now looking west along Route 7. It is marked by the Wick's sign in the distance. The peaked-roof building is the centerpiece of the Gurney Block. The Schenevus National Bank is between the Texaco gas pumps and the white two-story building. BOTH, SCOTT ROLAND COLLECTION. LOWER RIGHT: In a similar contemporary view to the one at right, a now-paved Route 7 passes the Wilber National Bank that replaced the Schenevus National Bank. Otherwise, the buildings remain pretty much as they were earlier and still provide some prosperity to the village. Walmarts inhabit Cobleskill and Oneonta, both some distance from still-rural Schenevus. Samuel Gurney's dry goods store that had been in the peaked-roof building currently is home to the village Post Office.

CLOCKWISE FROM LOWER LEFT: *When we arrived at Schenevus, this sign greeted us; the Chief watching every car that passed on Route 7. Until April 28, 1910, the Susquehanna House sat astride Schenevus' Main Street in the middle of the village. On that day, it burned to the ground, some say at the hands of an irate wife whose husband was spending too much time inside at the bar. At the time of the portrait of this 19th Century roadhouse, Mr. L. A. Pratt was the proprietor. According to the calling card (INSET) and the notation across the bottom of the scene (BELOW) the Hotel Potter was operated by J. Stanley Potter. This hotel, which also dates from the Nineteenth Century, began life as the Hotel Siver, then the Potter, and when the Westcott family acquired the building in 1945, Everett and Beatrice named it the Schenevus Hotel. Its life ended on March 28, 1954 when fire consumed the structure and it was destroyed.*

HOTELS AND TRADE CARD, SCOTT ROLAND COLLECTION.

AHA Member — Stop at Recognized Hotels — SERVICE FIRST

HOTEL POTTER
J. STANLEY POTTER, Prop.

American - European Plan   All Conveniences
Breakfast 6 - 9   Dinner 11 - 8   Chicken Dinner Sundays

ON SCHOHANNA TRAIL, ROUTE 7

PHONE 75   SCHENEVUS, N. Y.

Officially Inspected and Approved by Publicity Bureau

WELCOME TO SCHENEVUS

HOTEL POTTER, SCHENEVUS, N.Y.
J. STANLEY POTTER, PROP.

When the Albany & Susquehanna Railroad put the Schenevus depot construction out to contract, it called for the erection of a combination station whose footprint would be 30'X137', making it one of the two largest such buildings on the railroad. The other was at Otego. UPPER LEFT: On a winter morning years ago, a northbound passenger train is about to make its call at Schenevus where it appears it will board quite a number of men; some appear to be traveling salesmen. UPPER RIGHT: On a nicer day, ladies far outnumber gents walking between the depot and train. The track at right is a siding that served the two-story flour, feed, and grain dealer as well as the coal dealer beyond. ABOVE RIGHT: In a reversal of fortune, the Borden Creamery at Schenevus later became a property of Myron R. Kilmer's Schenevus Dairy. The wonderful cupola-topped building sat on the opposite side of the track from the depot and just a little further to the north.

UPPER LEFT, A. BRUCE TRACY COLLECTION. UPPER RIGHT AND BELOW, SCOTT ROLAND COLLECTION.

ABOVE: *With his back to the railroad, Frank E. Bolles photographed the Depot Street bridge that was built in 1889 to cross Schenevus Creek. Its little falls of water, and that of the upstream pond, will eventually empty into the Susquehanna River. The bridge has since been replaced by a modern span whose design is a throwback to the old Whipple bridges of yesteryear. SCOTT ROLAND COLLECTION. BOTTOM: On a wonderful summer morning in 2010, NS train 938 passes Schenevus depot where, unfortunately, weeds seem to have the upper hand. The right-of-way for the old low-grade line lies unseen at left.*

to call Schenevus home. But, lets finish our lunch so we can go over to the railroad and see the surviving station. So long, Rich, we'll see you again soon, I'm sure.

To get to the depot, turn onto Arch Street from Route 7, take Arch to Race Street (where a raceway from Schenevus Creek to an early mill was located nearby), then cross Schenevus Creek on a modern steel bridge that appears to be a throwback to the Whipple-designed bridges of yesteryear. Race takes us to Depot Street. Look to the right; there is the depot. It doesn't look anything like it did when it served the railroad, but it is nonetheless one of the two largest surviving examples of A&S station architecture; the other is at Otego. We'll see the latter later on.

The Schenevus depot was built in 1865 when the railroad opened on August 7 of that year. It is a survivor of many years of post-passenger train activity as well as railroad and private ownership. It had been a combination station, 30'X137' in size, built to the Albany & Susquehanna's standard design but lacking even the signature fascia boards along its roofline. Schenevus' station was a real monster in size. A&S depots didn't get any bigger than this one. The roof eaves overhung the building's size by eight feet all the way around. Its footprint may have been 30'X137', but the area under the roof was 46'X153.'

Schenevus agents Horace Chester (1870), Erwin R. Waelde (1880-1890), and John H. Wild (1900-1930) had an eighty-nine-foot-long freight room to rattle around in, but only a ten-foot-wide office where a bay window faced the tracks. The passenger waiting room was more spacious. It was twenty-six feet long with indoor plumbing for the ladies. (Men were only provided the more traditional outdoor "water closet.") All the rooms were, quite naturally, thirty feet wide.

Erwin Robert Waelde, by the way, lead a very active railroad career. Born in North Bay, NY

in 1852, he first worked as a telegraph operator in his hometown for the New York, Ontario & Western Railway. By 1880, he had joined the Delaware & Hudson and was running the depot in Schenevus. In the 1890s, he found employment with the West Shore Railroad (which had been leased by the New York Central in 1885) as the station and express agent at Milton and later at Marlborough, NY. He rounded out his career with that company as the express agent at Kingston (1910) and then at Saugerties (1920). Tragically, a leak from a gas stove caused the deaths of Waelde and his wife, Frances, at their Poughkeepsie home on April 29, 1940. Both are buried in Schenevus.

Looking at the Schenevus station today, which is used as an office/warehouse by an electrical contractor, it is somewhat difficult to appreciate the enormity, importance, and attractiveness of this one-time board-and-batten structure. But, during the days when tracks 1, 2, and 4 were all active, and augmented by a "house" track that ran by the depot's face, Schenevus depot was a busy and wonderful place. Besides the Borden's Creamery that was across the tracks and just to the north of the depot, there was a smattering of buildings scattered about the station grounds and Depot Street that relied on the railroad's and agent's services. Wooden buildings that housed coal, flour, feed, and grain, a storehouse, and a cattle pen all provided the D&H with enough revenue so that it could be happy that Schenevus was on its map.

Much like the depot, all of these ancillary structures still survive, albeit in various states of disrepair, giving the area an appearance similar to that of a western state's ghost town. Yet, there are those who still recall all of the activity that used to take place here. Jack Nagle, a retired superintendent of Schenevus Central Schools, told me that on Saturday mornings when he was a kid, he used to hang out around

Please don't hold it against me when I tell you that there is one good thing that happened when I-88 was built. At the location of its entrance and exit ramps, many existing roads—and some new ones—were built to go over the railroad, which was all the better for taking photographs. This may make up for the Findago Road bridge having been removed just south of Schenevus. RIGHT: Train 939 has just crossed over Schenevus Creek and is about to cross Depot Street at grade, the depot being only a short distance away. Track 4—the low-grade line—once passed through the notch in the pine trees at right. BELOW: The bleakness of a New York winter lies heavily on the land. The muted colors, washed with winter's stain, are punctuated by northbound CPRail train 253 as it passes through the old station grounds at Schenevus, with the station itself in the distance; the old Borden's creamery building is at left. Depot Street is just slightly more improved than the rutted lane at left that had been the location of the former low-grade's track 4.

the depot. Jack enjoyed watching a steam locomotive go about its duties providing switching service for the myriad consignees the railroad had here at Schenevus. "There was always something going on," he recalled, "boxcars and hopper cars getting moved about, horses and livestock coming and going, and it was always thrilling to watch the switcher get passed by another freight train. I wish everyday could have been a Saturday." Most school age boys would feel the same way.

I love everything about Schenevus: its small, but vibrant "downtown" along Route 7; its restaurant; its depot; and its legend. I hope you do too. Now we have to move along to another spot nearby that is one of my favorites. I want to show it to you, and tell you why it is a special spot along the railroad for me. To get there, we won't go back to Route 7; we could if we wanted. Rather, we'll take Depot Street to its end and then take Lake Road to Tannery Road where we'll turn right to get back to the railroad. Not far along Lake Road we pull abreast of Interstate 88, but it is higher than our road. Then we'll pass a Little League baseball field that is simple in design and cozy for players and spectators alike. In fields such as this is where baseball should be played. No artificial turf, or towering skyscrapers nearby; just a railroad that runs behind the

backstop. That's okay, though. Aren't baseball and train watching two of the great American pastimes?

Let's park the car near the Tannery Road grade crossing of the railroad, shut off the engine, and just listen. Hear anything? No? That's country quiet. And it is because of that quietude that we can hear a northbound train approaching long before it appears way down that stretch of tangent track. That signal off to the south will tell us when to begin listening. It is normally off (dark) unless a train is approaching. When it turns red, we'll know that a northbound train has passed the signal at Maryland two and a half miles away. Southbound trains are harder to hear approaching because they are going downgrade, this still being a part of Worcester Hill. But, again, that signal will help us. If it turns green, then we'll know a southbound train is coming.

Signals not only help the locomotive engineer, they also help visitors like us. Hey! It just turned red! Just listen. Wait a minute, then....you hear that? Off in the unseen distance a low monotone droning can be heard. That sound can only be made by something mechanical and powerful, like a speeding locomotive. Moment by moment the sound gets louder and is easier to hear, but to someone without our trained ear they may still be oblivious to the approaching train until its engineer

blows the air horn for the County Route 56 grade crossing at Chaseville. Are Manaho and Manatee listening, too, we wonder? Do they "see" the iron horse passing?

In another moment, our train curves into view just as it begins to cross the railroad-made embankment across Schenevus Lake, which is known today as Seward Lake. In one more moment, the train's 40 mph speed brings it into the location where WN Tower's interlocking plant could once be found. Then, the engineer begins his 2-longs, 1-short, and 1-long air horn warning for the Tannery Road crossing just as the crossing's gates begin to lower. Next, the train is upon us: noise, dust, sound, vibration. Thrilling. Wonderful. Locomotives pass with the sound we have been hearing having reached its peak crescendo. Now, intermodal platform cars begin to pass, telling us that this is train 938. Looking to the south, single and double stack containers keep coming around the curve from County Route 56 in seemingly conveyor-belt fashion. For nearly three minutes train 938 passes us, telling me that it is nearly two-miles long. Then, the marker-carrying final car passes, the crossing gates go up, and quiet again reigns supreme.

That, my friend, was exhilarating! But it's not the only reason I like it here about one-half mile south of Schenevus' depot. Another reason is the railroad's cross-

There are several reasons why I enjoy being at the Tannery Road grade crossing, not the least of which is waiting for a train to arrive, such as train 939 on October 10, 2010 (far left). The scenery is spectacular, it is quiet, and it is historic. Even nature's creatures seem to be comfortable and at ease here. This deer (near left)—whether doe or buck, I can't tell—has just come up from Seward Lake and looks both ways before crossing the track. The "dark" signal tells humans that no trains are near. Track 4 ran northward through the righthand portion of this scene near Tannery Road.

After parking the Neon near the Tannery Road grade crossing, a glance to the left reveals that the signal at CPF539.4 is "dark," (ABOVE LEFT) which tells us there are no trains nearby. Then, after a few moments, it blinks to a "red" indication (ABOVE RIGHT) telling us that a northbound train is approaching. To the right of the track is the out-of-service double-masted tower that at one time held the semaphore and targets for WN Tower's home signal. Beyond is the foundation for the tower and WN Cabin. Little by little, we begin to hear the sound of the train's hard working diesel locomotives. After several minutes its headlight comes into view. At 40 mph, the train's engineer quickly closes the distance between us. A crossing warning blares. Crossing gates go down and then train 938 (RIGHT) passes us with one car for SMS just behind the engines. Exhilarating? Yes. This is another reason why I like to be at Tannery Road.

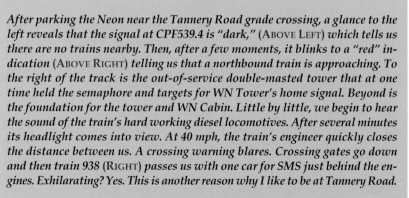

ing of Seward Lake, and still another is that the foundation that had supported WN Tower is still in place. Where DJ and JX towers had stood, nothing remains. But, here at WN its foundation remains as an historical marker to a bygone era of Delaware & Hudson railroading. WN Cabin is still there, too. Whether it had anything to do with the signal that alerted us to the imminent arrival of train 938 or not we do not know.

Before the low-grade line had been placed into service here in 1921, the railroad undertook ice harvesting from Seward Lake. Along its eastern shore, an elevator brought ice cakes up to a platform that had parallel tracks on each side. These two side tracks switched onto track 2 so that the ice could proceed on its merry way to milk stations, icehouses, and iceboxes alike. When the railroad began planning construction of the low-grade line's track 4, ice harvesting came to an end and the elevator, platform, and sidings were removed. In their place track 4 diverged off track 2, the switchwork being controlled by WN's towerman.

Then, when Centralized Traffic Control usurped the importance of WN Tower's local control, the tower was removed. Its foundation remained, and when we view it today it reminds us of how important this location once was; how a towerman made a living to support his family by working at this lonely outpost. Yet, he had the passing trains to keep him company. How many greetings, we wonder, were exchanged between towerman and engineman here, a wave of the hand that not only said "hello" but indicated that everything was okay. The human factor is gone from old WN interlocking; only one track remains to pass the tower foundation. In total, these are all the reasons why this location, at Tannery Road and Seward Lake, is a favorite spot for me. The sight and sound of contemporary railroading, combined with the historical significance of WN's foundation at the southern entrance to old track 4, draws me to this place regularly. The peacefulness and serenity of this area is also most welcome. I hope you enjoyed my taking you here.

We could use Tannery Road to return to Route 7, but we will continue on Lake Road, from which a wonderful view of Seward Lake can be enjoyed and where the immensity of the railroad's embankment across the lake can be appreciated. Lake Road ends at County Route 56. A right turn takes us across the railroad at grade near a point where it crosses over Schenevus Creek just to the south. County Route 56 then crosses the same body of water as well. It ends at Chaseville's Stevens Road, which is another segment of Route 7's earlier path. Going left, or right, will take us to modern Route 7, but by going left we'll arrive at Route 7 and Findago Road at the same time. Before Interstate 88 was built, Findago Road crossed the railroad via a scaled-down bridge similar to Brooker Hollow Road's old span. On an 1868 map, old Findago Road went to a saw mill and a cider mill. Findago Road dead ends now, although a railroad crossing sign remains.

It's only a mile or two to Maryland via Route 7, but when we get there, don't look for any vibrancy within the village or at the station grounds. Time has not been kind to either. There was never much to the village in the first place, just

ABOVE: WN Tower was put into service on April 11, 1923 as a thirty-two-lever electro-mechanical interlocking tower. In this view looking north, tracks 1,2 and 4 are shown as well as WN's home signal in the distance (shown out-of-service on the previous page). BELOW: Train 938 cruises past Seward Lake on an embankment fashioned by the railroad. The switch to track 4 came off track 2 just about where the locomotives are.
ABOVE, LAMBERT D. COOK PHOTOGRAPH.

Now that our friendly deer has crossed the track to graze along the northern tip of Seward Lake, rail traffic can once again pass by safely. Trains 939 (Below Left) and 938 (Below Right) are both splitting the signals — old and new — as they approach WN Tower's foundation and the Tannery Road grade crossing, respectively. With both trains "in the block" that signal had better be red and it is in both cases. Train 939 is powered by No. 2554, an SD70, while C40-9W No. 9147 and a sister unit handle the other consist. Left: Train 934 is running late on April 4, 2010. Bound for the Ayer, MA intermodal terminal, Norfolk Southern C40-9W No. 9848, a 2004 product of General Electric, and a matching trailing unit put their combined 8000 horsepower to work to make up time. The consist has just crossed Seward Lake's embankment and is about to pass WN Cabin and WN Tower's surviving foundation. Wonderful scenery and historical reminders of the past are two more reasons I enjoy being at Tannery Road and Seward Lake.

a couple of two-story wood frame stores, and a similarly designed—but three-story—Hotel Maryland that once sat on the corner of Route 7 and Depot Street (which has become known as Factory Street). Besides the railroad and its depot—and a creamery just to the north—the big show in town was the Maryland Wood Products Company which operated an acid factory on the east side of the railroad just a short distance away. A siding to the facility ran off of track 2 just north of the depot, but this track did not connect with the wood company's five private sidings that served the retort house and its wood storage shed. Nearby were a powerhouse and a two-story office building. All this is long gone, replaced by a few dwellings that may be gone shortly as well.

The depot had been another A&S standard design board-and-batten structure, sized 21'X81.' As late as the 1950s, Guy Maddalone used it for his feed and coal business. Now, only twenty-five feet of it is still (barely) standing; the 55-foot freight room has collapsed and fallen in on itself. It is very depressing to see the building in this condition. It has deteriorated far beyond being able to be restored. I don't say this often about old railroad depots, but this one should be humanely put

to sleep. We won't even get out of the car here as it is impossible to interpret the past when the present is in the condition it is. Further west we go on Route 7.

What a delight it is to be on Route 7 as it traverses the lower regions of Schenevus Creek. Here the valley is wide. Pastureland and farm barnyards are attractive. Homes are well-maintained. Schenevus Creek lies off to the south, curving to and fro and seeming to be in no hurry to get to Colliers where its existence will come to an end. The railroad is even further to the south. For the next five miles it will remain unseen as it travels through isolated countryside where only one dirt road (Leonard Road) will intersect it. At that grade crossing there is nothing remarkable to be seen except—just to the south—the railroad again crosses the creek for its next to last time. We won't see either until we arrive at Cooperstown Junction, which is just on the outskirts of Colliersville.

Prior to July 14, 1869, there was no such place as Cooperstown Junction. In fact, an 1868 map of the junction area called the location "South Milford." On that day, the Cooperstown & Susquehanna Valley Railroad began operations between Cooperstown and the Al-

bany & Susquehanna Railroad. Where the C&SV intersected the Albany & Susquehanna became known as Cooperstown Junction.

The C&SVRR was incorporated on February 25, 1865, which was just several months before the A&S opened its line to Oneonta on August 28, 1865. The imminent completion of the A&S to Oneonta was all the stimulus needed for Cooperstown folks to get caught up in railroad fever. It seemed to them that connecting their village with the A&S would be a rather simple affair since the railroad could follow the course of the Susquehanna River that got its start at Otsego Lake in Cooperstown. It took the C&SV four years to complete the line, but on that opening day in 1869, all the trials and tribulations were forgotten and only celebration ensued.

For almost twenty years, the 16.09 mile long C&SV merrily went about its business of providing adequate transportation between Cooperstown and the Junction. In 1888, promoters for an extension of the line from the junction down the valley of Charlotte Creek to meet the Ulster & Delaware Railroad at West Davenport divided the line's supporters. The pro-extension faction formed the Cooperstown & Charlotte Valley Railroad on

Summer finds northbound CP Rail train 253 on the Seward Lake embankment with covered hoppers in tow.

The last remnants of winter at still-frozen Seward Lake greet Norfolk Southern train 938 with a string of TOFC flats on the head-end.

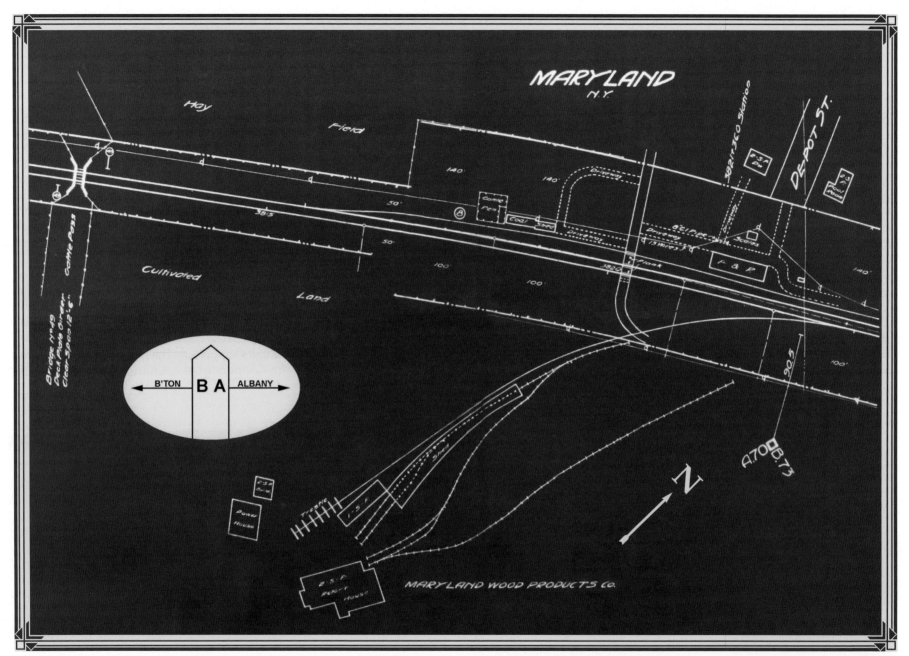

The railroad station at Maryland was situated just over seventy miles from Albany and was accessed by turning onto Depot Street from Route 7. Depot Street is now known as Factory Street. Both names are appropriate to where the street had gone during an earlier period. The big industry in town was the Maryland Wood Products company. This acid factory was located along the east side of the railroad which served it via a siding that ran off of track 2. NATIONAL ARCHIVES COLLECTION.

LEFT: *The village of Maryland was compact in size. Most of its commercial enterprises lined Depot Street, which led to the A&SRR-built station. Operated by A. C. Tallmadge, the Hotel Maryland sat at the intersection of Depot and Main (Route 7) and provided convenient overnight accommodations for visitors or those out-of-town lumbermen wishing to do business with the Maryland Wood Products Company — located beyond the station.*

BELOW LEFT: *The 21'X81' footprint of the Maryland depot made it a medium-sized stationhouse. Yet, the decorative bargeboards tell us that it was still a member of the Albany & Susquehanna's depot family. Robert E. Sperry, Emmett Sperry, George Lovell, Jason E. Wagar, Roy C. McCullough, and James E. Pratt all spent time here as station agents. It is not clear exactly which of those agents is flagging down this southbound passenger train so that a group of local folk can go shopping in Oneonta. An unimproved Depot Street (BELOW RIGHT) directs wagon traffic to the rear of the station where business is being transacted on both sides of the building. The community's creamery — a Borden's facility managed at this time by Otis C. Graham — is out of view to the left. South Hill provides the lofty backdrop.* LEFT AND BELOW LEFT, SCOTT ROLAND COLLECTION. BELOW RIGHT, A. BRUCE TRACY COLLECTION.

ROADS, RIVERS, AND RAILS

The hills around Maryland, NY once featured lush stands of hardwoods. That resulted in one of the region's more unusual industries: the Maryland Wood Products Company—as noted on the blueprint on Page 150. By 1908 the six Gaffney brothers of Bradford, PA—who had twelve wood products factories in that state—built a plant in Maryland to manufacture hardwood bobbins for shipment to New England textile mills. Later the Gaffneys expanded the plant by adding a wood acid factory which used beech, birch and maple cords to generate charcoal, wood alcohol (methanol), "acetate of lime," and wood tar oils. The D&H built a spur into the plant for deliveries of cordwood and lime while shipping carloads of wood chemicals. A narrow gauge railroad was used to shuttle cordwood cars into one of the four ovens which operated night and day. The fire-proof retort house is the large structure visible over the roofline of the D&H box cars. To its right are storage sheds with four empty "buggies" and a New York Central boxcar. The boiler house is at center. Part of the D&H mainline can be spied at the lower right. Maryland resident Emmons L. Peck laid a narrow gauge railroad from Burnsides Switch on the D&H, about a mile south of the acid factory, up Hazen Brook to the top of South Hill (in the background) where he harvested the forests for his lumber business (1909-1912). Peck reportedly used a homemade geared steam engine for this work. No physical connection between the logging line and the D&H at Burnsides Switch is known; logs were likely transloaded from narrow to standard gauge cars on a siding at Burnsides Switch. The Burnside family was also involved in the lumber trade. Peck logged the forest surrounding Gilbert Lake near New Lisbon, NY between 1906-1909 using another narrow gauge railroad and homemade locomotive. It is thought that after abandonment, Peck shoved that locomotive out onto frozen Gilbert Lake where it was allowed to sink to the bottom when the ice melted. Peck's two geared locos may well have been similar to lightweight vertical-boilered Shays. The Maryland Wood Products Company—pictured here in 1911—closed in the Great Depression year of 1932. It was started up again in 1938, only to cease operations for good in 1944. DEPOT SQUARE PUBLISHING COLLECTION.

April 29, 1888 and the very next day—through legal shenanigans—it gained control of the C&SV for a term of ninety-nine years. This legal wrangling that allowed the C&SV to be leased by the C&CV divided the residents of Cooperstown and began what came to be known as that community's Railroad War. The managers and supporters for the C&CV and its construction to the U&D held fast. When the extension down the Charlotte Creek valley opened on September 24, 1889 they claimed total victory over their detractors who mourned the loss of control of their railroad.

The reign of the Cooperstown & Charlotte Valley Railroad would not even last as long as that of the C&SV. On July 1, 1903, the D&H purchased the C&CV and began operating the line as its Cooperstown Branch.

Two months later, an operational improvement was made that allowed Branch trains to originate and terminate at Oneonta instead of at Cooperstown Junction. One month after that, the D&H abandoned the portion of the old C&CV that had been built between the junction and West Davenport when the bridge over Charlotte Creek was washed out. The D&H did not need that connection with the Ulster & Delaware anyway as both roads still interchanged at Oneonta, which was the U&D's northern terminus. The stone bridge abutments that had allowed the West Davenport extension to bridge the D&H mainline at the junction have stood without a purpose since the October 9, 1903 abandonment.

When the D&H installed a third track between Oneonta and Cooperstown Junction in 1917, it also placed

ABOVE: *From Schenevus to Maryland, Schenevus Creek comes between the railroad and Route 7. It cozies up with the roadway before becoming fickle and turning towards the railroad once again, as if not to play favorites. The view is east along Route 7.* LEFT: *NS train 930 accelerates southward through Maryland, passing the remnants of the old station.* UPPER RIGHT: *Time has not been kind to Maryland's depot; its freight room has collapsed and the remaining portion has had its boards and battens removed exposing the interior to the elements. Yet, the signature bargeboard that denotes this as being an A&S built depot still remains intact in places.*

The Albany & Susquehanna and Cooperstown & Susquehanna Valley railroads were both six-foot gauge affairs when this notable early photograph was taken from the shoulder of Route 7 at Cooperstown Junction. You may think that the gable-roofed building in the left-center of the image was the station. That is correct as it is noted that way by the map on the following page. For a time, the three-story Cooperstown Junction Hotel in the distance had offered ticket and waiting room services for those persons desiring to ride the cars. ONEONTA HISTORICAL ASSOCIATION COLLECTION.

into service N Tower, whose operator manned the tower's lever machine to regulate train interaction from the Branch onto the mainline trackage and vice versa. The tower was placed on the east side of the mainline tracks at the point where a switch on track 1 led to Cooperstown Junction's south leg of the wye. By that time, a small shelter (14'X25') had also been placed along the south leg of the Cooperstown Junction wye for use by passengers not desiring to travel beyond the junction, or for those needing to travel from the junction to Cooperstown or the line's intermediate stations at Portlandville, Milford, Hartwick Seminary, or Phoenix Mills. Both the south and north wye legs led directly to the Cooperstown Branch, but all passenger trains running between Oneonta and Cooperstown ran via the south leg.

The last passenger train to Cooperstown ran on June 24, 1934, and the following day the Branch was operated for freight service only. By that time, however, improved roads—especially New York State Route 28 that paralleled the line—allowed motor vehicles to siphon off increasing amounts of the line's freight. Eventually, service on the Branch was reduced to tri-weekly service, then as needed.

On April 6, 1971, the Cooperstown Branch was sold to Walter G. Rich. His previous railroading venture, the

DO (Delaware Otsego) Line, came to an end when New York State began acquiring property through Oneonta on which to build Interstate 88. New York State's Department of Transportation did not want to build a bridge over Walter's Oneonta-to-Mickle Bridge track, so eminent domain was used to acquire the railroad's property. While at first thought this appeared to be a setback for Walter's desire to become a railroad magnate, it proved to be a step in the right direction. Using the money that New York State paid him for the ex-U&D property, he bought the branch from the D&H and renamed it the Cooperstown & Charlotte Valley Railway. From this new beginning he eventually gained control of other branchlines and shortlines after the creation of Conrail on April 1, 1976, as well as the New York, Susquehanna & Western Railroad. Walt's Delaware Otsego System, of which he was President and Chief Executive Officer, was the corporate umbrella under which his collection of railroads fell.

While his railroad system grew, revenue on the old Cooperstown Branch plummeted. The line was sold to the Leatherstocking Chapter of the National Railway Historical Society. They now provide limited seasonal passenger service between Milford and Cooperstown, and very sporadic service to Cooperstown Junction where their headquarter office is located. They still fly the flag of the Cooperstown & Charlotte Valley.

Through all of these changes to the railroad, Cooperstown Junction has remained a junction. Only the north leg of the junction wye is still connected to CPRail's mainline. CP and NS trains regularly round the broad curve at Cooperstown Junction, with Schenevus Creek hard by the right-of-way to the west. The C&CV's collection of "antique" freight cars, locomotives, and a caboose lie to the east along Route 7. It is somewhat surprising to see when you arrive at the junction. One finds two ex-Pennsylvania Railroad GG-1 electric motors and two ex-New Haven FL-9 tri-power engines sitting forlornly upon the junction property. For now, they have been put out to pasture after having had lengthy careers handling trains in and out of both New York City's Pennsylvania Station and Grand Central Terminal. Their glory days are behind them, just as the

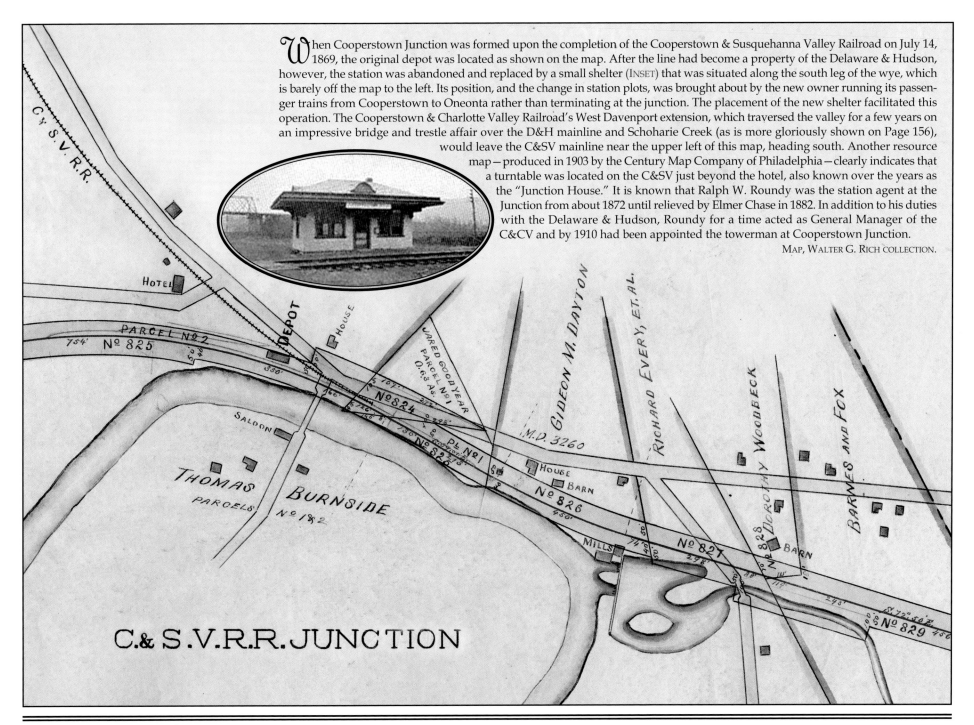

When Cooperstown Junction was formed upon the completion of the Cooperstown & Susquehanna Valley Railroad on July 14, 1869, the original depot was located as shown on the map. After the line had become a property of the Delaware & Hudson, however, the station was abandoned and replaced by a small shelter (INSET) that was situated along the south leg of the wye, which is barely off the map to the left. Its position, and the change in station plots, was brought about by the new owner running its passenger trains from Cooperstown to Oneonta rather than terminating at the junction. The placement of the new shelter facilitated this operation. The Cooperstown & Charlotte Valley Railroad's West Davenport extension, which traversed the valley for a few years on an impressive bridge and trestle affair over the D&H mainline and Schoharie Creek (as is more gloriously shown on Page 156), would leave the C&SV mainline near the upper left of this map, heading south. Another resource map—produced in 1903 by the Century Map Company of Philadelphia—clearly indicates that a turntable was located on the C&SV just beyond the hotel, also known over the years as the "Junction House." It is known that Ralph W. Roundy was the station agent at the Junction from about 1872 until relieved by Elmer Chase in 1882. In addition to his duties with the Delaware & Hudson, Roundy for a time acted as General Manager of the C&CV and by 1910 had been appointed the towerman at Cooperstown Junction.

MAP, WALTER G. RICH COLLECTION.

ABOVE: *The first passenger train—albeit abbreviated—of the Cooperstown & Charlotte Valley Railroad is returning to Cooperstown Junction from West Davenport on September 24, 1889. On locomotive No. 4 are Engineer Cornelius L. Vandervoort and Fireman Fred Pennington; Lawrence A. Kaple was the Conductor (that may be him at the end of the train standing on the bridge). The single through-truss span crosses the D&H track. What would become Route 7 passes under the trestlework at left.* BELOW RIGHT: *The nearest stone pier still survives along with its abutment that was put in after the trestlework had been filled and a steel bridge was used to cross Route 7.* BELOW LEFT: *Not quite as elderly as the abutments, there are many sections of rail such as this one that are still in place at the junction. Noted on the web of the rail are: LI&SCo (Lackawanna Iron & Steel Company), SW (steel wrought), Scranton (rolled at Scranton, Pennsylvania), and 3-95 (date of manufacture, March 1895).* ABOVE, GREATER ONEONTA HISTORICAL ASSOCIATION COLLECTION.

LEFT: *This is how Cooperstown Junction looked in 1904. The double-track D&H mainline passes under the ex-C&CV bridge, where it appears a train had just crossed. The north leg of the wye curves to the right as does the unimproved Route 7. The Cooperstown Junction Hotel—now under the management of George A. Evans—is still in place and it will remain so until falling victim to fire in 1922. The gable-roofed two-story building to the hotel's left is believed to be a general store owned by Evans. The new passenger shelter is hardly noticeable beyond the telephone pole at left center. The four-car train does not have an engine attached, and it may be a local train whose locomotive is switching about the junction trackage.* EDWARD P. BAUMGARDNER COLLECTION. BELOW: *Finally, Schenevus Creek is at left, as it still is today, to welcome train 938 to the junction.*

BELOW LEFT: *CPRail train 250 has just arrived at Cooperstown Junction from the north and is running along the bank of Schenevus Creek. This picture was taken from the embankment for the old Cooperstown & Charlotte Valley Railroad. Route 7 runs just in front of the white house in the middle of the scene. In both this picture and the one above the trains are passing ex-Pennsylvania Railroad GG-1 electric engines. One is destined for the Henry Ford Museum; the other is the property of the Leatherstocking Chapter of the National Railway Historical Society.*

ABOVE: *Cooperstown was named in honor of William Cooper who settled the area in 1786. His son, James Fenimore Cooper, made the region more popular and famous with his Tales of the Leatherstocking Country. Beyond Cooperstown's new station that was built in 1916, lies Otsego Lake from which the Susquehanna River was born. "Glimmerglass," as author Cooper called it, is the more romantic name for the lake.* ABOVE RIGHT: *A D&H train is at the new station, probably not long after it was constructed. It will be leaving for Oneonta via Cooperstown Junction in a few moments.* BOTH, DEPOT SQUARE PUBLISHING COLLECTION. CENTER RIGHT: *When the new Cooperstown station was put into service, it replaced this depot erected by the C&SVRR in 1870 that then became the freight house. It is believed the first agent was Washington Wilson. The building is currently the headquarters of the Delaware Otsego System. Before his untimely death, Walter G. Rich's office window was at the left on the second floor.* NATIONAL ARCHIVES COLLECTION. LOWER RIGHT: *A southbound train led by Mogul (2-6-0) No. 135 leads its four-car consist through the rural countryside of the Coopertown Branch near Milford, NY. The four cars are: combination, coach, milk, and baggage. Intermediate depots along the branch could be found at Phoenix Mills, Hartwick Seminary, Milford, and Portlandville.*

EDWARD P. BAUMGARDNER COLLECTION.

glory days of railroading on the Cooperstown Branch have waned. One of the GG-1s, however, is slated to go to the Henry Ford Museum in Dearborn, MI where it can certainly be more easily maintained and appreciated. We can only hope that the other three speedsters are as fortunate.

To Colliersville from Cooperstown Junction it is less than a mile to the Susquehanna River. From "Glimmerglass," James Fenimore Cooper's name for Otsego Lake, the Susquehanna has steadily gained strength, but here at Colliersville—just "Colliers" to the railroad—it will be given an infusion of water from Schenevus Creek, whose own course will come to an end. We have enjoyed its company since its birth at Dante, but its end here at Colliers is just the beginning of a more grand association with one of America's great and ancient rivers.

Colliers (and Colliersville) gets its name from the Collier family. The family's patriarch was Isaac who settled here in 1775. Two years later his son, Peter, was born. The family owned all of the land near the union of Schenevus Creek with the Susquehanna River, a tract that encompassed much more of an area than just today's Colliersville and Cooperstown Junction. While the Colliers were important to the area because they established a grist mill, several sawmills, a tavern, and pursued lumber rafting down the Susquehanna, it was Peter's interest in promoting the Otsego & Schoharie Railroad—along with Leonard Caryl whom we met earlier—that turned the family's attention towards railroad promotion. It was Peter's later son-in-law, Jared Goodyear, who used the family's influence to promote construction of the A&SRR. He built a hotel at Colliersville, too. These three families were pivotal in the development and prosperity of this village.

CLOCKWISE FROM ABOVE: The Leatherstocking Chapter, NRHS's collection of FL-9 locomotives, freight cars, and an ex-D&H caboose surrounds its office building (the former Elmer Chase homestead) at Cooperstown Junction. Route 7 runs by the front door. Mr. Chase had been the Junction's station agent from 1882 to 1904 and its postmaster—the post office was conveniently situated inside the original depot. He spent the last twenty-three years of his forty-five-year career with the D&H as the station agent for Otego. The white sign at left tells us that train 938 is passing Cooperstown Junction and the switch for the old north leg of the wye. On a cold day, train 930 pulls alongside the Howe Caverns billboard that appears on Page 33. From the same vantage point, train 252 rolls parallel to Route 7 beneath a heavy downpour. In the left distance is all there is to Cooperstown Junction.

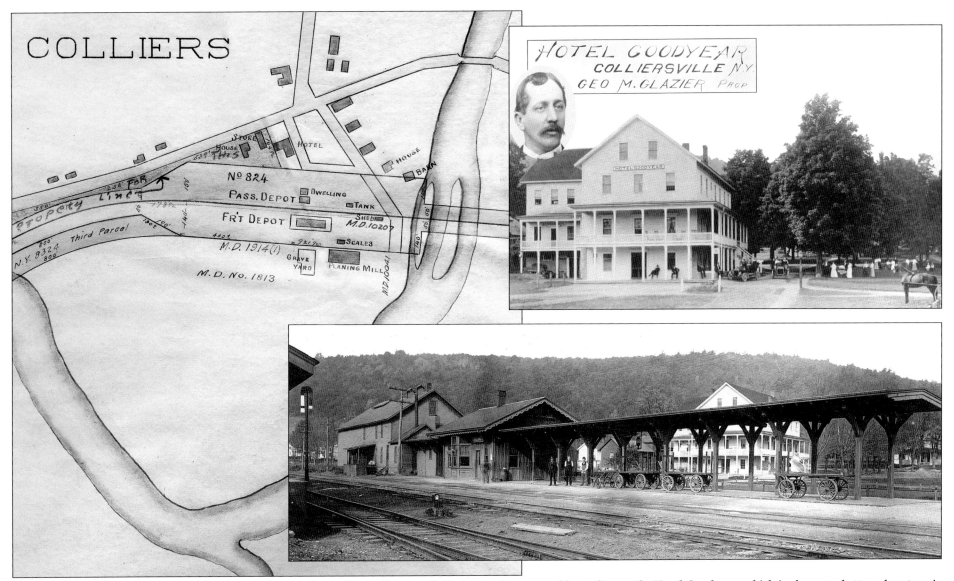

COLLIERS

HOTEL GOODYEAR
COLLIERSVILLE N.Y.
GEO M. GLAZIER PROP.

Schenevus Creek deposits its accumulated water into the Susquehanna River at Colliers, as shown at the bottom of the map, thereby helping the river to gain strength for its long journey still ahead. Also indicated on the map are the passenger and freight depots and the Hotel Goodyear—the only significant structures in the community at the time. The small passenger station, 24'X36' in size, was made to appear much more robust (ABOVE RIGHT) when canopies were added to both its ends in 1904, the north end "arcade" being of a greater length. Just a corner of the freight house's roof can be seen at left. South of the passenger depot, stands the Colliersville milk station and through the passenger platform at right we are able to glimpse the Hotel Goodyear, which is shown to better advantage in the top view. Although George M. Glazier was the proprietor at the time of the picture, the establishment was erected by Jared Goodyear in 1867. Mr. Goodyear, an influential force in promoting the need for the Albany & Susquehanna Railroad, had married Ann Eliza Collier in 1822. Her grandfather, Isaac Collier, was the namesake of the settlement. The hotel stopped taking guests in the late 1920s and afterwards the building hosted the local post office and a grocery store. It burned to the ground in April 1966. MAP, WALTER G. RICH COLLECTION. ABOVE, DEPOT SQUARE PUBLISHING COLLECTION. BELOW, A. BRUCE TRACY COLLECTION.

Jared Goodyear was another early supporter for the building of the Albany & Susquehanna Railroad. He became a long term director, vice-president, and temporary president of the railroad, whose board of directors laid much praise at his doorstep for helping to bring the railroad to life. In his honor, A&SRR locomotive No. 7 was named the "J. Goodyear." (I'll tell you a little more about Mr. Goodyear in the next chapter.) Also in thanks for Goodyear's efforts, the A&S constructed a 24'X36' passenger station on the west side of its track, and a separate 30'X110' freight house on the other side opposite the station in similar fashion to the arrangement at Central Bridge. Both railroad structures were located immediately south of the railroad's three-span through girder bridge (No. 4) that crossed the Susquehanna River. This 211' bridge is where the railroad met the river, and Route 7 is only a stone's throw away.

The year following the D&H purchase of the Cooperstown & Charlotte Valley Railroad, the company erected canopies (they called them "arcades" in those days) that were attached to both ends of the small passenger station, giving it the appearance of being a much larger facility. This was done so that passengers arriving from the branch who desired to go north on a mainline train, rather than south to Oneonta, could be better accommodated and

ABOVE: Route 7 crossed over the Susquehanna River at Colliersville using this covered bridge that was built by Jared Goodyear in 1832. As we arrive at Colliersville, we cross the river via a modern deck span that is a second generation descendent of this bridge whose timbers and wood sheathing were cut at the Collier-Goodyear sawmill nearby. SCOTT ROLAND COLLECTION.

LEFT: This is where the Albany & Susquehanna Railroad and the Susquehanna River first met. We are looking south through the two-span, 211-foot-long bridge No. 54 with a northbound train bearing down on us. Through the southward portion of the bridge the station at Colliers can be seen. Route 7 crosses the river just out of view at right. A. BRUCE TRACY COLLECTION.

ROADS, RIVERS, AND RAILS

protected from the elements. Station agents here included Mathew P. Van Deusen and Frederick C. Burdick—who both served the Delaware & Hudson for decades. When passenger service ceased on the branch in 1934, the Colliers depot lost whatever importance it may have had in providing revenue to the railroad. It was retired during the following year.

When we arrived at Colliers, we found little evidence that any railroad facilities—or the creamery that stood just to the south of the passenger station—had ever been here. Long vanished is the substantial sash and blind factory operated for years by Francis M. Fox and the dry goods and feed store once owned by Percy R. Southworth. Triple-track has reverted to just one, but the railroad still spans the Susquehanna, and abutments for the two removed tracks still survive. From here, Route 7 will tag along with the course of the river and right-of-way of the railroad until we reach Nineveh, proving that for those forty-four and a half miles three can be company.

We'll miss Chief Schenevus and his creek, but the flavor of his "scones" will no doubt last for quite a few miles more.

ABOVE: This single span deck bridge replaced the earlier through-truss bridge No. 54 shown on the previous page, and train 930 is using it to cross the Susquehanna River. Leading the way is NS No. 9218, a C40-9W which was the last unit among 120 similar diesels purchased from GE in 1997. At one time, three tracks had been in use here. RIGHT: Train 931, with NS No. 2666, an SD70M-2 on point, leans into a super-elevated curve with a mixed freight. It has just crossed the Susquehanna River bridge—about ten cars back—and is now hugging Route 7 as it proceeds northward into Cooperstown Junction on the single-track right-of-way.

At the Grave of Chief Schenevus

Beneath these pines, Schenevus lies,
    Chief of his Tribe – the Speckled Trout.

So runs the legend; and the place,
    Thick-sown with arrow heads, keeps trace,
        And memory of his warrior race.

Killed by his sons at his behest,
    Helpless and blind he longed for rest.
        Each pressed the spear which pierced his breast.

No more the feasting and the shout,
    No more the war dance and the rout.
        Victor and vanquished as Speckled Trout.

Yet, peacefully the stream flows by,
    And beautiful the woods and sky,
        Where old Schenevus chose to lie.

— The Reverend Henry Herbert Pittman
Rector of the Church of the Holy Spirit, Schenevus, NY (1906-1907)
First published by the *Elizabethtown* [NY] *Post & Gazette*, 1909

It is very difficult to leave Schenevus Creek behind as we have enjoyed its company all the way down Route 7 from Dante, were delighted by its valley's scenery, appreciated the opportunity to get to know the villages along its way, and marveled that while its course and valley were created so long ago that it can still be so beautiful and vibrant today. I suppose the old adage is true: things get better with time! RIGHT: *CPRail train 252, which is crossing County Route 58 in Colliersville, will lead us on to little Emmons and greater Oneonta whose nickname is the "City of the Hills." That's where the Neptune Diner is.*

CHAPTER 5
CITY OF THE HILLS

At Colliersville, it is easy to skip a stone across the Susquehanna River. But, further south, its width continually increases in size so that by the time the river reaches Harrisburg, PA, it takes forty-eight stone arches measuring seventy feet in length each for the old Pennsylvania Railroad's Rockville Bridge to cross the fully matured river. I'll do the arithmetic: that's 3,360 feet (3,820 feet with approaches). The Indians referred to the river as being "a mile wide but only a foot deep." They were not wrong. We are not going to go down the river as far as Harrisburg, of course, but even by the time we reach Oneonta—the City of the Hills—the Susquehanna has outgrown puberty and has reached its adolescent stage, more progressively at Sidney, Bainbridge, and Nineveh. We will get to the river at those communities tomorrow after an overnight rest at Oneonta's Hampton Inn.

The Susquehanna today is pretty much a lazy river, although it does drain water from 27,500 square miles of land and deposits it into the Chesapeake Bay. That is a pretty big job, I suppose, but other than that it doesn't do much else, especially within the geographic context of this story. The river does, however, put up with a yearly rowing regatta from its Cooperstown source to Bainbridge. It allows recreational fishermen to put their dinghies into its water followed by a hooked worm. The river is then supposed to give up one of its fish to the aspiring angler. Oh, it also helps to provide power for electricity generation at Colliersville's Goodyear Dam (RIGHT). Earlier it supplied water to the railroad terminal at Oneonta, but that was its avocation from the Twentieth and Twenty-first centuries. You could say that the Susquehanna is retired, and considering that it

could be 570 million years old, that retirement would seem to be well deserved. That is because when it was younger it was a noteworthy transportation corridor until roads and railroads replaced the need for its flowing water.

The Susquehanna, known as the Crooked River by the Susquehannock Indians who named it, was considered a channel that only a canal could tame and utilize. In 1737, New York State Surveyor General Cadwallader Colden, known as the Father of the American Canal System, envisioned building just such a project parallel to the river when he visited its source at Otsego Lake. That never came to pass, but the river's main job became a thoroughfare for commercial rafting, especially from Oneonta south, until the 1840s. As early as the mid-1700s, the river supported and transported rafts loaded with mostly lumber and some shipments of agricultural products. These rafts were much more than Huckleberry Finn-size; some were half the size of a football field! Imagine Mark Twain piloting one of these rafts down the river where curvature and depth were always obstacles to safe passage. Fortunately, there were no railroad bridges across the Susquehanna at this time, as bridge abutments—and their inherent spacing—would not have allowed rafts of this size to pass.

Piloting a raft 8-10,000 square feet in size down the Susquehanna was no small task as you can imagine. To

do so required a crew of 10-14 men between Oneonta and Bainbridge, and then only four crew members beyond as the ever maturing river provided additional width for the raftsmen to negotiate the channel. Regardless of how far the crewmen worked, to get back home they had to walk. This wasn't so bad for those men who left the raft at Bainbridge, but for those who continued on to

Binghamton, Harrisburg, and beyond a longer hike home was not much to look forward to. Yet, they were at least going back to their abode. Because of the lengthy time required for the experienced raftsmen to get home, generally one roundtrip per season was all they could undertake. In that one trip they earned their seasonal pay. More importantly, they got the shipment through so that the businessman who sent them off could also be paid for his lumber, etc.

Did some rafts "break-up" enroute with their cargo subsequently lost? Most certainly that occured. Did some raftsmen lose their lives during their journey down the river? Absolutely.

One such unlucky fellow was Asa Emmons who perished on the river in 1820. It was Asa, along with his brother Ira, who moved from Oneonta to an area midway to Colliers in 1800, and provided their name for the hamlet they helped to develop. When the Albany & Susquehanna Railroad came along, it was Ira who forged an agreement with the railroad for the perpetual operation of a station at Emmons. When the A&S began operating into Oneonta on August 28, 1865, Emmons was on the timetable some three miles from Colliers and a similar distance to Oneonta. By 1872, however—and regardless of the prior agreement—the Delaware & Hudson Canal Company discontinued service to Emmons, putting an end to the location being listed on the company's timetables. For the brief period of time that Emmons station was in operation, it appears that Zachariah Sloat had been the only agent to serve at the rural outpost (see below). One can only wonder what type of depot was erected there. Was it built by the A&S? If so, it would have been one of their smaller-sized standard board-and-batten stationhouses? Had Ira Emmons built the depot in order to obtain the A&S agreement to stop their trains there? If that were the case, then the "depot" may have looked more like a simple dwelling or barn. Regardless of appearance or size, there just was not enough business for the railroad's trains to continue serving Emmons. D&H trains then, and CPRail trains today, pass Emmons without so much as a blink of an eye.

The former site of Emmons depot is noteworthy in one regard, however, and that is because it is on the south side of Interstate 88, which means that the new

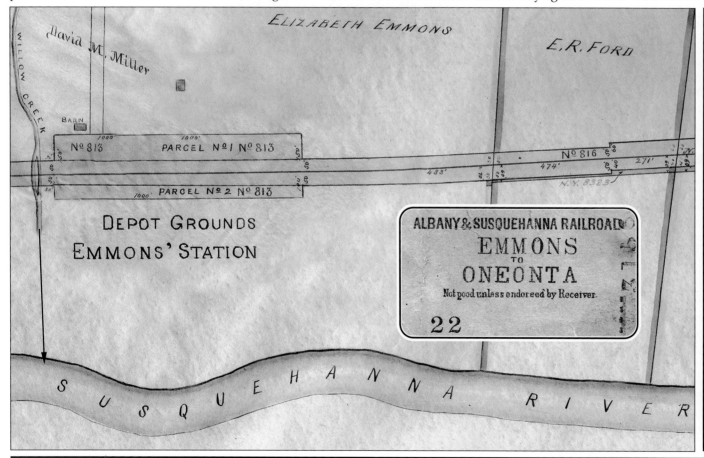

Ira Emmons negotiated an arrangement with the A&SRR for the perpetual operation of a station at Emmons, a deal that was not to last long. A depot of unknown design was used by the railroad for just seven years: 1865 until 1872. It was only three miles to either Oneonta or Colliersville. The depot grounds were situated as shown on the map at left, with the road running north through the name of "David M. Miller" going to the future Route 7. For the seven years of its operation, it appears that Zachariah Hawkins Sloat was the only station agent to be employed at Emmons until the last year when Ralph Roundy filled the role (prior to moving over to Cooperstown Junction). Sloat's hand probably passed the inset ticket to a passenger desiring to "ride the cars" three miles to Oneonta. Sloat was born in 1834 in Delhi; was a "student of divinity" as well as a farmer. He dabbled in Delaware County politics and served as a 1st Lieutenant in the 8th Battery of light artillery in the Civil War before entering his railroad career.

MAP, WALTER G. RICH COLLECTION.

and 551, indicates to an Oneonta-bound engineer what the dispatcher wishes to do with his train: proceed through Oneonta non-stop; meet an opposing train by holding the main track; or meet an opposing train by waiting within the passing siding. As for us? We are going into Oneonta to layover.

Leaving Colliersville, Route 7 takes to the high ground with Interstate 88 acting as a temporary interloper between us and the railroad. As we travel west, we can look down and see the interstate's crossover of the railroad as both head for Emmons. For the interstate highway there is an interchange at Emmons; for the railroad only single track where three tracks once held sway.

At Emmons, we come to a halt for the traffic signal at the intersection of Route 7 and County Route 47 that also acts as part of the I-88 Emmons interchange. This is the first traffic light we have seen since Richmondville. When the signal changes and allows us to proceed, we will enter Oneonta's East End, although technically we are still in Emmons. Of note here is the Brooks Barbecue (chicken) Restaurant that is a very popular eatery throughout the region. We could stop here to have

ABOVE: At Emmons, Interstate 88 — the Warren M. Anderson Expressway — crosses over the railroad, and in so doing comes between Route 7 and its railroad. The intrusion is short lived as it quickly passes over the railroad once again to take up its position on the railroad's east flank where it has been located all the way from Schenectady. The Susquehanna River is not far out of the scene at right. This is train 939 that is being powered by a pair of General Electric-built ES40DC Diesels on June 8, 2009, one day before the author's sixty-second birthday. The four-lane I-88 crosses overhead with Oneonta lying to the left.

roadway crosses the railroad. For its entire distance from near Schenectady, Interstate 88 was built on the south (railroad east) side of the ex-Delaware & Hudson track(s). Unlike Route 7, which has crossed over and under the railroad at Cobleskill (once each), and then over once again at Dante, I-88 waited until Emmons to cross to the other side of the track. That position was short lived, since in a matter of only a few miles, the interstate highway crosses back to the side it is more familiar with and will not meet the railroad again until its crossover at Dyes between Tunnel and Sanitaria Springs. Route 7, on the other hand, wishes to remain more intimate with the railroad so by the time it reaches Dyes it has said hello to the railroad five more times: Unadilla (twice), Bainbridge (twice), and Afton (once). Oh, Route 7 crosses under the railroad at Dyes, too, via a magnificent stone arch bridge that was built in 1889. We will get to all of these places tomorrow. Right now, we are heading for the "City of the Hills," and so is the railroad whose approach signal for Oneonta (at old MU Cabin) is located at Emmons. This signal, which is situated between CPF550

ABOVE: Looking north along the long tangent track at CPF551 reveals evidence of the existence of the triple-track that had been in place earlier between Oneonta and Cooperstown Junction. These three bridges, which are about to be assaulted by the onrushing train 939, pass over Willow Creek that is shown on the extreme left of the map on the previous page. The three tracks were reduced to two not long after diesels ousted steam engines in 1953.

RIGHT: *Proving that Senator Anderson's highway is good for something, this picture was taken from its eastbound shoulder and, no Virginia, this isn't Nebraska or Wyoming. Rather it is Emmons, NY. The brace of Union Pacific engines—with No. 7602 flying both winged emblem and patriotic flag—are about to lead northbound train 938 under Interstate 88 with headend autorack cars for SMS. The appearance of "foreign" locomotives is due to mileage and horsepower equalization agreements made between connecting railroads. In this case, UP is paying back Norfolk Southern. March 11, 2010.* LOWER LEFT: *As we saw previously at Delanson, and as we will see again tomorrow in Oneonta, safety signs have been placed at Emmons to remind crewmen to be careful during the performance of their duties. The signs not only remind trainmen, but also maintenance personnel who use the rutted, parallel lane where Oneonta to Cooperstown Junction track 4 had once been located. Norfolk Southern engines bring northbound train 931 through Emmons.*

LEFT: *Standing atop the County Route 47 bridge over the railroad has been a longtime favorite location to watch and photograph the passing railroad scene, at least since I-88 was constructed. Jerry Coyne did so during the D&H's final years capturing this southbound train passing milepost A79. This former triple-track section reverted to double-track in 1954, and would be further reduced to just one track after the arrival of CPRail. The second (open tri-level) car of the train sits upon the Willow Creek bridge shown in closer detail on Page 167. I-88 is just above the train, while Route 7 lies beyond the buildings at far left. This is where the expressway has come between Route 7 and the railroad. BELOW LEFT: At the same location, now single track and marked CPF 551, train 250 passes the Emmons depot site on August 27, 2010. BELOW: From the same vantage point, but now looking south, BNSF engines including C44-9W No. 5231 bring train 938 into Emmons. At this point the train's marker has cleared Oneonta's speed restriction and the engineer has opened his throttle to gain track speed and to overcome gravity on this slight uphill climb. Otsego's wonderful hills rise in the background in all three views.*

a tasty dinner but even though we have had a long day there is still daylight burning so please allow me to show you some of Oneonta's noteworthy sights and sites.

As we proceed further into Oneonta, a rash of convenience stores, fast-food restaurants, and several strip malls begin to line Route 7's curbside, and all the while the railroad is narrowing the distance between us. By turning to the left at Fifth Street we can wiggle our way down to Railroad Avenue, which parallels the

old D&H Susquehanna Division, now CPRail's mainline. Railroad Avenue is not named for its association with either the D&H or CPRail. Rather, Railroad Avenue was where the Ulster & Delaware Railroad built its Oneonta station when it arrived in town on September 25, 1900.

The arrival of the U&D at Oneonta was the culmination of many years—and various schemes—to connect the Hudson River valley with Otsego County's premier community. Early on, Oneonta was not planned to be the western (northern) terminus of the line. Originally, a group of railroads was envisioned so that the Hudson Valley would be connected with Syracuse, NY via a circuitous and rural route similar in fashion to that of the New York & Oswego Midland Railroad. In 1870, the Oneonta & Earlville Railroad was organized to be the "middle-man" between the Syracuse & Chenango Valley Railroad (Syracuse-Earlville) and the Ulster & Delaware Railroad (Oneonta-Kingston). It took the creation of the Delaware & Otsego Railroad in 1887 to eventually connect the stalled U&D at Stamford with the Delaware & Hudson at Oneonta, which turned out to be the end of the line —physically and literally.

LEFT: *Who has a better view of Electric Lake, the railroad's passengers or the two occupants of the canoe? This man-made lake was formed in 1898 when the Oneonta Electric & Power Company purchased fifty acres of land, diverted some of the Susquehanna's water on the east end, and then dammed the west end to provide water power that was used in the company's power plant. Besides providing electricity, the lake also was used as a picnic, swimming, and ice skating recreational area for Oneonta residents who benefitted from the lake's main purpose. In 1954, the power plant here was closed, and the lake was filled. Today, I-88 passes directly through the body of water at right. Admittedly, the train passengers have a better view of the lake, but I'd rather be in the rowboat so as to get a better look at the Oneonta-bound train!* DEPOT SQUARE PUBLISHING COLLECTION. ABOVE: *The Ulster & Delaware Railroad began service to Oneonta on September 25, 1900, with their terminus located at the community's East End, where it appears a train has just arrived from Kingston. The D&H tracks (foreground) connected with those of the U&D not far to the south (right).* EDWARD P. BAUMGARDNER COLLECTION.

The completion of the U&D may have been all the impetus the D&HCCo needed to abandon the Cooperstown & Charlotte Valley Railroad's extension from Cooperstown Junction to West Davenport in 1903. One connection with the U&D at Oneonta was all the D&H desired and needed. It was also the imminent completion of the U&D that would provide an all-rail routing for the D&HCCo's coal so that their canal to Kingston could be abandoned (which it was in 1899). The closing of the canal further provided the railroad a reason to request permission to change its corporate title from Delaware & Hudson Canal Company to (somewhat more) simply the Delaware & Hudson Company.

Although the D&H benefitted from the completion of the U&D, with little apparent loss through competition, Oneontans were not equally pleased, and their displeasure stemmed from the fact that the U&D depot on Railroad Avenue was located at too great a distance from the village business district that lined Main Street (Route 7) several miles away. Since the U&D and D&H tracks were physically connected at Railroad Avenue, why couldn't U&D (passenger) trains use the more centrally located D&H depot that was at the end of Broad Street just off of Main Street? (Broad Street is today the eastern extension of Chestnut Street.)

Well, Oneontans did get their "union" depot, but it took an act of war to do so. Still, the joint use of the D&H station by the U&D did not commence until nearly the end of World War One's hostilities. From 1918 until 1922, the Ulster & Delaware (now controlled and operated by the New York Central Railroad) passenger trains originated and terminated at the new Delaware & Hudson station that had been constructed in 1892.

When the Albany & Susquehanna Railroad arrived in 1865, Oneontans primarily attributed getting the railroad to Eliakim R. Ford, Harvey Baker, and Jared Goodyear. Did the community's residents actually think that the A&S would pass them by? Their village had been the pre-eminent center for business and commerce ever since the Susquehanna's water flowed past their doorstep. Turnpikes such as the Catskill, Charlotte, and Franklin had made it feasible for overland travel

Oneontans did get the union depot they wanted, but they had to wait until eighteen years after the Ulster & Delaware's arrival. By that time, the D&H's new station had been built and decorated with an attractive garden. The D&H didn't mind hosting U&D passengers (the New York Central assumed control in 1932), but it wanted them to know whose station this was. The Romanesque-style station was constructed during 1892, and opened to the public on October 20 of that year. In its construction, Howe's Cave limestone was mostly used with locally procured sandstone trimmings. Its size was thirty-one feet wide and 128 feet long, and besides providing rooms for passengers and the ticket agent, it also featured a restaurant within the north wing (at left in picture), and a baggage room at the south end. For conductors and the restaurant manager, several rooms were provided on the second floor. GREATER ONEONTA HISTORICAL SOCIETY COLLECTION.

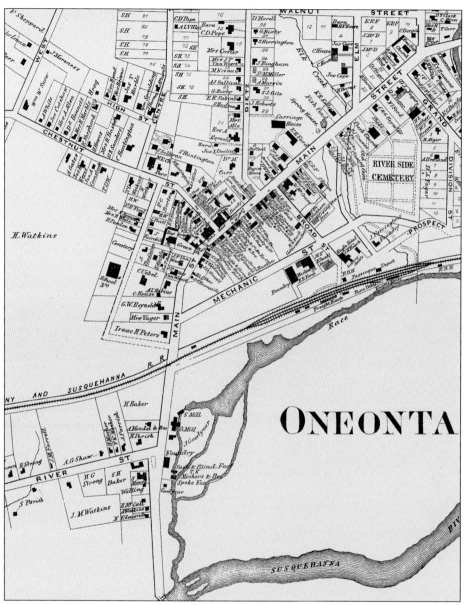

UPPER LEFT: *In 1877, D&HCCo. employees posed outside the original brick car repair shop and wooden blacksmith shop with their hometown locomotive, "Oneonta," that has just been converted from wide to standard gauge. The caboose at left has yet to be similarly re-gauged, but the track it is upon has been dual-gauged for that eventually.* LOWER LEFT: *The original eleven-stall roundhouse (left center) opened in January 1871. It was enlarged to twenty-two stalls in 1876. The second roundhouse (right center) contained fifteen stalls and began service* on January 7, 1882. The preponderance of shop buildings lie between and beyond the two roundhouses in this westward view. ABOVE: *Oneonta's original roundhouses, yard, and shops will be built on the large plot owned by Hezekiah Watkins ("H. Watkins") shown to the left of center on this 1868 map. Note that the freight house, turntable, and engine house were situated across the mainline from the depot which stood at the foot of South Main Street (center right).* ALL, GREATER ONEONTA HISTORICAL SOCIETY COLLECTION.

LEFT: *By 1876, the village of Oneonta had become the railroad center Harvey Baker had envisioned by becoming the recipient of the D&HCCo. shops and roundhouse. The company's primary shops are behind the roundhouse.*

RIGHT: *Six years later, a second roundhouse (far right) only reinforced the community's statue as the premiere terminal for the railroad. The substantial stock of construction supplies suggests that additional buildings or expansion are also underway. Both views look down the Susquehanna River valley with Franklin Mountain at left, and Table Rocks not far out of the scenes at right.*
BOTH, GREATER ONEONTA HISTORICAL SOCIETY COLLECTION.

LEFT: *While the Oneonta shops could—and did—build a steam locomotive, its main emphasis was rebuilding and repairing both engines and cars. The Delaware & Hudson relied almost exclusively on Consolidation-type engines, such as No. 175 shown here; Oneonta's facilities and shopmen helped keep them in tip-top shape. This double-cab 2-8-0 has just been released from the shops for a return to service. Posing proudly with it are, left to right, Engine Dispatcher Charles Owen Beach and Master Mechanic John R. Skinner. Born locally in 1843, Beach worked on farms around the area. By 1870, the census recorded him as an engineer for the D&H. Skinner, who was an Englishman, worked at the shops. He was assigned as Superintendent of Stores in 1905. The substantial, multichimneyed machine shop serves as the backdrop for this scene.*

RIGHT: *Not too many years after the opening of the new roundhouse in 1882, an enterprising lensman hiked to the lofty heights of Table Rocks to photograph the terminal area that caused Oneonta to become widely known and increasingly populated. The Susquehanna River lies near the base of distant Franklin Mountain, while Chestnut Street—the future Route 7—is located at the base of this hill within the foreground tree growth. Oneonta's future is still on the rise, but it would have to wait until the Twentieth Century for further growth and prosperity.* BOTH, GREATER ONEONTA HISTORICAL SOCIETY COLLECTION.

since 1802, 1834, and 1835 respectively. Before then, Oneonta's Main and Chestnut streets, the two thoroughfares upon which its business district is situated—and where Route 7 is now signed—had been Indian trails. The river supported Oneonta's earliest industry: lumbering. The turnpikes made trade possible for Oneontans with the entire surrounding region. What Ford, Baker, and Goodyear did was speed up the railroad's arrival at Oneonta; its natural setting dictated the railroad would call there.

Besides building several portions of the A&SRR (for thirty-two miles east of Oneonta and over Richmondville Hill, and from Afton to Harpursville), and developing the Howe's Cave Lime & Cement Company, Harvey Baker had also been an Oneonta village president (1853) and town supervisor (1858). He preferred to be known as a contractor since it was he who built the preponderance of grist and lumber mills throughout the area—including those operated by Peter Collier and Jared Goodyear. Mr. Baker, however, envisioned that when the railroad came to Oneonta it might need land for terminal facilities. And, he was right. Yards, shops, and roundhouses would later be built upon property he brokered to the railroad. That may have been a reward for his signature upon the railroad's charter and for being an original stockholder. To a lesser extent, it may have been due to moving a single-stall enginehouse from Harpursville to establish Oneonta's first engine facility.

Jared Goodyear, you may recall from the previous chapter, had married the daughter of Peter Collier and built a hotel at Colliers. Goodyear owned all the land there, too. Basically, Colliers was all his, especially after his father-in-law died. But, Goodyear lived in Oneonta where he was also a leading businessman and shopkeeper. His support for the railroad was acknowledged by an agreement with the railroad that the A&S shops would be built on his Colliers property. A locomotive—number 7—carried his name. But, Eliakim Reed Ford had Goodyear beat, because the A&S also named a locomotive in his honor, and that engine number was 2; that locomotive was built three years prior to the railroad's arrival at Oneonta.

E.R. Ford, along with Peter Collier, Leonard Caryl of Worcester, and Sherman Page of Unadilla, were all early supporters of Otsego County railroads: Otsego & Schoharie and Cooperstown & Colliers in 1832; Cherry Valley & Susquehanna Valley in 1836; and Cherry Valley & Cooperstown the following year. It was expected then that these men would promote and support the A&SRR, and they did. Ford, a businessman, store and land owner, came to Oneonta in 1822, became the justice of the peace in 1829, town justice in 1831, town supervisor in 1844, and was considered by Oneonta's 650 residents to be the community's foremost citizen in 1848. When the A&S was chartered, he invested heavily in the road—both physically and financially—and was on the railroad's board of directors until he died in 1873. That was what you had to do to get a locomotive named in your honor in the 1860s.

Ford also owned substantial property in Oneonta. When the time came to select a site for the railroad's depot, Ford and his friend Harvey Baker picked an appropriate location on a parcel of Ford's land. In fairness, though, it was prime real estate, being just

Oneonta's first station had been completed in time for the opening of the A&S on August 28, 1865. This picture, however, was taken sometime after 1874 when the foreground section was added to the original north end. It may have been taken by either Charles J. Freiot or William Sherwood, both Oneonta photographers of the day. This edifice was one of the three original stationhouses that were built with stone—making it a more substantial building to reflect the efforts expended by Harvey Baker and Eliakim R. Ford (whose land the building sat upon) in securing the railroad for the community. The scene looks north. According to the May 6, 1873 issue of the Utica Weekly Herald, Charles Wadsworth was the station agent here and his younger brother, Paul, was the train dispatcher. Standing among the crowd of curious onlookers could be the Wadsworths (Paul succeeded Charles as station agent); Emulus A. Reynolds, express agent; Jay Tucker, telegraph operator; Charles H. Butts, freight receiver; and Alonzo Wood, baggageman. Paul Wadsworth had a colorful career with the D&H. He began as a telegrapher at Cooperstown Junction in 1871, then transferred to Binghamton where he was also the ticket agent. After his stint in Oneonta, he moved to Albany. While living there, he served as the local freight agent (1877), assistant general freight agent (1889), and finally, as general freight agent. EDWARD P. BAUMGARDNER COLLECTION.

several stone throws off of Main Street (later to be Route 7). Four years later, Ford and Baker teamed up once again to convince Goodyear to void his agreement with the railroad for shops being located at Colliers. This was easy for Goodyear to agree to do since he also owned land in Oneonta that he thought was more suitable for the railroad's shops. But, he had been hoodwinked. Baker knew that Goodyear's Oneonta property was inferior in location to property owned by Hezekiah Watkins, and it was the Watkins land that Baker acquired to become the middleman between Watkins and the railroad. This most likely came to pass because of Baker's close association with the railroad's Master Mechanic, Robert C. Blackall. The railroad considered other sites at Unadilla and Sidney, but Blackall favored Oneonta. (You do remember Blackall, don't you? He's the fellow who saved the railroad for Joseph Ramsey from Jay Gould and James Fisk at Tunnel, and who was

played [loosely] by Gary Cooper in the Hollywood movie *Saratoga Trunk*. Blackall died in Albany on August 31, 1903, as Supervising Mechanical Engineer.) Regardless of the method Baker used in locating the roundhouse here and later the shops, it was always his utmost desire that Oneonta should get the facilities and not Colliers.

Thus, it was Baker, Goodyear, and Ford who led the effort in bringing the railroad into Oneonta, ahead of time, and it was Ford's locomotive that led the celebratory train into town on the opening day of railroad service, August 28, 1865.

As we roll along down Oneonta's Main Street on our beloved Route 7 it is easy for us to recognize that there is much vibrancy, life, and excitement still within the business district. Stores for all kinds of merchandise, restaurants for all tastes, banks, a post office, church, and hotel, all line Oneonta's main drag. There is nary a

vacant building to be seen. Along the way we pass Ford Avenue, named—of course—for E. R. The sign for his street reminds me of another story of how Ford helped to bring about (indirectly) the dominance of railroading, not on a local level, but nationally.

It was during 1849, the year of America's Gold Rush, that Mr. Ford "staked" another local shopkeeper so he could move to California. This recipient of Ford's generosity had been born on October 22, 1821, and twenty-two years later he came to Oneonta along with his brother Solon. The brothers opened their general store, and before long the Huntington brothers reveled in the sweet aroma of success. Solon's brother, Collis, petitioned the village to incorporate in 1847 (which was done on October 27, 1848), and became Oneonta's first fire chief that same year. The next year he became the community's first street commissioner, and then the following year he accepted Ford's monetary stake along with that of his brother and set out on his overland trip to California.

Once in the Golden State's capital of Sacramento, Collis Potter Huntington quickly and efficiently established his business which—as you may imagine—succeeded above all expectations, primarily due to gold rush miners. Within a short period of time he had become an influential member of the community. His financial success placed him in the same class as Charles Crocker, Mark Hopkins, and Leland Stanford. In California at that time but especially in Sacramento, it was these four men—Crocker, Hopkins, Huntington, and Stanford—who rose to the forefront in developing America's westernmost frontier into a thriving state. It was only natural that when surveyor and visionary Theodore Judah envisioned the construction of a cross-continent railroad that he solicited the interest and financial support of these men, who became known in railroad lore as the Central Pacific Railroad's "Big Four."

Although he was a continent away from Oneonta, C. P. Huntington never forgot where he had started. He was a continual supporter of the community's improvements. He dabbled forever in real estate speculation. Huntington even continued his subscription to the local newspaper until his death on August 15, 1900. As you probably already know, C. P. Huntington became quite wealthy. During his lifetime it was said that he could travel across the length and breadth of the United States by using only railroads he controlled.

It was George Mortimer Pullman who built Huntington two private cars. They were named the *Oneonta*, and the *Oneonta II*. And, of course all wealthy men of the period also owned an Adirondack estate, and C. P.'s was on an island within Raquette Lake. How did he get to the island? By steamer of course, and it was named *Oneonta* as well. When he died, Huntington's wealth was estimated to be two-hundred million dollars. Keep in mind, that was when a penny was worth something.

E. R. Ford may have been Oneonta's most prominent citizen in 1848, but it may well be that C. P. Huntington is Oneonta's most favored son today. They think so at the Huntington Library on Chestnut Street. The building was provided for them by a descendent of C. P., no relation to CPRail, of course.

Oneonta is the most bustling community along the CPRail's ex-D&H Susquehanna Division today, and that vitality comes from its being a college town, a seat of higher education and not from being a railroad town as in the past. It is college students that are shopping and dining al fresco along Route 7's sidewalks, not railroaders trundling back and forth from the shops, roundhouse(s), and depot. Both Hartwick College and a campus of the State University of New York (SUNY) call Oneonta home. That may seem appropriate, as the office for SUNY's chancellor is located in the ex-D&H Plaza building in Albany, but is it fair for education to take over a railroad town and then the railroad's headquarters, too?

Of the two schools, Hartwick is the most senior, although it didn't get its start in Oneonta. Named for the Rev. John C. Hartwick, it began in 1816 on property he had owned before his 1796 death. The school was called Hartwick Seminary then, but when it planned a move to Oneonta in 1927 the Seminary became a College. A science building went under construction during 1928. The next year Hartwick College opened its doors to higher education, which seemed appropriate because its campus—then and now—can be found upon one of Oneonta's hills. Although the school has increased in size and enrollment, its territorial expansion includes Table Rocks, which overlooks Oneonta's West End. Table Rocks is noteworthy for several reasons. First, geologic formations that were found there may be the Indian meaning for the word "Oneonta." No one really knows the derivation of the name. Some claim that Oneonta was a lesser known daughter of Chief Schenevus.

Left: *Table Rocks rises high above Oneonta's West End where distant views of the railroad and the ancient Susquehanna valley and Otsego hills can be equally appreciated. Unfortunately, Interstate 88 occupies a portion of the view, while Route 7 passes unseen at the bottom of the hill. The railroad approaches Oneonta from the south in the middle distance where—earlier—the nearly four-mile-long yard began. Lutz Feed Company is in the middle of the scene in a location referred to as the "Hole." That was where the Southern New York Railway had earlier interchanged with the D&H; at least it did so until 1971.*

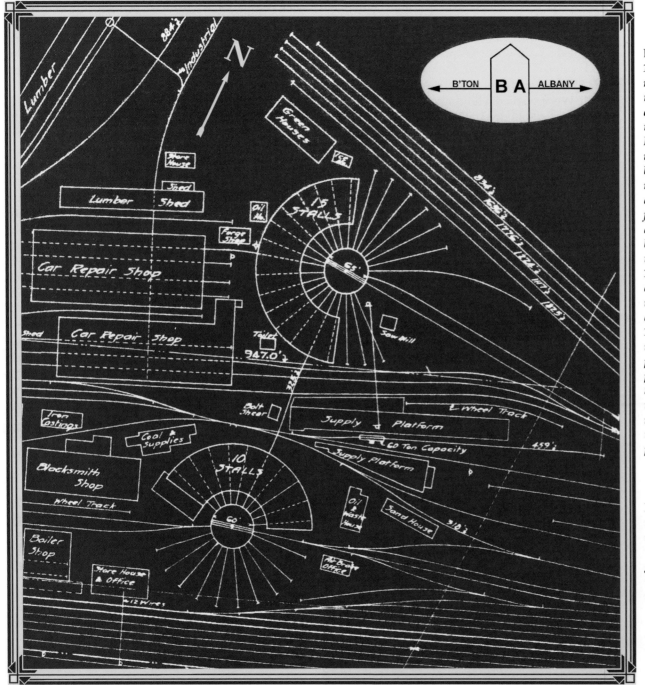

LEFT: *When Oneonta received the railroad's shops and 1871-1882 roundhouses it had secured its status as a railroad town and terminal. It would not be until the new fifty-two-stall roundhouse (facing page) was put into operation during May 1906 that the community achieved the fame that Harvey Baker had always thought it should have. By the time these Interstate Commerce Commission valuation maps were drawn in 1919, the new roundhouse had been in operation for thirteen years, while the original roundhouse had been reduced from twenty-two to ten stalls, and the 1882 roundhouse still displayed its original configuration. Both roundhouses, however, still had other open-air radial tracks emanating from their turntables. These two buildings — along with the shop buildings that surrounded them — were situated (railroad) north of Fonda Avenue. The 1906 roundhouse was built on the south side of Fonda Avenue. When the new fifty-two-stall roundhouse was opened it was proclaimed "The Largest Roundhouse in the World," and rightly so. With dimensions of 428 feet in diameter and 1,344 feet in circumference it was no small structure. Yet, with its completion, its most important purpose was achieved: providing adequate, efficient, speedy, and safe care and repair for the railroad's ever increasing steam locomotive fleet. Still, when viewed from Table Rocks (inset on facing page) the magnificent, large roundhouse paled in size to its surroundings, while at the same time it blended in and enhanced them all. In both maps, the apex of the directional milepost points toward the site of Table Rocks.*

FACING PAGE, INSET: *In this view (from Table Rocks) of the two-year-old "Largest Roundhouse in the World," the residential area along River Street on the far side of the tracks had yet to blossom. The yard itself was only beginning to spread southward. Both would eventually take place creating a larger classification facility for the railroad that, in turn, would help to bring about a population boom for Oneonta.*

BLUEPRINTS, NATIONAL ARCHIVES COLLECTION.

ROADS, RIVERS, AND RAILS

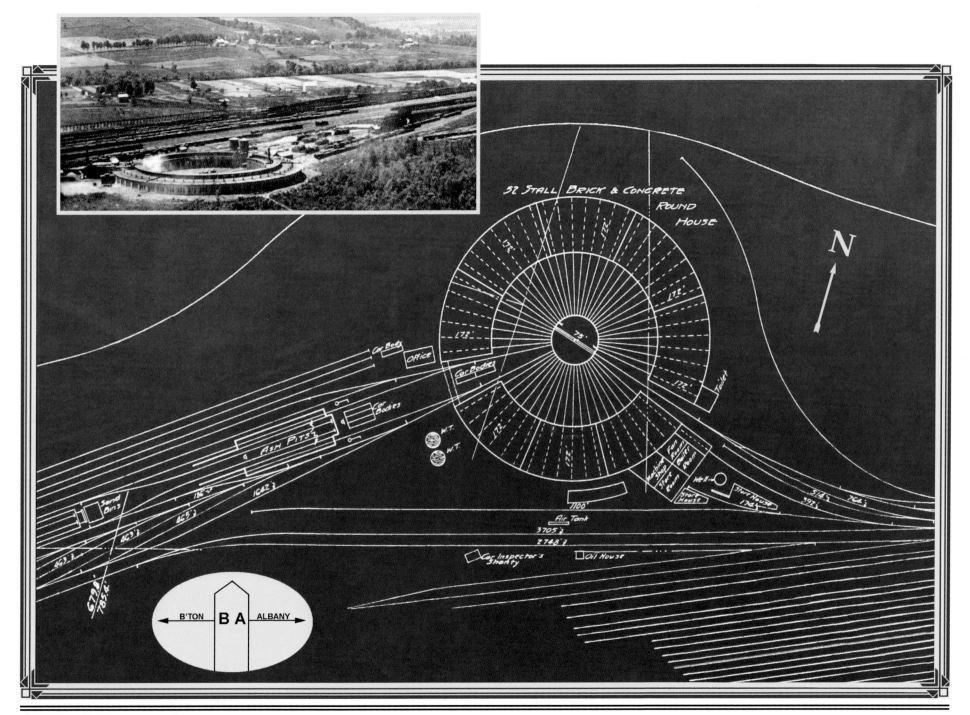

52 STALL BRICK & CONCRETE ROUND HOUSE

N

172'

172'

172'

172'

172'

172'

172'

172'

172'

75'

Toilet

Car Body

Office

Car Bodies

Car Bodies

W.T.

W.T.

Ash Pits

Machine Shop

Store Room

Boiler Room

Fan Room

Store House

Well

Store House 174'

Sand Bins

186'

1642'

465'

463'

1100

Air Tank

3705'

2748'

574'

597'

762'

Car Inspector's Shanty

Oil House

6198'

7854'

B'TON ← B A → ALBANY

BELOW: *Although Oneonta's roundhouse was the largest in the world (for about 24 years) it was three stalls shy of being completely circular. Two stalls were omitted so that two tracks could be used for locomotives to enter the facility, and another stall on the opposite side of the building was omitted so that engines could be dispatched via that track. The roundhouse cost $150,000, and for that money the railroad got fifty-two stalls, each eighty feet in length, and an attached machine shop and toilet room that sat abreast of the outbound track. In this view, which was taken from the coaling trestle, we're looking at the inbound opening to the roundhouse with the gable-roofed master mechanic's office located just outside stall No. 1. The two water tanks each held 80,000 gallons of water and just to their left is stall No. 52. Barely noticeable is the seventy-five-foot turntable, and ash pits where engine No. 797 and an unidentified locomotive are having their ashpans cleaned.*
LEFT: *Despite the as-built stall length, increasingly larger locomotives dictated longer stalls. Twenty-seven were lengthened to 100 feet by 1927. Nineteen more stalls were lengthened in 1942 and 1944 to 117 feet to accommodate the 116-foot-long J class Challengers with No. 1506's tender hanging outside the structure. Also to accommodate the larger engines, the turntable was lengthened to 105 feet in 1924.*

BELOW, A. BRUCE TRACY COLLECTION. LEFT, LEN KILIAN COLLECTION.

ROADS, RIVERS, AND RAILS

LEFT: *The sheer size of the Oneonta yard complex is effectively displayed here. The view also pinpoints lofty Table Rocks within the left corner of the frame. In the upper center the roundhouse can be discerned beyond the 500-foot-long elevated coal trestle (INSET) from which the lower picture on the previous page was taken. The trestle was wide enough for two tracks. Up to ten hopper cars loaded with coal could sit atop the structure before dumping their load into bins from which engine tenders would be chute-loaded. On March 13, 1946, this trestle was destroyed by a spectacular fire that unfortunately killed two D&H employees, and injured nine others. (ABOVE) Three months later, a modern coaling facility was under construction. When it was completed during December 1946 the concrete tipple could store 450 tons of coal, and distribute it into three locomotive tenders simultaneously. Its cost was $250,000, almost twice the price tag for the roundhouse that was built forty years earlier! In this view, Challenger No. 1500 is taking coal in preparation for another journey north or south on the Susquehanna Division. On the other side of the coal tipple—and barely discernible through its opening—were a pair of sand towers that were also used for providing an engine with sand for adhesion out on the road. This new coal and sand facility was built slightly further to the (railroad) south than had been the coaling trestle.*

LEFT, DEPOT SQUARE PUBLISHING COLLECTION.

ABOVE: *After Fonda Avenue was severed so that it did not cross the yard trackage any longer, the railroad erected a footbridge there in 1916. Pedestrians no longer had to walk across the tracks. From that footbridge the two views that look south (left and below) were taken, albeit during different eras. The 160-foot-tall smokestack seen in the distance in both views marks the location of the new powerhouse that was built in 1913 next to the fifty-two-stall roundhouse. Despite the different periods (circa 1920 left, and 1976 below) the yard appears to be very active in both scenes. For those of you with keen eyesight, the new coal tipple can be discerned just to the left of the smokestack in the view below. A corner of FA tower's roof can also be seen at lower right.*

LEFT: *The railroad built a highway bridge over its yard trackage at Richard's Crossing after closing the Fonda Avenue grade crossing. This bridge, which was constructed in 1906, allowed vehicles to cross from Oneonta's South Side to its West End so that the Main Street viaduct would not have to be used. Local folks called this bridge at Richard's Crossing the "Lower Viaduct" From it we look south, with the railroad's yard extending around the eastward bend all the way to Pony Farm at Glen's Bridge. All of the trackage has since been removed so that today's CPRail utilizes only one main line and one passing track. LEFT AND ABOVE LEFT: GREATER ONEONTA HISTORICAL SOCIETY COLLECTION. ABOVE, JERRY COYNE PHOTOGRAPH.*

ROADS, RIVERS, AND RAILS

Prior to 1904, Oneonta's Main Street crossed the railroad at grade with the station lying a short distance to the north, and the yards, shops, and roundhouses situated a slightly greater distance to the south. But, in 1904, the Main Street viaduct was built over the tracks; the D&H paid one-half its cost, Oneonta and New York State paid the other half. Both of these views, again from different eras, look south. The scene above was taken from the 1904 viaduct, and shows MX tower at right, and the railroad company's earlier coaling trestle in the distance; the roundhouses are just out of view behind the trees at right. Approximately one hundred years later, Norfolk Southern train 938 was photographed from the "new" Main Street bridge (built in 1979) headed north on CPRail's main track on February 13, 2010. The Oneonta passing siding, whose north switch is directly under the bridge, extends four miles to CPF557 at Glen's Bridge. The difference in the railroad's activity, trackage, and facilities of both eras is quite striking.

ABOVE, GREATER ONEONTA HISTORICAL SOCIETY COLLECTION.

With the railroad's ever expanding terminal facilities, a greater number of men and women were needed. They ran the roundhouses, shops, towers, station, and offices. Yardmen made up the trains so that engineers, firemen, trainmen, and conductors could take them out on the road to Albany, Schenectady, Binghamton, Carbondale and all points in between and beyond. LEFT: Engine tenders — or maybe shopmen — appear to be cuddling up to a warm D&H Consolidation on a cold winter day. BELOW LEFT: Trainmen and a conductor will soon be boarding their four-wheel bobber caboose for another trip over the line. RIGHT: These men staffed the dispatcher's office upstairs within the divisional offices above the freight house; the chief of course is sitting at the desk. BELOW RIGHT: These fellows pose for their picture within one of the D&H "Armstrong"-actuated interlocking towers at Oneonta. These towermen — maybe within FA or MX towers — used the levers in the foreground to change switches and signals so that trains and switchers could be routed correctly and safely. All of these men helped to bring prosperity to Oneonta, and a larger population as well.

ALL, GREATER ONEONTA HISTORICAL SOCIETY COLLECTION.

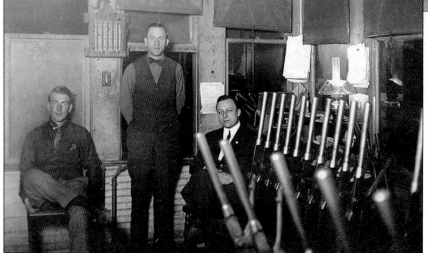

Regardless of how Oneonta got its name, Table Rocks has been there since before human habitation. From its heights, a marvelous view of the Susquehanna Valley unfolds to the west, and an equally marvelous perch it was to view the Susquehanna Division terminal of the Delaware & Hudson Railroad—especially the fifty-two-stall roundhouse that was built in 1906 and claimed the title of "Largest Roundhouse in the World" for a brief period of time. That's the second noteworthy feature of Table Rocks. Before 1906 and the big roundhouse, the land that Harvey Baker had brokered supported two smaller roundhouses: one originally built with eleven stalls, the other with fifteen. Both were only a large "slice of the pie" rather than a full circle like their big brother replacement. From Table Rocks, both of the earlier locomotive facilities could barely be seen as they were further to the north, but viewing them wasn't as awe inspiring as the sight of one big circular roundhouse with only two small slivers cut out of its 1,344-foot circumference so engines could enter and exit the roundhouse, after a spin on the seventy-five-foot turntable, of course.

The other institution of higher education in Oneonta cannot claim that its property affords a great view of the railroad, but it can claim that it got started before Hartwick College. It was one of the founding colleges for SUNY when that system was formed in 1948. But, the Oneonta Normal School first opened in 1889 as the third Normal School in the state. It was that institution that was the forerunner of SUNY Oneonta.

It is the students from these two colleges—supported by parental resources to be certain—that are doing the shopping and dining, keeping Route 7's sidewalks busy. It is from them and their colleges that Oneonta derives its vitality today. One cannot help but wonder, however, if that financial well-being is commensurate with that provided by the railroad's workers one hundred or more years ago.

When the railroad came to town in 1865, the population of Oneonta was listed as being 744 persons. Six years later, after the erection of roundhouse No. 1—an eleven-stall affair, and the shop buildings, as staked out by R. C. Blackall and H. A. Fonda, Oneonta's population had swelled to 1,787 people. Many of the newly located 1,043 people surely worked for the railroad. They built at least one locomotive there: 4-4-0 No. 237 in 1898. Repairing locomotives, however, was to be their forte, and the railroad provided robust facilities for them to do so. The original roundhouse that had opened on January 18, 1871, had eleven additional stalls added in 1876. Six years later a second roundhouse, encompassing fifteen stalls, was also built on the Watkins property nearby the first roundhouse. Additionally, the railroad erected buildings where machine work, boiler repair, blacksmithing, forging, casting, carpentry, and freight car and passenger car repair could be undertaken. These buildings were the "shops." Even a greenhouse would be added to the complex so that the men could work amongst flower gardens, no matter how out of place the greenery seemed.

LEFT: Oneonta's Lower Viaduct at Richard's Crossing was still under construction by the railroad when this picture was taken in 1906. ABOVE: That same year, its two spans crossed the railroad and allowed vehicles to cross from the community's South Side to the West End. The narrow gauge track was used to fill the embankment that would become the bridge approach from the South Side. At right above, the roadway dropped into the "Hole."

LEFT, DEPOT SQUARE PUBLISHING COLLECTION. ABOVE, A. BRUCE TRACY COLLECTION.

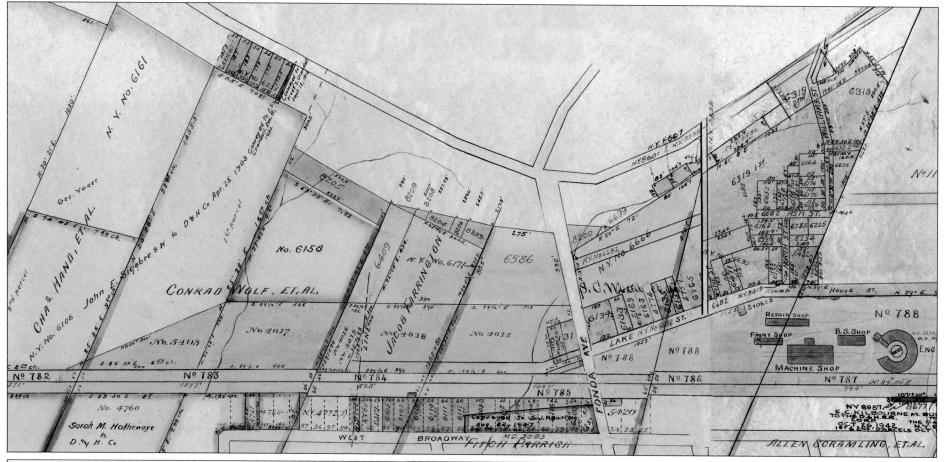

ABOVE: *Although this hand-drawn, colorized map is from an earlier period when only the original roundhouse was present, it adequately portrays the scope of the area from which the railroad extended from the passenger station (facing page, right) to where the 1906 roundhouse would be located at the extreme left. Additionally, it also displays the area where Jared Goodyear's Oneonta property was (far right) that was rejected for use for the roundhouse and shops area, as well as the relationship of the business district (tan color) to that of the railroad's facilities (light red).*

LEFT: *When the community's 1892 passenger station was still new, flower gardens, shrubbery, and manicured lawns all enhanced its Howe's Cave limestone appearance and conveyed to passen-*

ROADS, RIVERS, AND RAILS

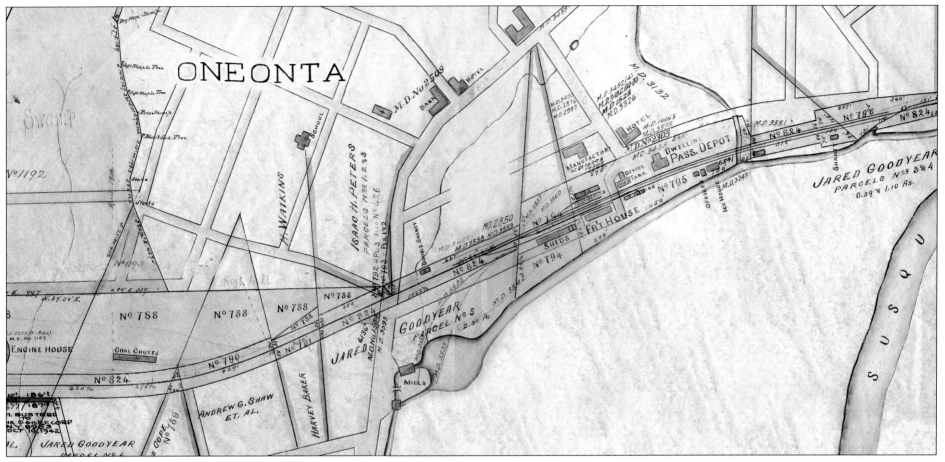

ONEONTA

SUSQU...

gers the feeling that Oneonta was a prosperous community that was on the move. And, it was! All of the flowers and shrubs were grown at the railroad company's greenhouse that was located in the shop area. Its personnel tended to all the lawns and gardens throughout the Oneonta terminal area. RIGHT: As time wore on, the economies of the Loree era caused a downgrading in the once impeccable appearance of the depot, which created a more business-like environment for the railroad's setting. Still, a double-track mainline, a siding closest to the depot, and an abundance of sidings in the coach yard all substantiated the fact that the Delaware & Hudson Company was providing timely, efficient, and superior passenger service on its Susquehanna Division.

MAP, WALTER G. RICH COLLECTION. FACING PAGE, A. BRUCE TRACY COLLECTION.
RIGHT, DEPOT SQUARE PUBLISHING COLLECTION.

ABOVE: *On Page 183 we were treated to southerly views of the railroad from the Main Street viaduct, so on this page we compliment them with northerly views from the 1904 viaduct and 1979 bridge. In the vintage scene, a two-car passenger train has just departed Oneonta's station (obscured by the steam plume) on a cold winter day. The trackwork in this downtown area is extensive, and contrasts sharply with what remains today, at right: only a single track mainline.* RIGHT: *Although this view is also a wintertime scene, there is no vapor to hide the appearance of the passenger station-turned Stella Luna Restaurant and the two-story ex-freight house that has been heavily modified for college student housing. The upper floor of the freight house was added in 1939 to accommodate the Susquehanna Division offices that had earlier been located within rooms of the Central Hotel. Norfolk Southern train 939 is slowing as it prepares to enter the passing siding whose switch is directly under the photographer's vantage point.*

ABOVE: A. BRUCE TRACY COLLECTION.

Delaware & Hudson President Leonor F. Loree, despite his "day's work for a day's pay" edict, thought that flower gardens would help attain his workmen's goal and beautify the terminal at the same time. He was right; now if he only had stokers applied to his steam engines that would make all of the firemen happy, too.

Just as certainly as manpower had increased at the shops and roundhouse, it was the employee's salaries that caused merchant prosperity along Main Street. Without the railroad and its workers Oneonta would not have been able to prosper and grow, a condition that became an ever increasing reality by the time 1,500 men—out of Oneonta's 8,000 residents in 1940—were employed by the railroad. By then, the D&H presence in Oneonta had reached its zenith. The shops, roundhouse, and yard had all been enlarged and modernized so that the railroad's footprint extended from the Main Street viaduct over the railroad (that replaced a crossing at grade in 1904) to beyond Richard's Crossing (the so-called "Lower Viaduct" that was built by the railroad in 1906) all the way to Glen's Bridge near the Pony Farm—a total distance of just over four miles in length. At its widest point, the railroad's facilities nearly occupied all of the land between Chestnut Street's "Chinese Wall" (that was built to hold back the mountain below Table Rocks) and River Street, a distance of over one-half mile. For these dimensional reasons, the D&H at Oneonta can be favorably compared to that of the New York Central Railroad and its Selkirk Yard of the same period, or the Pennsylvania Railroad's Enola Yard at Harrisburg, PA, or even the Norfolk & Western Railroad's Schaffer's Crossing terminal at Roanoke, VA, all of which are noteworthy railroading centers.

At its height of activity, the D&H's Oneonta freight terminal saw the arrival and departure of over 4,000 freight cars a day. It was where 134 engineers, 148 firemen, 209 trainmen, and seventy-four conductors called home. That was in 1924. Over at the passenger station (in 1931) four northbound and four southbound trains made stops at the new station on a daily basis; two trains each way on Sunday. Except for its passenger trains from Albany to Montreal, the D&H could never be considered a "passenger" railroad as it was coal and freight that paid the bills and employee salaries. Oneonta was always first and foremost a freight terminal, especially after the D&H purchased 350 acres of land (beginning in 1906) to enlarge the yard mostly south of Fonda Avenue. When Howard W. Hontz hired out on the D&H as an Oneonta assistant yard clerk on January 15, 1942, the hump yard was classifying over 2,000 cars a day! (That was during the early World War II years, so activity at the yard would certainly increase.) Forty years later, he had risen through the ranks to become Assistant to the President of the railroad. A little later on I'll tell you more about Howard, Jean Ward (his wife), and Table Rocks.

Metropolitan Oneonta (it became a city in 1909) is today a little over four square miles in size and residentially spread out as opposed to yesteryear's neighborhoods. Regardless, the railroad's property commands at least one of those four square miles. So, keep in mind, that as we drive along Main and Chestnut streets and are pleased to see that Oneonta is thriving, it was the Delaware & Hudson Company that had first elevated the community to financial well being. Just imagine what Oneonta

would be if its railroad terminal facilities were still thriving, too! But, they are not. The D&H's "new" depot is over one hundred years old but now it houses a fine restaurant named Stella Luna. The Ulster & Delaware's station is over a hundred years old and it's a restaurant, too: "The Depot." The D&H brick freight house that lies just to the north of the Stella Luna, where a second floor was added to accommodate Susquehanna Division offices, is now an apartment complex. The dispatcher who controlled the 1940 CTC installation was located on the second floor of the freight house, too. And, I hate to tell you what's happened to the shops, roundhouse, its new 105-foot turntable (that was installed in one day on January 7, 1924), and the yards: they are all gone. Just a single mainline track, and a pass-

ABOVE: *In 1972, Howard W. Hontz (center) was the D&H Railroad's Superintendent. With him are General Superintendent H. J. Farley (left) and Superintendent of Transportation F. W. Hewitt.* HOWARD W. HONTZ COLLECTION. BELOW: *On January 29, 2010, southbound train 939 is passing through Oneonta's East End along Railroad Avenue, and is abreast of the ex-U&DRR station that is now a restaurant known as The Depot. Compare this view with the historic picture on Page 170.*

How to Install a Turntable in One Day

When "The Largest Roundhouse in the World" was completed in 1906, a seventy-five-foot "balanced" turntable rotated locomotives into and out of the fifty-two-stall roundhouse. By 1923, however, steam engines had lengthened. This prompted the D&H to provide the facility with a longer turntable while also extending the roundhouse stalls. The difficulty was not the installation of a new turntable; it was doing so as quickly as possible to avoid service disruptions at the busy Oneonta terminal. Plans were adopted for a 105-foot-long turntable, the materials were acquired, and all feasible pre-installation work was completed. January 7, 1924 was chosen as the date for the removal of the old turntable and the placement of its successor. On that day, electric power to the condemned sev-

enty-five-foot turntable was shut off. Seven hours and thirty-eight minutes later, the new 105-foot turntable was completely installed and handed over to the Operating Department for use. The heart of the Oneonta terminal had hardly skipped a beat. FACING PAGE: Prior to cutting the power, Class B-1b double cab 0-6-0 No. 21 performs some last minute work as the last locomotive to utilize the old turntable. ABOVE LEFT: At 8:07 AM, workmen prepare the turntable for removal. Its thirty-foot-longer replacement is being positioned beside the shorter span. ABOVE RIGHT: Cranes hoist the old turntable from the pit and slowly move it to the side so that its two-piece, non-balanced replacement can be installed. BELOW LEFT: The new turntable has been lowered into position and is being readied to receive

the electricity that will bring it to life. BELOW RIGHT: Soon after power was restored, Class P 4-6-2 No. 600 is called upon to test the turntable's operation, thus becoming the first locomotive to use it. Despite the added length of the new span, the 116-foot Class J 4-6-6-4s could not be turned without first disconnecting their tenders. This extra step required twice the work to attain the desired result. We wonder what President Loree would have thought of that additional time and manpower. But, he had vacated the presidency two years before the arrival of the Challengers, which were delivered from ALCo with mechanical stokers — a device not within the vocabulary of L. F. Loree.

At about the same time that the railroad was building shops and roundhouses on the Watkins property, less than a dozen homes lined the unimproved lane that was named for H. A. Fonda. In this view (LEFT) that looks north towards Table Rocks, the foreground wye leads right to the original shops area, the left fork will lead to the future site for the "big" roundhouse. Behind the photographer, Fonda Avenue crossed the railroad's tracks at grade, a circumstance eventually causing the closure of the road and the building of the Lower Viaduct. Ten years later, the railroad erected a footbridge (LOWER LEFT) to keep pedestrians from walking across the track. Its cost was $19,054.91—no small sum in 1916. The footbridge passed just behind FA Tower (BELOW), which was built during the railroad's yard expansion south during the first decade of the Twentieth Century. The car shop is visible below the bridge in this 1950s scene

LEFT, GREATER ONEONTA HISTORICAL SOCIETY COLLECTION.
BELOW, LEN KILIAN COLLECTION.

ing siding that extends from CPF553 to 557, remain. Current owner CPRail does have a small maintenance facility where the shops had been off of Fonda Avenue, but the old shop buildings themselves have been mostly razed. All that does remain of the once superlative terminal facilities can be seen from Table Rocks: the footprint (foundation) of the big roundhouse, the 160-foot-tall smokestack built in 1913 when a new power-house was erected, and the 1946-built coal tipple that replaced an earlier coaling trestle destroyed by fire on March 13 of that same year. The new coaling facility was constructed at a cost of $250,000, which was $100,000 more than it cost to build the fifty-two-stall roundhouse! The price for many things, it seems, had substantially increased between 1906 and 1946.

Fonda Avenue, named for H. A. Fonda who assisted Blackall in laying out the shop/roundhouse area in 1871, at one time connected Oneonta's West End Chinese Wall along Route 7 with the South Side's River Street. That meant that the street crossed nearly the full width of the yard at one time. It was a nice shortcut for buggies and pedestrians to get from one side of town to the other. But, as the yard complex became more active Fonda Avenue was severed. That is why the rail-road built the new Lower Viaduct in 1906 so that a short-cut across town could still be made, albeit a little further to the south. Mr. Fonda's name had also been perpetu-ated by an interlocking tower initialed and coded FA. It stood where his street had earlier crossed the yard's throat. Although the Lower Viaduct was supposed to replace the Fonda Avenue crossing at grade, and it did for buggies and later cars, people still could walk across the yard tracks to get from the West End to the South Side. The railroad put an end to this "trespassing" by erecting a steel footbridge across the yard during 1916 at a cost of $19,054.91. After that, persons could pass safely, and the railroad could go about its business se-curely, too. But, the footbridge and the tower are both just memories today as well. Footings for the bridge, and a foundation for the tower are all that remain in place. The footbridge, acting in much the same fashion as the Brooker Hollow Road bridge, did double-duty as a platform for railroad photography. And, the tower

actually still exists—in part. It was dismantled by the Leatherstocking Railway Historical Society (who oper-ate the Cooperstown & Charlotte Valley Railroad ex-cursion trains) and its pieces were taken to Cooperstown Junction where they lie in a pile in the weeds with the slate roof still trying to protect the remains from the elements. One day, I'm told, the LRHS plans to re-erect the tower.

Besides the Delaware & Hudson and the Ulster & Delaware (New York Central) there was another rail-road that came to Oneonta beginning in 1885. This was then a horse-powered trolley line that got a name,

Oneonta Street Railway, in 1887 and rails in 1888. The rails were laid within Main and Chestnut streets—right where we are riding now—from Oneonta's East End (where the horse barns were) to Fonda Avenue, 2.25 miles distant.

In 1897, the trolley line changed owners and names for the first of six times, and the Oneonta & Otego Valley Railroad was extended and electrified to West Oneonta. Then, it was the Oneonta, Cooperstown & Richfield Springs Railway that further extended the line to Cooperstown (1901), Richfield Springs (1902), and on to Mohawk and Herkimer (via the Utica &

ABOVE: Not long after the 1908 formation of the Otsego & Herkimer Railroad (successor to the O&O, OC&RS, and O&MV) an electrified 90-series car has come to a stop on Oneonta's Main Street to pick up riders in front of the Central Hotel. Regardless of era, pedestrians were always on the move around the city's business district.

DEPOT SQUARE PUBLISHING COLLECTION.

Mohawk Valley Railway) in 1904 and 1906 respectively. Ultimately, Herkimer and Oneonta were the termini. A branch from Index served Cooperstown. Shops were built at Hartwick Seminary.

By the time the OC&RS reached Herkimer, it had simultaneously reached the end of its (corporate) line and run out of electric power, too. The Oneonta & Mohawk Valley Railway, another new corporate title, soldiered on admirably by building a new electric generating station at Colliers that was envisioned to supply electric power for the entire line. The Susquehanna River was dammed so that a lake was formed over the property of the Collier family grist mill, but the name, Goodyear Lake, was a remembrance of Jared rather than Isaac or Peter. Despite the facility's completion in 1907, and a healthy supply of electricity coursing through its wires (and some "juice" being used by online villages) the O&MV failed the following year and was re-organized as the Otsego & Herkimer Railroad. Then, in 1916, another corporate name change to the Southern New York Power & Railway Company, a name that better applied to the purposes of the corporation. But that name may have alerted the federal government to their dual role as a supplier and user of power. In 1924, the government dictated that railroads and power companies could not own each other, so the railway had to divest itself from power generation. Naturally, the company floundered once again, and a final change of title took place that same year to the Southern New York Railroad.

Prior to 1924, however, the electric line had already begun to suffer from the same malady as steam railroads: the intrusion of motorized vehicles and improved roadways. Consequently, it abandoned service to Richfield Springs in 1917, curtailed service on Oneonta's Main and Chestnut streets in 1923, and ended all Oneonta local service in 1931. Two years later, all remaining passenger service was discontinued and the line became freight-only from the D&H connection in the "Hole" at Oneonta's West End to the north.

In 1939, the H. E. Salzburg Corporation took over operation of the SNY, and they curtailed service to Cooperstown in 1940 as well as the entire line north of

West Oneonta the next year. Somehow, the SNY was able to stay in business even after the New York Central had cut back its ex-U&D line from Oneonta to Bloomville during July 1965. But even the SNY eventually died from a lack of freight revenue in March 1971. In Oneonta, there isn't much left of the old Southern New York Railroad, and that's because the Lutz Feed Company facility in the "Hole" has consumed the entire interchange area where the SNY got its cars from the D&H. The Lutz company, by the way, is one of only three feed dealers along CPRail's line that receives cars and switching services from the railroad. The feed mill in the "Hole" is situated at the north end of the old Lower Viaduct at Richard's Crossing.

It was only a year or two after the New York Central discontinued service into Oneonta that Unadilla railroad historian, Jean Banta, had suggested to Walter Rich that the Oneonta-to-Bloomville portion of the old Ulster & Delaware might make for a profitable excursion operation. Walter embraced the idea, and negotiated a deal with the NYC to acquire the Oneonta-to-Mickle Bridge portion of the discontinued line. Being an historically-minded person, Walter named his new enterprise the Delaware Otsego Line (DO Line for short), and from this beginning he set out on his pre-destined course to become a railroad magnate, which he successfully accomplished. The DO Line, however, was not to be long lasting as it was in the way of New York State's plans for construction of Interstate 88. When Conductor Billy Galpin called the final "all-aboard" in November 1970, the DO Line operation ceased and moved to the ex-D&H Cooperstown Branch the following year with the City of the Hills then becoming only a one railroad town again. And, it still is.

I've been driving as slow as I can down Main Street while I told you all about Oneonta's glorious railroad history. Fortunately, a handful of traffic lights have helped by giving me time to do so. But, it's beginning to get late so let's head over to the Neptune Diner for supper. Afterwards, we will watch the sunset from Table Rocks. It's a good place for doing that, too.

There are a lot of fine restaurants in Oneonta, and I suppose it would be appropriate if we had dinner at

ABOVE: *During the final years of its operation, the Southern New York Railway used engine No. 5 (and a near identical brother) to operate from West Oneonta to the D&H interchange in Oneonta. The railroad's trainmen are in the process of running down into The Hole to pick up cars from its Class One supplier. The boxcar sits on a team track awaiting unloading. Beyond it is the approach to the Lower Viaduct from the West End side. Lutz Feed Company now occupies this site.*

LEN KILIAN COLLECTION.

ABOVE: *Walter Rich's DO Line No. 2 is outbound from Oneonta to Mickle Bridge in October 1970. The locomotive is an ex-Army 0-6-0. The railroad proper is the ex-Ulster & Delaware mainline. During the following month operations out of Oneonta will cease, and the entire enterprise will move its headquarters to Cooperstown to be run as the Cooperstown & Charlotte Valley Railway.*

the Stella Luna, or at my favorite restaurant, Michael's, over on River Street, but I like the Neptune Diner for its home-style menu, its old-fashioned hospitality, its considerate pricing, and its being a reminder of many similar diners on Long Island. One time, when Dad was taking us on one of his patented Sunday drives, we ended up at the Islip Diner, on Montauk Highway just across the road from Islip's town hall. Rich and I both ordered hamburgers, something Mom never made at home. It was a real treat to have a hamburger then, as the first McDonald's we knew—which was also located in Islip—had yet to be built or maybe even envisioned by Ray Kroc. I think you will agree, that diners make the best burgers and hot dogs, too. Tomorrow we'll stop at Bob's Diner in Bainbridge for their Foot-Long Super Dog!

ABOVE: *An excellent example of public or private re-use of a former railroad station is shown here. The D&H's centerpiece in Oneonta has been converted into the popular Stella Luna restaurant, where today, northbound Norfolk Southern train 938 forms the backdrop with a string of autoracks bound for interchange with SMS at Delanson, NY. The old freight house is at left.*

ABOVE: *As the DO Line's No. 2 simmers near its Oneonta depot (far right) while awaiting its next run to Mickle Bridge, two of the Delaware & Hudson's celebrated PA ALCo-built passenger engines strut by headed south with a business train bound for Binghamton. Because of turbocharger "lag" when the throttle for the PA's 244 ALCo diesel engine was being advanced, excess unburned fuel caused black smoke to be exhausted, which provided the locomotives with their title of "Honorary Steam Locomotives."* PHOTOGRAPH BY WILLIAM S. YOUNG.

The Neptune Diner is located on Route 28 within Oneonta's South Side. To get there, we'll stay on Main Street, which crosses the railroad on a new viaduct built in 1979. Directly below this overpass is CPF553 where the north switch for Oneonta's passing siding begins. By looking to the right here (railroad south) you can glimpse the vacant land where the 1871 and 1882 roundhouses had been located. They haven't been there since being taken down in 1927. Then, we will pass River Street on the right, and the entrance to Neawha Park on the left (that's where the Brotherhood of Railroad Brakemen (later Trainmen) caboose No. 10 memorial is located.

At Route 28, a turn to the left will take us to the diner where along the way Oneonta's modern business district is situated: Hannaford's, Home Depot, the South Side Mall, and a number of other fine restaurants (Sabattini's is another favorite). Our diner is just across the road from the mall.

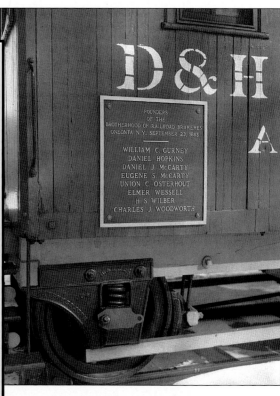

Oneonta can lay claim to the facts that it was where Collis P. Huntington got his start; that it housed The Largest Roundhouse in the World and the largest turntable, too. While both of these historical facts center around railroading, there is a third. On the evening of September 23, 1883, eight Delaware & Hudson brakemen met in four-wheel bobber caboose No. 10 to discuss the need for an organization to protect themselves and other members of their craft. After this informal meeting, the men met formally in Oneonta's Blend Hall to draft the constitution and by-laws for creating the Brotherhood of Railroad Brakemen that was ratified by thirty-three other attending brakemen. Thus, the BofRB was formed, and this group of D&H workers who formed the brotherhood was named Grand Lodge No. 1. The eight founding fathers of the BofRB were: William C. Gurney, Daniel Hopkins, Daniel J. McCarthy, Eugene S. McCarthy, Union C. Osterhout, Elmer Wessel, H. S. Wilber, and Charles J. Woodworth. On October 20, 1884, the 1st annual convention of the BofRB was held in Oneonta; five years later the organization's name was changed to the Brotherhood of Railroad Trainmen. What became of caboose No. 10? It was eventually taken out of train service and brought to Glen's Bridge where it became a truck-less tool house. It languished there for many years until a memorial was desired for the group's founding. In 1924, No. 10 was brought to the shops where it was refurbished and readied to be put on display in Oneonta's Neawha Park.

On September 24, 1924, the caboose was enshrined undercover in the park (ABOVE LEFT), and placed upon it was a plaque that listed the eight founding fathers of the brotherhood (ABOVE RIGHT). On that day, three of the eight men (along with one man of the group of thirty-three ratifiers) posed in front of the historic caboose (RIGHT). They were: Gurney, Woodworth (whose assigned caboose had been No. 10 at the time of the informal meeting), Martin Ryan, and Elmer Wessel.

ABOVE LEFT AND RIGHT, DANTE TRANQUILLE PHOTOGRAPHS. RIGHT, GREATER ONEONTA HISTORICAL SOCIETY COLLECTION.

By the time that the Soaring Sixties came, the once timely scheduling of passenger service on the Susquehanna Division had been reduced to just one single roundtrip daily. Every day, train 205 left Binghamton, and after its arrival at Albany Union Station's lower level, the southbound version, train 208, made its way back to the Parlor City. On August 24, 1962 (ABOVE) northbound train 205 is stopped at Oneonta's station. While it appears at least three persons will be boarding the train, Railway Express Company business is being conducted from the train's baggage/parcel car. In the Delaware & Hudson's annual report for that year, stockholders were advised (ABOVE RIGHT) regarding the company's passenger service on both the Champlain and Susquehanna divisions. The last four lines are particularly telling: "…we will do everything possible to operate this service as attractively as possible, with the hope that patronage will warrant its continuance." But, that would not be the case. During 1962, several meetings were held in Albany where the railroad made its case for the discontinuation of trains 205-208. The railroad advised the Public Service Commission members, and other interested parties, that it had lost $35,777 on Susquehanna Division passenger service in 1961, and that during the first half of 1962 it had already lost $33,823. Additionally, the railroad provided Greyhound officer A. D. Betts to advise the members that it was providing more than adequate service should the railroad cease running its trains. Speaking for the public were Senator Warren M. Anderson, Brotherhood of Locomotive Fireman & Enginemen Chairman Lewis H. Baisden, representatives of the BofRT, REA, Town of Afton Supervisor Ernest Poole, and Floyd Conklin who represented several communities along the line affected. Their pleas for continued service were not persuasive enough to keep Judge Jacob C. Rothstein from setting aside January 24, 1963 as the last day for Susquehanna Division passenger service. On that wintry day, train 205 was delayed leaving Binghamton because of a frozen steam generator in the train's locomotive, and another engine had to be sent down from Albany. While the replacement engine was added to the train, Susquehanna Valley Historical Society members loaded a symbolic coffin into the train's baggage car (RIGHT). The men were (clockwise from lower left) John J. Young, Jr., Tom Carter, Richard Allen, Clarence Tharp, and Horace Boyd. Unfortunately, the word "passenger" was misspelled.

ABOVE, GREATER ONEONTA HISTORICAL SOCIETY COLLECTION. RIGHT, BROOME COUNTY HISTORICAL SOCIETY COLLECTION.

"Because of reduced patronage, the Public Service Commission of New York, upon application by the Delaware and Hudson Railroad, permitted discontinuance last fall of the only commuter trains operated by the Delaware and Hudson between Saratoga Springs and Albany. Then upon further application the Commission granted authority to discontinue the last passenger train service operated between Binghamton and Albany. Thus, the only passenger train service remaining consists of a day train and night train operated between New York City and Montreal in conjunction with the New York Central. While patronage on these trains has decreased during the last three or four years because of air line and private automobile competition, we will do everything possible to operate this service as attractively as possible, with the hope that patronage will warrant its continuance."

BELOW: *Once the train got to Albany, the coffin was taken off—and then put back on—the train. In so doing, (l/r) Tharp, Allen, Carter, Young, and Boyd pause for a moment while an unknown bugler blows taps. Too bad Worcester Civil War bugler Seth Flint was not around to perform "last call" now as he did at Appomattox.*
ABOVE, JOHN J. YOUNG, JR. PHOTOGRAPH.
BOTH, SUSQUEHANNA VALLEY
HISTORICAL SOCIETY COLLECTION.

ABOVE: *On January 24, 1963, the last train 205 stopped at Oneonta where a multitude of folks are getting on and off the train. Even at this late date, the Railway Express Agency is still conducting business with the railroad. What will REA and these people do tomorrow? Take Route 7, of course, as I-88 did not exist.*

I'm going to have a 'burger, and while we wait for our meals let me tell you more about Howard and Jean Hontz. I previously mentioned that Howard hired out on the Delaware & Hudson as an assistant yard clerk on January 15, 1942. But, this story really begins long before then, back to the previous generation of two families: the Hontzes and the Wards.

George L. Hontz, Howard's father, was born in Shickshinny, PA on August 20, 1887. Hontz ancestors began arriving in America not long after William Penn started settling an area that would become the state named for him. At about the age of 23, George started railroading with the New York, Ontario & Western Railway at nearly the same time the road was receiving its new W-class 2-8-0 engines in 1910 (nicknamed "Long Johns"). Being an O&W fireman based out of Mayfield, PA did not satisfy the new railroader. By 1915 he had switched employment to the Delaware & Hudson at Carbondale. Five years later, George married Bessie Fay (on October 4, 1920). Within a year or two of that blissful day, he was promoted to engineer, but not "set up" yet. Thus, he was still firing locomotives, while running off the "extra" board. Eventually Hontz became an engineer, moving to Oneonta with Bessie, where Howard was born. A brother, Glenn, was born in Plattsburg in 1928; George moved the family there to become the railroad's Champlain Division Road Foreman of Engines. William "Bill" Wallace was the Division Superintendent at the time. When Wallace was re-assigned to become the D&H Susquehanna Division Superintendent, he took the Hontz family with him to Oneonta. (Bill Wallace, you may recall was the fellow all the way on the right in the back row of that grouping of Eastern Signal Engineers.) At Oneonta, George Hontz became the division Road Foreman of Engines with his office overlooking the railroad from the second story divisional offices above the freight house.

Meantime, while Engineer Hontz was successfully pursuing his career with the D&H, so was Russell S. Ward, who had been born in Wales in 1885. Russell's father, William, was a coal miner there, but immigration to America took place not long after Russell was born. Being a coal miner, it was only natural for William

ABOVE: Around the age of 23, George (center left) went railroading with the New York, Ontario & Western Railway. This was about the same time (1910) that the O&W was receiving its new W-class 2-8-0 engines—referred to as "Long Johns." RIGHT: George Hontz at his office in Oneonta. BOTH, JEAN AND HOWARD HONTZ COLLECTION.

to bring his family to the Lackawanna Valley of Pennsylvania where anthracite coal mining was then King. Russell, however, did not take to mining as it was machinery that intrigued him. So, he went to the D&H at Carbondale where Charles Norris was the Master Mechanic, and applied for a job. He got much more than that. So did Mr. Norris, who not only got a good worker but a son-in-law as well.

Not long after Russell Ward married Frances Norris, the couple moved to Oneonta where work in the roundhouse(s) and shops there were somewhat of a promotion for him. But, by the time the couple's daughter, Jean, was born in 1922, Russell had become a foreman in the "big" roundhouse. The next year, Howard was born, and after a few years the two toddlers would both begin attending school: Jean in Oneonta and Howard in Plattsburg, where the Hontz family moved in 1927. The two had yet to meet.

When Jean was a young girl, she and her girlfriends liked to go to the top of Table Rocks, which was handy for Jean because that was just a short (uphill) hike from her West Street home. Sometimes the girls would go up to Table Rocks just to play, sometimes to pick For-

get-me-nots to use in making May baskets, and sometimes Jean would go there with just a peanut butter and jelly sandwich and look down at the roundhouse where her father worked.

It was 1938 when Bill Wallace brought the Hontz family back to Oneonta, and by that time Howard and

Jean's father, Russell S. Ward, takes a break outside the D&H shops at Carbondale, PA. (All images on this and the following page are from the Jean and Howard Hontz collection.)

Jean Ward, age 11

Jean Ward Hontz and Howard W. Hontz on their wedding day, October 3, 1943.

Jean were teenagers. And, it was just about that time that Russell Ward had been promoted to General Foreman at the roundhouse. All fifty-two stalls were his domain. Whether boss or worker, being in the roundhouse was a hot and dirty place to be, but sometimes during the summer Jean and her mother would bring homemade ice cream to help keep Russell's day cool. Both Russell and George knew and respected one another, even though their offices were across town from each other. George made sure engineers didn't abuse their locomotives, which pleased Russell, and if the engines did require fixing, Russell's men repaired them, which pleased George.

With both families now in Oneonta, and Jean and Howard being teenagers, it was only natural that girl and boy would meet, and that occurred at one of the school's proms. Neither had a date, and neither would go unless they had one. A friend advised Howard that "Jean Ward didn't have a date," but soon she did and she went to the prom on Howard's arm. That was the beginning of their life together. They were married on October 3, 1943, when Howard was home on leave from his military duty. He could have gotten a deferment because he worked for the railroad, but he chose to serve his country. Instead, he served in Europe with the 12th Army Air Force's 310th Bomb Group—Jimmy Doolittle's Boys.

During those war years, Howard's father was diagnosed with leukemia and he had to step down from his duty as Road Foreman. He was, however, appointed the D&H System Rules Examiner, and provided car No. 653, a former pay car, in which to tour the system to provide rules instruction and examinations.

When Howard returned to Oneonta and Jean, after being discharged on November 10, 1945, he beat a path home and resumed his $149 per month duties at the D&H yard. Constant promotions were a part of his future. On November 11, 1949, he was promoted to Relief Yardmaster at Binghamton, and in 1955 he and Jean were back in Oneonta. He was Assistant Trainmaster beginning May 16; she, an employee of Wilber National Bank. (We went by that Main Street bank earlier.) George Hontz was not able to celebrate his son's return to Oneonta; he had passed away on May 2, 1951 having never taken a vacation or even a few days off! George Hontz was a proud company man through and through. Russell Ward retired sometime shortly after George's death.

On July 1, 1958, Howard was appointed Trainmaster at Carbondale; then Chief Trainmaster-System exactly one year later. This latter promotion took the Hontz family to Albany where, with his next promotion to Assistant Superintendent of the Railroad (May 15, 1971), it provided him with an office in the tower of the railroad's Plaza Building headquarters. Russell Ward had died three years previously. Then, in quick succession, Howard rose to Superintendent of the Railroad (February 1, 1972), General Superintendent-Operations (July 1, 1973, the Plaza Building was sold the following month; his office was in the new headquarters building located at 40-44 Beaver Street in Albany), Vice-President-Operations (October 1, 1973), and finally to his most lofty position, Assistant to the President (K. P. Shoemaker) on March 1, 1981.

The following year, on July 7, 1982, Timothy Mellon's Guilford Transportation was given permission by the Interstate Commerce Commission to acquire control of the Delaware & Hudson Railroad. With that impending transfer of ownership, which eventually occurred on January 5, 1984, Howard decided that it was time to retire. Casting aside pleas from President Shoemaker to remain to assist the railroad in its transition to Guilford, he retired effective March 30, 1983. Thus ended the family's association with the Delaware & Hudson Railroad, an association formed by George Hontz and Russell Ward over sixty years earlier. Jean and Howard were blessed to have two children; Robert an Air Force officer in Colorado, and Brian who is currently the Regional Director of the Federal Railroad Administration in Washington, D. C. It is their grandson, Todd, however, that is continuing to associate the family name with the ex-Delaware & Hudson Railroad. He's a CPRail engineer working out of Saratoga Springs, NY.

Guilford and CPRail would eventually cause the complete shutdown of Oneonta's yard and shops on February 16, 1996, but it was the D&H who began that process in 1954, the year after the railroad became fully dieselized. On

Glenn, Howard, and George Hontz in July 1943 when George was the D&H System Rules Examiner with car No. 653 at his disposal.

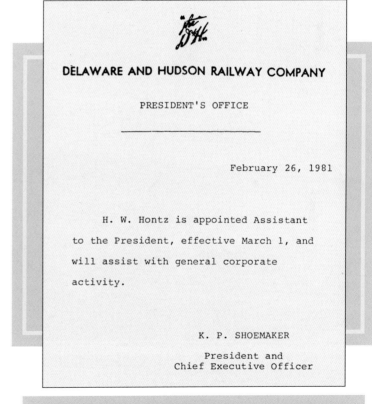

DELAWARE AND HUDSON RAILWAY COMPANY

PRESIDENT'S OFFICE

_____

February 26, 1981

H. W. Hontz is appointed Assistant to the President, effective March 1, and will assist with general corporate activity.

K. P. SHOEMAKER

President and
Chief Executive Officer

ABOVE: *This announcement informed all employees that Howard W. Hontz had been promoted to Assistant to the President.*

December 2nd of that year, the partial demolition of the one-time "Largest Roundhouse in the World" commenced. When the razing was finished, only sixteen stalls remained: three for use by the railroad's Bridge & Building Department, the other thirteen by a local aluminum—and later a fertilizer—company. Afterwards, with the D&H gone, and the fertilizer company departed, the pared down roundhouse fell into disuse and disrepair. It remained to become owned by CPRail, who mercifully removed it from the landscape several years after their 1991 purchase of the railroad.

The 'burger and fries were good, and I hope you enjoyed your meal, too. I'll take care of the bill—please leave the tip—and then let's end our day up upon Table Rocks. To do so, we'll retrace our path along Route 28 and Main Street, and then after crossing over the railroad, we will turn left onto Chestnut Street which is Route 7. We will stay on Chestnut until we reach West Street—that's where the Ward's lived—and then turn right to head up into the Hartwick College campus. At the first parking lot the trail to Table Rocks begins, so after parking the Neon we'll head up the still well-worn path that Jean Ward and her girlfriends used so many years ago. Back then, there were many outcroppings of rock from which to view the railroad yard and Oneonta's West End, but today only the highest table of rocks still affords a grand view. Once there, the West End, the railroad, the Susquehanna, and even Route 7 disappear off to the south and west, depending on whether you are employing railroad or highway navigational directions.

From our lofty perch, we can see the "big" roundhouse foundation footprint, the once 160-foot-tall power house smoke stack that has lost a course or two of bricks at the top, the Lutz Feed Company that is in the Hole where SNY met the D&H until 1971, and the Hampton Inn where we will spend the evening to recharge our batteries for another long and interesting day tomorrow.

The sun is just touching the top of one of Oneonta's western hills. The shadows it creates as it drops lower in the sky first darkens the West End, then the railroad and its forlorn, vacant old yard, and the Susquehanna's valley. Finally those shadows begin to gobble up Franklin Mountain from bottom to top. The day of our journey from Albany and Schenectady to Oneonta has turned to dusk and by the time we get to the Hampton Inn it will be dark. Once inside, we will not be able to hear anything of the railroad like we would at the Worcester-Whitehouse Inn. There are only three grade crossings in Oneonta. CPRail engineers will blow warnings for each of them but they are several miles away. Whatever railroad activity that goes on tonight will happen without our notice.

Jean Ward Hontz has not been to Table Rocks in many years—more years than her marriage to Howard, which in 2011 celebrates sixty-eight years. Their marriage that united two D&H families has stood the test of time, and so have the Forget-me-nots up on Table Rocks. They still bloom every spring even though folks don't make May baskets to give to friends any longer. Their emergence every year signals the return of fair weather and yet another endless summer, but Oneonta's railroad slowly declined with each passing summer. When the wrecking ball first touched the roundhouse bricks beginning in 1954, the end was decided. The unassailable inevitability of the demise of the Delaware & Hudson's shops and the one-time largest roundhouse in the world was at hand. While the remaining mainline and a few ancillary tracks are still in use, they pale in comparison to what was once there. Still, the memories linger for those employees and families that were fortunate to live and work at the facilities during their zenith. There will be no glorious revival of Oneonta's great railroading past now, but at least a dozen or so trains still pass through the City of the Hills on a daily basis, recalling a bit of the grandeur that once was. Maybe tonight, unseen, Todd Hontz will be at the throttle of engines leading a CPRail train through town.

As we end this part of our tale, the second part of our journey beckons tomorrow. We will begin our travels anew shortly, when we will continue down the "Roads, Rivers, and Rails" through Otego, Wells Bridge, Unadilla, Sidney, Bainbridge, Afton, Nineveh Junction, Belden, Tunnel, Sanitaria Springs, Port Crane, and finally Binghamton, the "Parlor City."

Howard and Jean Hontz on March 20, 2011. They'll be married sixty-eight years in October. Thank you for a wonderful story full of love, railroading, and memories!

ABOVE: *People still climb the steep path to Table Rocks heights in order to enjoy one of the Susquehanna Valley's most fabulous panoramas. I'm pleased that I got to bring you here at the end of our long day, and thanks for taking a picture of my "best side" while I was contemplating this view that was made possible by Mother Nature and time.* RIGHT: *The partial footprint of "The Largest Roundhouse in the World" can be seen. It is being kept company by the 160-foot-tall — minus a few brick courses — smokestack that was put up by masons seven years after the birth of the roundhouse. In the middle of the scene is the Hampton Inn where we will spend the night. Many years have passed since Jean Ward was here. If we employ our imagination we can still see smoke rising out of that mighty chimney, and hear the sounds of railroading that once rose from the innards of the roundhouse. There is no yard today, but back in Jean's time it would have been full of cars waiting to be taken out onto the Susquehanna Division, pulled by engines repaired by Russell, and driven by men who worked under George's guidance. Yesterday: what a great time to be alive.*

Although Oneonta is no longer a railroad town, and proclaims itself to be the City of the Hills, it perpetuates the memory of its one-time life blood of steam and steel by exhibiting this mural within the walkway that leads from the city's parking garage to its Main Street—Route 7. From the upper level of the garage you can look out on the CPRail mainline, and watch folks entering and leaving the Stella Luna restaurant. Many things have changed in Oneonta since the "BIG" roundhouse was in operation, but as long as this mural remains on the walkway wall Oneonta will never be completely a college town. ARTIST, J. WILLIAMS.

ROADS, RIVERS, AND RAILS

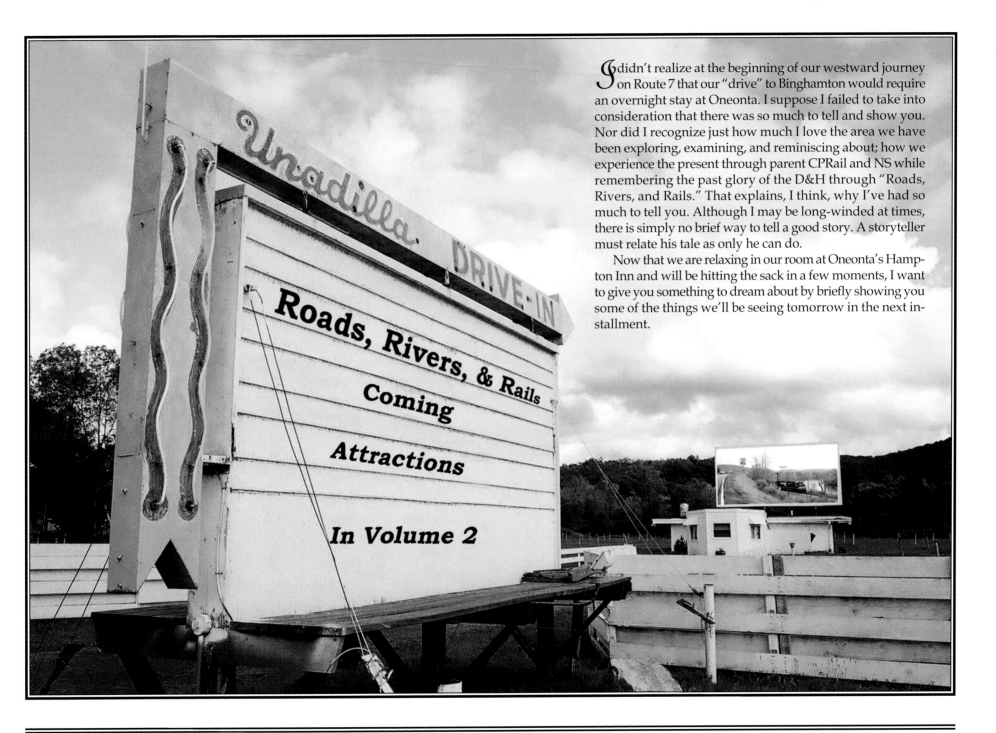

I didn't realize at the beginning of our westward journey on Route 7 that our "drive" to Binghamton would require an overnight stay at Oneonta. I suppose I failed to take into consideration that there was so much to tell and show you. Nor did I recognize just how much I love the area we have been exploring, examining, and reminiscing about; how we experience the present through parent CPRail and NS while remembering the past glory of the D&H through "Roads, Rivers, and Rails." That explains, I think, why I've had so much to tell you. Although I may be long-winded at times, there is simply no brief way to tell a good story. A storyteller must relate his tale as only he can do.

Now that we are relaxing in our room at Oneonta's Hampton Inn and will be hitting the sack in a few moments, I want to give you something to dream about by briefly showing you some of the things we'll be seeing tomorrow in the next installment.

Inbound excursion at Oneonta, NY.

CPRail action along the Susquehanna River near Otego, NY.

1867 D&H stone freight house, Unadilla, NY.

D&H PA No. 18 leads "Director's Special,"
Wells Bridge, NY

7

NS train at Main Street crossing,
Sidney, NY.

Belden Hill tunnel at Tunnel, NY

CLARENCE THARP

NS train approaching private residence crossing near Afton, NY.

CPRail at Port Crane, NY

A. BRUCE TRACY COLLECTION

Sanitaria Springs, NY depot

Harpursville, NY trestle

Nineveh Junction, NY

BIBLIOGRAPHY

BOOKS

Busbey, T. A. *Biographical Directory of the Railway Officials of America*. Chicago, IL: The Railway Age and Northwestern Railroader, 1893.

Carlisle Historical Society. *History of the Town of Carlisle*. Scotia, NY: Velocity Print, 2008.

Carmer, Carl. *The Susquehanna*. Rinehart & Company, 1955.

Child, Hamilton. *Gazetteer and Business Directory Of Otsego County, NY For 1872-3*. Syracuse, NY: Self-published, 1872.

Child, Hamilton. *Gazetteer and Business Directory Of Schoharie County, NY For 1872-3*. Syracuse, NY: Self-published, 1872.

Conklin, R. S. *Along the Great Rivers of Central New York*. Self-published, 2009.

Cooper, J. F.; Hollis, H. H.; Littell, W. R.; Shaw, S. M. *A History of Cooperstown*. Cooperstown, NY: New York State Historical Association, 1976.

Crist, Ed & John Krause. *Delaware & Hudson, Challengers and Northerns*. Newton, NJ: Carstens Publications, 1988.

Cudmore, Dana D. *The Remarkable Howe Caverns Story*. Woodstock, NY: Overlook Press, 1990.

Delaware & Hudson Company. *Century of Progress*. Albany, NY, 1925.

Delaware & Hudson Company. *Passenger and Freight Stations*. Albany, NY, 1928.

Doughty, Geoffrey H. *New York Central's Stations and Terminals*. Lynchburg, VA: TLC Publishing Co., 1999.

DuFresne, Marilyn E. *Tri Valley–Cobleskill to Colliersville*. Charleston, SC: Arcadia Publishing, 2001.

Edson, William D. et al. *New York Central System Diesel Locomotives*. Lynchburg, VA: TLC Publishing, 1995.

Frost, James A. *Life on the Upper Susquehanna 1783-1860*. New York, NY: King's Crown Press, 1951.

Funk, Robert E. *Archaeological Investigations in the Upper Susquehanna Valley*. Buffalo, NY: Persimmon Press, 1993.

Grabau, Amadeus W. *Geology and Paleontology of the Schoharie Valley*. Albany, NY: New York State Museum, 1906.

Greene, Nelson. *The Old Mohawk Turnpike Book*. Fort Plain, NY: Nelson Greene Publisher, 1924.

Hunt, William L. *Unadilla–The Village Beautiful*. Unadilla, NY: Rotary Club, 1957.

Kerr, James W. *The Official 2007 Edition Locomotive Rosters &*

News. St. David's, ON: DPA-LTA Enterprises Inc., 2007.

Kilian, Len. *Smoke Under Vroman's Nose*. Rotterdam Junction, NY: ELESKAY Publishing, 2011.

Leuthner, Stuart. *The Railroaders*. New York, NY: Random House, 1983.

Loudon, Jim. *The Oneonta Roundhouse*. Cooperstown, NY: Leatherstocking Railway Historical Society, 1993.

Loudon, Jim. *Leatherstocking Rails*. Cooperstown, NY: Leatherstocking Railway Historical Society, 2005.

Milener, Eugene D. *Oneonta: Development of a Railroad Town*. Deposit, NY: Courier Printing Corporation, 1983.

Newland, David R. *Mineral Resources of the State of New York*. Albany, NY: New York State Museum, 1921.

Official Hotel Directory of the United States. New York, NY: Official Hotel Red Book and Directory Company, 1902.

Olenick, Andy and R. O. Reisem. *Historic New York*. Rochester, NY: Landmark Society of Western New York, 2006.

Pierce, Harry H. *Railroads of New York, A Study in Government Aid*. Cambridge, MA: Harvard University Press, 1953.

Pollard, Ray F. *Along the Country Road*. Cobleskill, NY: Cobleskill Times Press, 1941.

Roscoe, William E. *History of Schoharie County*. Albany, NY: D. Mason & Company, 1882.

Ryder, Charles L. *The Man, the Railroad, and the Bank*. Albany, NY: National Commercial Bank, 1960.

Shaughnessy, Jim. *Delaware & Hudson*. Berkeley, CA: Howell-North Books, 1967.

Smith, Alfred E. *Progress of Public Improvements*. Albany, NY: Governor's Office, 1927.

Sullivan, Dennis. *Voorheesville, New York–A Sketch of the Beginnings of a 19th Century Railroad Town*. Voorheesville, NY: Village of Voorheesville, 1993.

Taibi, John R. *Rails Along the Oriskany*. Fleischmanns, NY, Purple Mountain Press, 2003.

VanDiver, Bradford B. *Roadside Geology of New York*. Missoula, MT: Mountain Press Publishing Company, 1985.

Van Schaick, Jr., John. *Nature Cruisings*. Boston, MA: The Murray Press, 1928.

Wettereau, Richard and Ron Ziel. *Victorian Railroad Stations of Long Island*. Bridgehampton, NY: Sunrise Special Ltd., 1988.

Yates, Austin H. *Schenectady County*. Schenectady, NY: New York History Company, 1902.

Zimmerman, Karl R. *A Decade of D&H*. Oradell, NJ: Delford Press, 1978.

ANNUAL REPORTS

Delaware & Hudson Canal Company (1825-1899).

Delaware & Hudson Company (1900-1967).

INTERNET SITES

Ancestry.com

Fultonhistory.com

Google Earth

Historic Map Works, Residential Genealogy

OTHER MATERIAL

Interstate Commerce Commission valuation documents and maps, VS4, 5, 6, 7a, b, c, 1916-1920.

Interstate Commerce Commission, D&H roadway report, 1942.

PERIODICALS AND NEWSPAPERS

Fairchild, Herman L. *The Susquehanna River in New York*. Albany, NY: N.Y.S. Bulletin No. 256, January 1925.

Povall, George. *Railfanning CP's D&H*. Railpace Newsmagazine, April and July 2005.

Schenectady Gazette, various issues.

The Altamont Enterprise, various issues.

The Evening Leader (Corning, NY), various issues.

The Freeman's Journal (Cooperstown, NY), various issues.

The Otsego Farmer, various issues.

Utica Weekly Herald, various issues.

UNPUBLISHED MANUSCRIPTS

Dana, H. T. *Early history of the Albany & Susquehanna Railroad*, 1903.

Sherry, John. *History of Richmondville & Surrounding Hamlets*, 1976.

Delaware & Hudson Railroad, Traffic Department Annual Report, 1967.

Ferguson, William Fern. Various photographic and historic textual notebooks maintained at the Worcester Historical Society.

ℐNDEX